ECONOMIC DEVELOPMENT AND PROSPECTS IN THE ASEAN

Also by Tran Van Hoa

NATIONAL INCOME AND ECONOMIC PROGRESS (*editor with D. S. Ironmonger and J. O. N. Perkins*)

THE MACROECONOMIC MIX IN THE INDUSTRIALISED WORLD (*editor with J. O. N. Perkins*)

Economic Development and Prospects in the ASEAN

Foreign Investment and Growth in Vietnam, Thailand, Indonesia and Malaysia

Edited by

Tran Van Hoa
Associate Professor of Economics
Wollongong University
New South Wales
Australia

First published in Great Britain 1997 by
MACMILLAN PRESS LTD
Houndmills, Basingstoke, Hampshire RG21 6XS and London
Companies and representatives throughout the world

A catalogue record for this book is available from the British Library.

ISBN 0–333–67024–8

First published in the United States of America 1997 by
ST. MARTIN'S PRESS, INC.,
Scholarly and Reference Division,
175 Fifth Avenue, New York, N.Y. 10010

ISBN 0–312–17607–4

Library of Congress Cataloging-in-Publication Data
Economic development and prospects in the ASEAN : foreign investment and growth in Vietnam, Thailand, Indonesia and Malaysia / edited by Tran Van Hoa.
p. cm.
Includes bibliographical references and index.
ISBN 0–312–17607–4 (cloth)
1. Investments, Foreign—Asia, Southeastern. 2. Asia, Southeastern—Economic conditions. 3. Economic forecasting—Asia, Southeastern. I. Van Hoa, Tran.
HG5740.8.A3E27 1997
332.6'73'0959—dc21 97–3275
CIP

---

10 9 8 7 6 5 4 3 2 1
06 05 04 03 02 01 00 99 98 97

Printed and bound in Great Britain by
Antony Rowe Ltd, Chippenham, Wiltshire

To dearest Souraya, Danielle and Cybele

Contents

List of Contributors ix

Preface xi

Acknowledgements xvii

1 Vietnam's Recent Economic Performance and its Impact on Trade and Investment Prospects

Tran Van Hoa, University of Wollongong 1

2 Foreign Investment and the Macroeconomy in Vietnam

Le Dang Doanh, CIEM 44

3 Foreign Investment Law in Vietnam: Legal and Economic Aspects and Comparative Analysis

Luu Van Dat, RIFER 87

4 Priority Areas to Attract Foreign Investment Capital to Vietnam: Present Conditions and Prospects

Nguyen Quang Thai, Institute of Development Strategy 98

5 Current Patterns and Future Trends in Trade and Foreign Investment in Vietnam: The 1995 Business Survey and an Econometric Analysis

Tran Van Hoa and Pham Quang Thao, ICTC 113

6 Vietnam Tourism, 1995 to 2010: Development Strategy and Plan

Le Nhat Thuc, RIFER, and Tran Van Hoa 159

7 Foreign Investment and Growth in Some Developing Economies in Asia Pacific: Leading Patterns for Vietnam?

Tran Van Hoa 179

8 Foundation for Better Forward Planning Policy in Developing Economies: Improved Forecasts of Macroeconomic Aggregates

Tran Van Hoa 198

9 Health Care in Thailand: Present Systems and Future Trends with Applications to Other Developing Economies

Sirilaksana Khoman, Thammasat University 223

Index 262

List of Contributors

Vice Minister Le Dang Doanh is President of Vietnam's economic think-tank, *The Central Institute for Economic Management (CIEM)*, a permanent member of the Prime Minister's Consulting Group for Economic Reforms in Vietnam, and an economic adviser to the Secretary General. He is a graduate from the USSR and the FDG, an internationally well known expert on macroeconomic policy in transitional economies in Asia, and a much sought after speaker at national and international forums. Mr Le Dang Doanh has written a number of policy reports on macroeconomic reforms and international cooperation for the government of Vietnam, and has co-authored a number of commissioned country reports with staff from the World Bank, the UNDP, the Asian Development Bank, etc.. Currently, Mr Le Dang Doanh is collaborating with Professor Tran Van Hoa on a major international research project, *Foreign Investment in Vietnam,* funded by the Australian Research Council and the Research Institute for Foreign Economic Relations (RIFER), Ministry of Trade, Vietnam.

Professor Luu Van Dat, a graduate in law from France, is a senior adviser to the Minister of Trade in Vietnam and a former Director General of RIFER. He has been recognized by international organizations and expatriates alike as a leading figure in the legal process of economic reforms in Vietnam in recent years. Professor Luu Van Dat was the chairman of the committee responsible for the drafting of the Law on Foreign Investment of 1987 which, with some minor amendments, is still the principal legal document on the subject matter. Being a jurisdicial lawyer and President of Vietnam's Law Association, Professor Luu Van Dat has in fact been responsible for drafting numerous other policy documents on trade and investment and business operation with foreign governments and corporations for the government of Vietnam.

Professor Le Nhat Thuc is currently Director General of RIFER and a Director of the International Consulting and Training Center (ICTC), a commercial arm of the Ministry of Trade, in Vietnam. A graduate from the USSR, he taught for many years at the Foreign Trade University in Hanoi, and is a well known authority on international economic relations. Before coming to the RIFER, he also headed Vietnam's Tourism Department. Professor Le Nhat Thuc has carried out research and published widely on many aspects of economic and tourism developments in Vietnam.

Dr Pham Quang Thao, a graduate in economic and marketing management from the USSR, is currently Executive Vice Director of ICTC. He has carried out research on business accounting, investment capital management, industrial investment expenditure, non-state financed systems, labour cooperation, trade, and trade promotion in Vietnam. Dr Pham Quang Thao has also provided consulting to a number of transnational corporations doing business in Vietnam.

Professor Nguyen Quang Thai gained a BA and PhD in Operations Research from Hanoi University and the National Center for Scientific Research in Vietnam. In 1986, he received a DSc degree in Macroeconomics. Professor Nguyen Quang Thai has taught and done research at a number of universities and research institutes in Vietnam (for example, the National Economics University, the Ministry of Energy, and the State Planning Committee) and in the USSR (for example, the Moscow Institute for National Economy). Currently, he is Vice President of the Institute of Development Strategy and Director of the World Economy Department in Vietnam.

Dr Sirilaksana Khoman is an Associate Professor in Economics and the Foundation Director of the BE International Program, Faculty of Economics, Thammasat University, Thailand. A graduate in economics from the Australian National University in Australia, and Hawaii University in the USA, Professor Khoman has extensive teaching experience and has carried out research and published widely in the field of health economics. Dr Khoman has also been a consultant to the World Health Organization and other private research institutes in Thailand.

Preface

The book is the first in a series of books and monographs we plan to prepare and, for the benefit of a wider readership who are interested in the subject matter, to publish in order to provide a soundly researched and concisely presented analysis in two areas of contemporary economic and business significance: (a) the current economic growth, development and performance in the major economies (the economic tigers and dragons) in the Association of South-East Asian Nations (ASEAN) and Asia Pacific in recent years, and, (b) the prospects of future growth, development and performance on investment, trade, and business between these economies and other countries in the region and beyond in the context of both bilateral and multilateral international economic relations.

The content of the analysis essentially covers important aspects of micro and macroeconomic structure, determinants of production, consumption and trade, government policy, domestic infrastructure, international outlook, social and health policy, and particularly the trends and patterns of economic growth and development and the up-to-date high level methodologies to study them in the major ASEAN and Asia Pacific economies.

More importantly for practical governmental and commercial policy studies, the present book and the series have the purpose of providing a timely and authoritative assessment of the impact and the opportunities of these trends and patterns, and their forecasts on investment, trade and business between these economies and other countries in a global context, to the early part of the twenty-first century.

In terms of a more specific focus, the present book is a collection of the results of recent high level economic research, prepared and presented by three groups of well known academic and government economists in Australia, Vietnam, and Thailand. The two main themes of the book are (1) the process of economic growth and development in the past few decades in two major countries in the ASEAN, namely, Vietnam and Thailand (and, to a lesser extent, Indonesia and Malaysia), and also (2) the commercial, cooperative, political stability, and mutual welfare prospects arising from this process in these countries vis a vis Australia and other developing, newly industrialized (NIC), and developed countries in the Asia Pacific and beyond to 2010. The year 2010 is selected as the target date because it is the year when most reforms as proposed under the current Asia Pacific Economic Cooperation (APEC) forum are expected to be in place for APEC members.

The book consists of two parts. The first part covers important aspects of economic development and trade, investment, and business prospects to 2010 in Vietnam in particular and, in addition, current issues of health care in Thailand. The second part focuses on the causes and effects of growth, inflation and external debts and how to forecast them better for policy analysis in Thailand, Indonesia and Malaysia in the ASEAN and Korea in the Asia Pacific in general.

The first part contains six chapters, and it is based on the research findings in 1995 from the research project, Foreign Investment in Vietnam. This project was funded in part by the Australian Research Council (ARC) and in part by the Research Institute for Foreign Economic Relations (RIFER), the Ministry of Trade, in Vietnam. The research work was jointly undertaken by the senior academic staff of the ASEAN Business and Economics Studies Research Program at the University of Wollongong (UOW) in Australia, and senior researchers, government advisers, and policy makers from the RIFER and other institutions in Vietnam.

The second part contains three chapters and it is based on some of the recent research work on the Asia Pacific economies by Professor Tran Van Hoa and by eminent economists from the University of Thammasat in Thailand.

All chapters deal with both theoretical and empirical (or observed) aspects of economic growth and development, and their forecasts. The forecasts, whenever made and used, are based on either official or soundly researched independent economic research. The book has therefore all the elements of important relevant background research for use in formal studies of development economics in developing and transition countries, or in further theoretical and applied economic and social research work. It also has practical and up-to-date information on feasible investment, trade, and business opportunities which are useful for informed discussions, for monitoring and planning strategies, and for policy formulation and implementation by government agencies, institutions, corporations, and the individuals in the business community.

On Vietnam, Chapter 1, written by Professor Tran Van Hoa, gives a concise account of Vietnam's contemporary history starting from the end of the Second World War to the present time. Vietnam's macroeconomic performance and microeconomic reforms in the past decade or so are then broadly discussed, and Vietnam's blueprint for economic development as well as possible obstacles to achieve its targeted level are described. Prospects as perceived by private and government agencies in Vietnam for investment, trade, and business by foreign companies and investing individuals in the fifteen separate sectors of Vietnam's economy (that is, from agriculture to mining, construction, forestry, etc.) to the year 2010 are finally discussed. These prospects are then presented as reference information for use by foreign companies and investing individuals in the formulation and implementation of general or specific investment, trade, and business policy.

In Chapter 2, Vice Minister Le Dang Doanh provides a survey of foreign direct investment (FDI) in major East Asian countries in the recent years, the reasons for its growth, and its effects on other aspects of the economy, domestic and international. FDI in Vietnam since after the promulgation of the Law of Investment in 1987 is then analysed first by the countries investing in Vietnam and secondly by the sectors where FDI takes place. The chapter is a detailed account with supporting high level policy evidence by a senior adviser to the government of Vietnam of the documented activities resulting from FDI into Vietnam. This account would give us an invaluable amount of information on the investment and operation status of FDI as it is today in Vietnam and its prospects in the future, and would provide a good guide to international investment strategists.

In Chapter 3, Professor Luu Van Dat, a senior adviser to the Minister of Trade in Vietnam, who has been responsible for the drafting of various investment laws in the country, describes in detail the genesis to the now famous Law on Investment (29 December 1987) in Vietnam, and the subsequent amendments in order to improve its effectiveness in attracting FDI into Vietnam. Legal and economic aspects of the Law including law implementation and enforcement, dispute resolution and compensation are also discussed within the political framework of the renovation or Doi Moi. A comparative analysis of the Law in relation to other relevant laws in operation in other countries in Europe and North America is finally made. The chapter gives an authoritative account of the rationale of the Law, traces its common international character, and how it has been adopted in relation to all FDI matters in Vietnam since 1987.

Chapter 4, written by the Deputy Head of the Institute of Development Strategy in Hanoi, deals with the commercially relevant problem of FDI, namely, the priority areas of foreign investment currently supported by the government in Vietnam in its national economic development policy. The rationale of the present conditions and the prospects of FDI and FDI-based projects are also analysed. Five categories of FDI projects are identified in the chapter: branch or sector, territory or locality, scope or scale of operation, forms of FDI, and the structure of investing companies or countries. FDI priorities are also described in more detail in terms of four indexes of preference. The direction of FDI for the period 1996 to 2000 is also discussed. The list of FDI priorities is finally given and briefly discussed.

A comprehensive analysis of an important survey of Vietnamese businesses and their FDI requirements and the future orientations carried out early in 1995 in Hanoi forms the content of Chapter 5. The format of the survey questionnaires was designed by Professor Tran Van Hoa in collaboration with Dr Pham Quang Thao and staff from the International Consulting and Training Center (ICTC), Research Institute for Foreign Economic Relations (RIFER), the Ministry of Trade, in Hanoi, Vietnam. In this survey, up to sixteen categories of Vietnamese businesses were interviewed. In addition, thirteen aspects of business organization, scale, operation, infrastructure, information base, planning of Vietnamese companies, FDI requirement, and prospects for investment, trade, and business for foreign companies and investing individuals are investigated in detail. The information we gathered for all classes of companies and for all levels of company operation from the survey is a first hand knowledge on the state of business in Vietnam and provides a good indicator of where FDI activity will be likely to be heading for in the near future. All analysis is based on the results of cross tabulation of the returned questionnaires, processed by the SPSS-PC software package.

Chapter 6 is written by a former Director General of Vietnam's Tourism Commission, Professor Le Nhat Thuc, with the collaboration of Professor Tran Van Hoa. The chapter is concerned mainly with an analysis of the natural and man-made attributes to attract tourists (both domestic and international) in Vietnam, the flows of these tourists in recent years, and the likely trend of these flows in the coming years. A useful comparative analysis of tourism in Vietnam and in other South-East Asian countries is also given in detail. The analysis provides invaluable information on infrastructure in the tourism industry, technical support for tourism, shortage of skilled and experienced staff, and the inadequacy or not of state management in the tourism industry in Vietnam. Plans for tourism development by sector, by location, and by product differentiation to the year 2010 by the government in Vietnam and the preferred areas for development are also discussed. The chapter finally deals with the problem of improving tourism management, and discusses ways to achieve the target.

Focused mainly on a formal analysis of economic growth and its causal nexus to FDI activity in a number of ASEAN countries, the motivation of Chapter 7 written by Professor Tran Van Hoa is to provide an empirical study of this nexus, and whether this nexus, if statistically present, would be able to give us some useful information or experience to adapt to the situation and conditions of Vietnam and other transition economies. The methodology of the chapter is a formal econometric long-term causal (or Granger-Engel and Sargan cointegration) investigation based on time series data. The questions we wish to answer in a significant manner are whether growth has affected FDI or vice versa in major ASEAN countries in recent times, and whether growth and FDI have in fact contributed to high inflationary pressure or, equivalently, to a more costly standard of living of the people in these countries. We thus attempt here to bring about the quantifiable measurement of the costs and benefits of FDI in a macroeconomic context, and to provide econometric evidence to support a balanced national policy of growth and investment and its possible economic and social costs as far as the flow of FDI into a country is concerned.

Chapter 8, written by Professor Tran Van Hoa, is an essay with empirical support on planning methodologies in economics and business, and has two purposes. First, acknowledging the important advances in information technology (IT) and their useful applications to almost routine economic and business modelling and forecasting issues in recent years, the chapter is aimed at providing a concise survey of recent major advances in modelling and forecasting methodologies which have been used in shaping, in an important part, forward planning strategies by the governments, the corporations, business economists, academic researchers, and economic advisers in developed countries. Second, it is aimed at exploring the extent to which these IT-based methodologies can be best adapted for use in formulating and implementing better and more credible policy or in quantifying the prospects on economic development, growth, trade and investment promotion, and business expansion in the developing and transition economies especially in the Asia Pacific region.

In Chapter 9, Dr Khoman gives a concise discussion on the economic-theoretic foundation (the case of market failures or inefficiency and the need for a social policy befitting high economic growth countries) for the intervention by the government in the health care scheme in Thailand, and also a description of the various programmes and their expenditures on health care and health services which have been introduced in Thailand in the past few years. Using the experience gathered from private and public health providers in Thailand during this period, Professor Khoman also presents a critical evaluation of these programmes on the basis of economic and social costs (prices) and benefits (effects). The lessons learned from health care schemes in Thailand, which is still a developing country by international standards, would undoubtedly provide valuable lessons for an implementation and management of similar schemes (intraregional exports of services) for other developing countries in the Asia Pacific as well as the transition economies in the region. Some of these economies include Vietnam, Cambodia, Laos, and Myanmar.

Acknowledgements

The present book is a result of two important international collaborations in theoretical and applied economic research on current regional and global economic issues with formal academic interest and practical commercial applications.

The first collaboration is a pioneering joint research work involving institutional cooperation in the international research project, Foreign Investment in Vietnam, undertaken by the ASEAN Economic Studies Research Program at the University of Wollongong, headed by Professor Tran Van Hoa, in Australia, the International Consulting and Training Center (ICTC), headed by Professor Le Nhat Thuc and Dr Pham Quang Thao, and the Research Institute for Foreign Economic Relations (RIFER), the Ministry of Trade, in Vietnam. The project funding is supported in part by the Australian Research Council and in part by the RIFER.

The second collaboration is between leading economists in Australia and Thailand and focuses on issues in economic development and growth in the ASEAN and their likely impact on regional developing and transition economies. Staff involved in this international cooperation in economic research include Professor Tran Van Hoa, senior academic staff of the Faculty of Economics at Thammasat University, and the Economic Modelling and Forecasting Research Program at Chulalongkorn University in Thailand.

The editor wishes to thank these institutions for their support, financially or logistically. Thanks are also due to academic and general staff of these institutions for their generous contributions to the research work done, the laborious translation of research papers from Thai and Vietnamese into English, the word-processing undertaken, the necessary liaisons and networking carried out for an effective management of a major research project of international nature and scope, and other general administrative arrangements.

Part of the preparation of the book was done at the Asian Business Centre, Institute of Applied Economic and Social Research, the University of Melbourne, during the editor's sabbatical leave early in 1996. He wishes to thank Professor Peter Lloyd, Director of the Centre, for his support. Associate Professor Duncan Ironmonger, Director of the Households Research Unit at the University, was also helpful with encouragement on the book's subject matter. Last but not least, the editor is indebted to Mr T. M. Farmiloe of Macmillan in the UK for useful suggestions on editorial challenges which I was only too glad to accept.

The editor and the contributors alone are nevertheless responsible for the content and defects of their contributions to this book.

Tran Van Hoa
Melbourne

1 Vietnam's Recent Economic Performance and its Impact on Trade and Investment Prospects

Tran Van Hoa

1 INTRODUCTION

The contemporary economic history of Vietnam and especially its relative economic success in recent years have amazed a number of economists, political scientists, and historians alike, in the Western or market-oriented countries, in the former USSR states, and in the mixed economies such as Japan, Singapore, and South Korea.

From the geo-politico-institutional and commercial perspectives, Vietnam's economic success has generated a climate of optimistic future opportunities. For many international organizations (such as the World Bank, the International Monetary Fund [IMF], the Asian Development Bank [ADB], the Association of South-East Asian Nations [ASEAN], the Ford Foundation, the Fulbright Foundation, the Sasakawa Foundation, the Swedish International Development Agency [SIDA], the Canadian International Development Agency [CIDA], AusAID, and so on), the opportunities are within the context of global political stability and mutual economic prosperity within or without the region. For many international corporations (the so-called multinational or transnational companies), the opportunities are within the context of business, trade, investment, profits or strategy potentials.

The wider implication of the relative economic success of Vietnam in recent years has also been that it (the success) has produced a number of interesting or even testable hypotheses on the survival theory of the socialist state (including especially the Commonwealth of the Independent States [CIS] of the former USSR) and its ability to accommodate free market ideas in the pursuit of economic development, of modernization of the country, of expanding individual freedom, of opening up for foreign investment and trade, and, from an almost abject poverty level a few years ago (with a per capita income of much less than USD 200 per year or about USD 1,162 in terms of the purchasing power parity [PPP] criterion) in the late 1970s and the early 1980s, of achieving an increasing standard of living (of about 0.4% per annum in terms of GDP growth in 1984, to 3.9% in 1988, 8.3% in 1992, and 7.5% in 1993 – Sources: Statistical Yearbooks, Vietnam's Economy 1986–91, and State Planning Committee [SPC], and other privately compiled sources) for its inhabitants.

It has been predicted that by the year 2000, Vietnam will leave the Philippines behind in terms of its gross domestic product (GDP) or gross national product (GNP) per head, and by the year 2010, it will by the same criterion catch up with the majority of the developing economies in the Asia Pacific region. The prospects are therefore enormous for the economies in the Oceania, the Asia Pacific and beyond trading with Vietnam.

While a study of the reasons for this economic success for Vietnam is attractive or even imperative for political scientists in the Western and in the Eastern blocs alike, such a study has been regarded by international experts as being monumental in its scope and limited (or restricted) to only a few scholars with particular specialisms and with a long-term research programme.

In this report, we therefore are concerned only with a brief description and explanation of Vietnam's macroeconomic performance in recent years, and provide some summary evaluation of the directions of trade and business and prospects in Vietnam vis a vis other trading countries in general and *vis-à-vis* Australia in particular to the year 2010.

The implications of these prospects for developing a strategic research programme or a commercial and aid blueprint on aspects of investment, business, trade, finance, and economics for Vietnam with an Australian perspective and specific interests are also discussed.

2 VIETNAM: BACKGROUND TO ECONOMIC DEVELOPMENT

In 1993, the population of Vietnam was 70,874 million, which is a fairly large market even by the standard of Asian countries. In 1995, the population was about 73 million. The ethnicity of the Vietnamese population consists of 87% Kinh or Vietnamese, and 13% other races including Chinese, Mong, Thai, Meo, Khmer, Tay, and Hao.

Vietnam has a land area of 331,041 square kilometres, and, in 1992, the population density was relatively high with 209 inhabitants per square kilometre. As with some other non-city state countries, the population is not uniformly distributed throughout Vietnam. It has been estimated that about 43.8% of the population are concentrated in the two deltas: the Red River delta in the North (21.4%) and the Mekong River delta in the South (22.4%). Both deltas represent only 17.2% of the area of the land with 5.2% in the North and 12% in the South. (Quinlan, 1995).

Vietnam is an agrarian economy and, in 1990, it had a per capita income of about USD 200 (in 1992, this income was USD 220), which is among the lowest level of income in Asia and the Subcontinent. By comparison, in 1992, the per capita income was USD 6,300 for South Korea, USD 7,380 for Taiwan, USD 1,575 for Thailand, USD 2,700 for Malaysia, and USD 625 for Indonesia. It has to be remembered that Vietnam has made great progress in the past few years (more precisely since 1980) in achieving positive per capita income (GDP) growth rates. These can be split into industrial and agricultural output growths, with the industrial component far outweighing the agricultural sector (a 10%/3.1% ratio in 1993). In 1992, about 78% of the population lived in the rural area, and the remaining 22% in the urban area. In the two major urban areas, the capital Hanoi has a population of about 2.1 million, and the principal commercial centre Ho Chi Minh City has about 4.1 million people.

Vietnam's total labour force was 31.8 million people in 1992. Between 1985 and 1992, the agricultural sector employed on average about 72% of Vietnam's total labour force. Agriculture's average share in national production (GDP) was 38.2% in 1992, which is roughly the same as services' share (37.2%). This share from agriculture is too high when compared to that of other countries such as Indonesia (17.9%), Malaysia (16.1%), or Thailand (13.1%). In Vietnam, the annual growth rates of agricultural output were 2% in the period 1976–80, 5.2% during the years 1980–85, and about 4.76% on average during the period 1986–93. In these later years, the growth rates were fluctuating however, from 0.3% in 1987 to 10.7% in 1990.

While Vietnam is densely populated, it is relatively rich in minerals and other natural resources which are necessary for economic development and sustainability, and which also make the country attractive to foreign investors especially in the manufacturing sector. Chief amongst Vietnam's advantages is its favourable geographical location, in that it lies along the major shipping routes in the South China Sea, and has a long coastline particularly suitable for fishing and aquaculture. In fact, seafood exports, in the same way as coal exports and oil shipments, have increased rapidly over the past few years. Unfortunately Vietnam's other natural reserves, including wetlands, forests, mountain and seaside resorts are unevenly distributed and remain mostly untapped either for recreation or for tourism.

Most of Vietnam's mineral resources such as coal (with a reserve of between 3.5 to 6.5 billion tons, and an annual production of between 4 and 7 million tons), chromate, iron, tin, copper and nickel ores are found in the North, while the South is well known for its gas reserves as well as its ricebowl in the Mekong delta. Minerals which have been discovered throughout the country include zinc, manganese, gold, precious stones, and bauxite. Minerals which have been used as industrial inputs include clay, kaolin, graphite, and talcum. In addition to these resources, Vietnam also is known to have large and proven oil reserves located offshore in the southern continental shelf as well as in fields in the Red River and Mekong River deltas. While the French began searching for oil in Vietnam in the 1930s, it was not until 1986 that the country became an oil producing state. Nowadays, crude oil exports have become the government's major source of revenue and a top hard currency earner. Finally, the climate and soil of Vietnam are suitable for growing treecrops such as rubber, coffee, tea, and other products. One of the new economic zones which has made a fortune in coffee and tea growing and trade is Bao Loc in the South.

As has been mentioned above, on the per capita basis and after allowing for great positive growth rates, Vietnam is not at all well endowed. The country has a very large population relative to its resources, implying that the country has to set its priority right from the start of the process of economic development. That is, Vietnam has to concentrate on economic growth first, and then to develop the basics of human resources second rather than natural resources (Nguyen Thi Van Anh, 1995). In addition, it will be a challenge to preserve the resource base in the face of pressure from the population itself. Vietnam's population growth rate of 2.2% is rather high on the current international level. A reduction of the population growth rate to 1.7% would have the effect of increasing output growth per head substantially.

Another important issue concerning Vietnam's endowment of basic resources is that there is a large regional imbalance. Compared to the North, the Southern part of Vietnam has relatively more agricultural land. The average area per farm worker is 0.24 hectare in the North and 0.46 hectare in the South. The South also has a greater entrepreneurial tradition due to its exposure to a capitalist market and mechanism even on a war footing. It has easier access to capital from overseas Vietnamese which amounts to USD 2.5 million at the moment, and better infrastructure since the economy there had followed the market oriented management system until 1975.

One of the noteworthy features of Vietnam is that most of its social indicators have been quite good, despite the country's very low income and a long history of wars. Compared to China which opened up about 15 years ago after the thawing out of US–China relations after President Nixon's historic visit in 1972, Vietnam today (1992) has slightly better social indicators in areas such as an infant mortality rate of 36/1,000 (38/1,000 in 1991, and 42/1,000 in East Asia on average), life expectancy of 69 years for females and 67 years for males, and a literacy rate of 88%, and an adult female literacy rate of 16.4%. In 1990, the education expenditure to GDP ratio was 3.9%, and the health expenditure to the GDP ratio was 4.3%. Also in the same year, the primary school enrolment as a percentage of the age group was 103%, and the secondary school enrolment ratio was 33%.

It has been agreed among Asian experts that China has outstanding social indicators for a low income country, and Vietnam is in the same league. Unfortunately, progress in the social sector stalled in the 1980s, as macroeconomic crises had produced the subsequent results of facing insufficient resources to provide quality health care and education. While the literacy rate is around 88%, drop out and repeater rates are also high, due to poor teaching, insufficient supplies of teaching materials, and a poor learning environment (World Bank, 1983).

The country still lacks an adequate physical infrastructure.The transport system, namely, roads, railways, and ports, has never been well developed in the North which functioned as a war economy for decades. In the South, the infrastructure has not been properly maintained although it was far better than in the North.

3 VIETNAM'S MACROECONOMIC PERFORMANCE

Vietnam's economic development path in its contemporary history in the past 50 years can be divided into three periods marked by significant political or economic change: the 1945–75 period is characterized as a war economy, 1976–85 as a period of macroeconomic crisis, and 1986 to the present day has been hailed as a period of significant economic reforms and also of remarkable economic performance.

3.1 Vietnam Before Thong Nhat – The Reunification – (1945–75)

France intervened in Vietnam during its turmoil war years early in the 1800s as an ally of the Nguyen Dynasty which was involved in internal struggles with other rival Vietnamese groups for control of the country. After defeating the local factional Vietnamese internal war-wearied imperial army and the renegade expatriated Chinese troops stationed in Vietnam in the late 1800s, France took over the country and ruled Vietnam for about 80 years as a colony and a French territory.

Following a century of factional fighting, the period of French rule was characterized by relatively slow economic development and minimal social reforms, particularly when compared to the experiences of major economies (for example, France, the United Kingdom) in Europe after the Great Industrialization in Great Britain in 1850. In fact, it has been argued that many policies adopted by France in Vietnam in this period could be regarded as repressive.

At the end of the Second World War, or more precisely, on 19 August 1945, Vietnam started its revolution against the French and about two weeks later declared its independence as the sovereign state of the Democratic Republic of Vietnam (DRV). A few weeks after that, the first Indochina war began between the Vietnamese nationalist forces (Viet Minh) and the French legionnaires and expeditionnaires and their local recruits (the so-called Bao Hoang troops). It was not until 1954 that the war came to an agreed end after the famous battle of Dien Bien Phu when the Geneva Agreement was signed between the French and Vietnamese delegations with the result that the country was divided into two separate regions at the 17th parallel, and the French had to completely withdraw from North Vietnam. This effectively set up Vietnam as the two sovereign states with two different political and economic systems which lasted for 20 years.

In the North, the government of the DRV adopted the socialist economic model which was a centrally planned economy. In principle, the economy was developed, like some other countries such as India and Thailand at about the same time, under the guidelines of a five-year economic development plan. After the reconstruction programme (1955–57) and the socialist transformation stage (1958–60), the first official five-year economic development plan (known as the First Five-Year Plan) was launched in 1961. The US bombing campaign that began in early 1965 disrupted the implementation of the Second Five-Year Plan.

The main features of the economic development strategies that were based on the socialist economic model can be summarized in two objectives as follows (Nguyen Tien Hung, 1987):

1. First industrialization priority is assigned to heavy industry. The heavy industry is the industry that produces the means of production such as machinery and equipment. This means that the major share of the state investment is allocated to this sector and not to other sectors such as the light industry which produces consumer and household goods such as textiles, clothing, electrical appliances, etc..

2. A centrally planned economy is adopted. This means that both the production and its distribution are controlled by the state through collectivization of agriculture and nationalization of industries and commerce.

During this period, the economies of the North and the South were, as mentioned earlier, on a war footing. The data for these years are in most cases not available for analysis.

In contrast to the North, the government of South Vietnam which was formed in 1954 after the partition of the country into two separate parts, adopted, with massive aid from the US and other allies, the market economic system. Although the South also had the experience as a war economy during the 1954 to 1975 period, it did, as a result of its allies' incoming aid, develop its infrastructure to some significant extent. In addition, the South organized labour unions, upgraded its manufacturing, construction, and consumer goods sectors, modernized its agricultural production base, and used fairly successfully the capitalist management and pricing system.

In April 1975, the partition of Vietnam into two parts came to an end after the battle for Saigon. The reunification (Thong Nhat) of Vietnam took place shortly after that.

3.2 The Macroeconomic Crisis Period 1976–85

In the years following 1975, there was an effort to incorporate the South's economy into the socialist system. After 1976, there was in fact a socialist transformation process in the southern part of the country. This was manifested in at least two ways.

1. First, the industrial sector was nationalized and, second, the agricultural sector was collectivized. This transformation of the South came

about after the North had adopted such policies 20 years before. Whether the socialist transformation both in the North and in the South was an economic success is still subject to debates.

2. Vietnam's Second Five-Year Plan (1976–80) was drawn up for the country as a whole for the first time. In other words, the central planning economy was applied for both the northern and southern parts of Vietnam as a whole. During the implementation of the Second Five-Year Plan, the Vietnamese economy performed very poorly and achieved an annual growth rate of only 0.4% for the national income (Tran Hoang Kim, 1992). This was far below the projected rate of 13–14% for the Plan (General Statistical Office of Vietnam, various issues). In the late 1970s, the economy plunged into a crisis. For the years 1979 and 1980, the growth rates were negative. In fact for the period 1976 to 1980, GDP per head was −1.8%. Most damaging was the fall in food grain production from more than 13 million tons in 1976 to only 12 million tons in 1978. The grain (rice) output per capita for the period 1976 to 1980 was 169 kg per year. The target set by the Second Five-Year Plan at the end of its implementation period in 1980 was 21 million tons (*Statistical Yearbook*, 1983). Between 1976 and 1980, food production increased only 6.45% while the population grew by 9.27%. This forced the Vietnamese government to import 8–9 million tons of food during this period.

Over the whole 1976–80 period, industrial production increased by a mere 0.1–0.6% and it even decreased during the years 1979 (9,382.6 million VND at 1970 prices) and 1980 (8,413.6 million VND) from 9,674.5 million VND in 1978.

This state of affairs in Vietnam can be explained partly by a number of factors, internal and external (Nguyen Thi Van Anh, 1995). First, the consequence of nearly 40 years of war, a number of natural disasters, the worsening external political climate surrounding Vietnam since the late 1970s, all led to the shortage of manpower skills, capital, infrastructure, and other ingredients and resources necessary for promoting and sustaining economic development.

Second, there were serious shortcomings in management and leadership (such as the distorted incentive regime, the ambitious targets, poorly trained cadres, arbitrary management, administrative inefficiency, and bureaucratic inertia [Tran Hoang Kim, 1992, p. 22]).

The overall effect was the decline in the living standard of the people in Vietnam. During the period 1976–80, national income at constant 1970 prices increased by only 0.8% while population grew by 9.2%.

As a result, per capita income dropped from 258.1 VND in 1976 to 233.7 VND in 1980, a decrease of 9.4% (*Statistical Yearbook*, 1982) or 1.8% per year. The average inflation rate for this period was 22% per year. This macroeconomic crisis led the Vietnamese government to find new approaches to rectify the problems and to avoid an economic collapse. The suggestions made at the Fifth Plenum (Fourth Party Congress) of the Vietnamese Communist Party in July 1979 were to liberalize the economy.

In what follows, we will see that the reforms initiated at the Fifth Plenum amounted to what economists in the Western or free market economies call microeconomic reforms. This phenomenon was well known in Australia in the past thirteen years or so (since 1983) under the government of the Australian Labour Party. It is our opinion that these reforms, because of their successes and gains in the economy, gave impetus later on to the launching of further economic reforms in Vietnam.

These further collective economic reforms come under the name of Doi Moi which is literally translated as New Changes. Often, this new policy is known as the renovation policy of the government of Vietnam. These reforms will be discussed in the section below.

The most dramatic change in the microeconomic reforms of the Fifth Plenum initiated policy was in the agricultural sector where restrictions in production and distribution were abolished, and in their place, the production was based on the so-called 'three points contract' aiming at stimulating farmers' incentives. Until the change in policy, the production and distribution in the agricultural sector had been strictly under the guidelines of the planned targets. The key instruments to achieve planned targets were collectivized organization of production, state-owned marketing monopolies, and price controls. Under this system, cooperatives were the main production units and farmers could only sell their marketable surpluses to state agencies at artificially state fixed low prices. This system discouraged the farmers to work and use inputs efficiently. A main feature of the new liberalizing economic policy was to make the household the basic economic agent in farming in place of the farm cooperatives. The households were allocated specific plots of land on short-term contracts. In return, the households' obligations were to sell a certain proportion of their production to the state trading agencies at fixed prices and to pay an agricultural tax. The surplus in production however was at the disposal of the households. There were no longer market restrictions.

These new incentives from the new policy in conjunction with other favourable factors such as good climatic conditions significantly contributed to the steady increase in agricultural production in the following years after 1979.

During the Third Five-Year Plan (1981–85), similar microeconomic reforms were introduced into the manufacturing sector. Until that time, all activities of the state enterprises were strictly under the controls or guidelines of the annual plans and targets. The resources (inputs) were allocated from the state budget to the manufacturing sector and the outputs of the sector were sold to the state distribution organizations at state-controlled prices. The new regulations allowed state enterprises to find other resources than from the state-allotted budget and to market a proportion of their production at market prices. This policy stimulated the firms' incentives to increase their production significantly.

During the period 1981–85, national income rose by 6.4% against the projected rate of 4.5–5%.

Also during this period, the production in the agricultural and manufacturing sectors increased by 5.2% and 9.5% per year, respectively (Tran Hoang Kim, 1992, p. 38). The projected rates for this Third Five-Year Plan were 6–7% and 4–5% respectively (Quinlan, 1995). The increase in industrial output is about 100% more than that targeted in the Plan.

3.3 The Doi Moi (Renovation) Period 1986

The success in higher growth rates for the manufacturing and agricultural sectors of the limited microeconomic reforms initiated in 1979 were primarily short-term gains, and could not have sustained long-term results.

This assessment is due to the fact that the structural and management problems of the Vietnamese economy remained unsolved (Nguyen Thi Van Anh, 1995). Until 1985, all reform measures adopted by the government were chiefly aimed at creating an incentive system, but the economy still remained a rigidly and centrally planned economy, although to a lesser extent than before (Tran Hoang Kim, 1992, p. 39). The government recognized that the earlier microeconomic (and, in tandem) macroeconomic reforms had saved the Third Five-Year Plan from the economic failure of the Second Five-Year Plan. As a result, a programme of more far reaching micro and macroeconomic reforms needed to be implemented. The reform programme known as Doi Moi was adopted in 1986, and was the turning point for the success of the reforming process in Vietnam.

The main measures adopted in Doi Moi were designed to reconstruct the economy along free market lines. And these were manifested in two specific ways:

1. First, state subsidies to the state sector to cover its operating losses were to be gradually phased out. State enterprises were to be responsible for their own profits and losses.

2. Second, the subsidization of prices and wages would cease and there was to be a sharp reduction in internal trade barriers and a liberalization of foreign trade.

The reforms were hampered by inflation caused by inappropriate wage and price policy introduced in 1985, government budget deficits, and the inability of the banking system to enforce credit discipline. The situation worsened as Soviet aid was scaled down and financial assistance from non-socialist countries was not yet available. As a result of this crisis, the government adopted in 1989 a more radical measure to accelerate the reform process: the remaining elements of central planning were effectively removed, the decision making of producers and consumers was to be governed by market-determined wages, prices, interest rates, and foreign exchange rates, and fiscal adjustment and enterprise reconstruction.

One can distinguish four specific features of the Doi Moi programme:

1. The socialist industrialization model giving top priority to heavy industry at the expense of agriculture and light industry which had been used for thirty years in Vietnam was now dismantled and reversed.

The industrialization programme had resulted in shortages of daily necessities and raw materials for industry. It is fair to say that there was a strategy shift in policy towards agriculture after 1979, but huge state investment still went to heavy industry. Under the Doi Moi, state investment outlays had to be adjusted, with top priority being reversed to agriculture and light industry and then to heavy industry. During the Fourth Five-Year Plan (1986–90), the 'Three Major Economic Programs: the production of foodstuffs, consumer goods, and export products' accounted for almost 70% of total state investment.

2. The market economy was accepted as a new policy and measures were taken to make sure that the market mechanism could work.

Before 1986, it was the belief that a planned economy was incompatible with a market economy. After the adoption of market economics, price control was eliminated, except in the cases of electric power, fuel oil, and transport fares. The currency exchange rate was liberalized in 1989, and interest rates were raised to an above inflation level to encourage savings.

Subsidies to state enterprises were limited, and tax reforms were introduced to increase the government tax base and to reduce delays in collecting revenue. As a result of these measures, the state budget deficit declined from 8.4% of GDP in 1989 to 1.7% in 1992.

3. Private ownerships were allowed in all activities.

Before the Doi Moi, the socialist economic policy which was adopted in the North and then extended to the South permitted only semi-private ownership and private ownership only in handicraft sectors. In 1988, the development of the private sector started. The Company and Private Business Laws were enacted in 1990 to liberalize controls of ownerships. In 1992, the government's pilot programme to privatize some profitable state-owned enterprises in non-strategic sectors was proposed and it listed seven of these companies for privatization. Although private ownership of land is still not permitted, various incentives have been introduced to boost agricultural production: the cooperative system was dismantled, land leases were changed from annual contracts to 15 years with lease extension and right-to-use transfer options, market and price controls were eliminated. As a result, Vietnam has substantially increased its agricultural production and has become the third largest rice exporter in the world market since 1989 (Nguyen Thi Van Anh, 1995).

4. An 'open door policy' in foreign economic relations was adopted giving emphasis to foreign trade, commercial relations, and economic, scientific, and technical cooperation with the rest of the world.

Under this policy, export expansion, which is one component of the 'Three Major Economic Programs' of Doi Moi, was given top priority. To support this policy, the Foreign Investment Law was promulgated in 1987.

During the Fourth Five-Year Plan, national income rose by 4.3% against a target of 8%. Agricultural and industrial production also rose by 1.4% and 5.6% respectively. These results are against the targets of 6.2% and 9% however.

Partly as a result of the successes of the Doi Moi programme in terms of the fairly substantial positive growth rates in GDP, agriculture, and industry, the Seventh National Congress of the Communist Party of Vietnam has decided to push the programme further as an economic development strategy for Vietnam in the current Fifth Five-Year Plan (1991–95) until the year 2000.

The main focuses of these reforms are:

1. Further macroeconomic reforms via key ministries to improve economic management and tax revenue.

2. Reforms of the public sector by speeding up privatization of state enterprises, selecting priorities for public investment especially in infrastructure, education, and health care.

3. Development of legal and other regulatory framework to support the activities of the market economy.

4. Promotion of further development of the private sector.

5. Strengthening of the outward programme by further liberalizing the trade regime and promoting foreign direct investment. This is to be achieved through simplification of procedures for issuing trade and investment permits and licences, and tax codes.

3.4 Vietnam's Current Macroeconomic Performance (1987–95)

Since the micro and macroeconomic reforms of the Doi Moi period starting in 1986, the economy of Vietnam has overcome a long period of recession, established the basis for a market economy, supported the freedom to make business according to the laws, opened up its economy to trade with the world, and is currently moving to a new stage of economic development that emphasizes sustainable growth, industrialization and modernization.

Some of the performance of the economy of Vietnam since 1986 can be assessed via the movements of major economic indicators such as prices, food supply, industrial and agricultural growth, overseas trade, economic structure, international economic relations and finance (Le Dang Doanh, 1995). In the case of prices, the rising trend of super inflation as occurring in the mid-1980s was curtailed. More specifically, since 1986, the case of super high inflation of 800% per year in 1988 has been reduced to 5.3% in 1993. The consumer price index for 1994 was a mere 14.4%. Chronic food shortages of the 1970s and 1980s have been surmounted. Vietnam now can not only provide a stable supply of food to its 73 million people, but also has acquired the status of the third largest rice exporter in the world.

During the 1970s, economic growth in Vietnam can be said at best to have stagnated, and in the 1980s, it was around 5% per year. However, the annual growth rate has increased to 6.3% in 1991, 8.3% in 1992, and 8% in 1993. In 1994, the rate of increase of GDP was 8.7%, and this was expected to be 10% in 1995.

Industrial output in Vietnam reached an average growth rate of 12% per year from 1991–93. In 1994 however, this output reached 13% as compared to the targeted rate of 11%. Agricultural production had increased on average by 4.5% per year in the same period, and for 1994, it reached 4.5% despite the big losses of crop due to natural disasters in Vietnam.

In the late 1980s, Vietnam lost the traditional markets of the former USSR and the East European countries which had taken a share of 65% of Vietnam's exports and 75% of its imports (in 1990). As a result, there is a need for finding new markets for Vietnam's products and their trade. Nowadays, Vietnam is trading with about 100 countries in the world, including the USA. About 85% of Vietnam's foreign trade is conducted with countries in East Asia. In the past three years, exports have reached an average growth rate of 20% per year or about USD 3,600 million. During the years 1995 and 1996, Vietnam's exports (at the annual growth rates of 22.2% and 23.5% respectively) have been predicted to exceed the increases in exports of all major ASEAN countries such as Indonesia, Malaysia, the Philippines, Singapore, and Thailand (Tan, 1996). In fact, these export growth rates exceed those in all NIC, NAFTA, and CER economies, as well as Japan, China, Chile, Colombia, and Peru (Tan, 1996, p. 4). Imports for this period were however USD 4,500 million.

Domestic government revenue has increased very rapidly. Domestic government revenue in 1993 increased by 55% over the previous year and 280% over 1991. In 1994, it continued to increase by about 39.2% over the year 1993. In relation to all government current expenditures, domestic government revenue share was 12.8% in 1991, 16.7% in 1992, 20.2% in 1993, and 22.7% in 1994. The contribution from domestic government revenue to national savings was about 10%. In spite of these improvements in government revenue, government budget deficits were 1.9% of the GDP in 1991, 2.4% in 1992, 5.8% in 1993, and 3.56% in 1994.

In contrast to the fast changes in the economic indicators above, the economic structure of Vietnam has only changed slowly. The share of industrial output to GDP rose from 18.8% in 1990 to 19.5% in 1991,

20.2% in 1992, 21% in 1993, and 22% in 1994. Agricultural output fell on the other hand from 42.7% in 1980, 40.4% in 1990, 38.9% in 1991, 38.2% in 1992, to 36.6% in 1993. In 1994, the share was 38.2%.

In terms of sectoral development, the state sector has been expanding both in absolute and relative terms. In 1991, its share of GDP was 35.8%, and has been increasing at 39.9% in 1992, 37.4% in 1993, and 42% in 1994. The private sector on the other hand has been increasing more rapidly. This has contributed significantly to the higher output growth rate of the economy. As a result, the effect of all this change is that the general living standard and conditions of the people have been improved. There is a general agreement within Vietnam that all groups of people in the country strongly support the economic reforms brought about by Doi Moi. This includes both urban and rural populations. The performance of the economy has been seen as remarkable. The achievements of the economic reforms have also been acknowledged as irrevocable and irreversible, due in part to their momentum and deepening impact throughout the various sectors of the economy.

Further reforms are considered moreover to be irresistable when the prospects of Vietnam's economy both on the domestic and international levels are taken into account. On the international front, the normalization of the relations between Vietnam and the IMF and the World Bank has opened the way to the world's capital markets for the Vietnamese economy. The Donors Conference in November 1993 promised Vietnam to have access to USD 1.86 billion in soft loans and in official development assistance (ODA). The Paris Club has accepted a programme of rescheduling Vietnam's USD 4.5 billion in hard currency debts. The lifting of the US embargo on Vietnam in February 1994 has also opened commercial relations between Vietnam and the USA. At the Consultative Meeting in November 1994, another USD 2 billion was promised to Vietnam for the year 1995. The World Bank, the IMF, and the Asian Development Bank have provided credits for reconstruction of the economy.

For its part, Vietnam has made a strong effort to be integrated economically with the world economy. It has received the status of an official observer at GATT, APEC and PECC, and has applied to join the World Trade Organization (WTO). Recently, Vietnam has signed a framework agreement with the European Union. Vietnam officially became a member of the ASEAN on 28 July 1995.

The activities above will surely help to create a favourable environment for economic development and progress (a blueprint for developments) in Vietnam in the foreseeable future.

4 VIETNAM'S BLUEPRINT FOR DEVELOPMENTS

Vietnam's prospects to the year 2010 and beyond can be assessed in terms of its present structure, economic activity, planning strategies, and, more importantly, micro and macroeconomic performance in all sectors of the economy in the past few years. The patterns, movements, changes, trends, growth strategies and economic activity of Vietnam – its blueprint – will help to direct its future path for planning, development, investment, business, trade, and cooperation.

While the blueprint for Vietnam's economic development and modernization is officially or unofficially in place, a number of possible obstacles have also been identified as being present and capable of impeding to some extent the planned development and modernization. Some of these obstacles are described below, as are some of the possible solutions to the problems.

4.1 Obstacles to Economic Developments

Despite the tremendous progress in the past three years, the economy of Vietnam is still a newly developing and transitional economy in an agrarian set-up which has been trying to exploit mainly its natural resources.

Per capita GDP, production and consumption on such basic goods and commodities as electricity, fuel, steel, cement, etc. are among the lowest in the the world. While foreign direct investment (FDI) has been regarded as the driving force of economic development and expansion especially in developing economies, Vietnam still lacks the required capital to support its various development programmes. This lack of capital has forced Vietnam to move to attract overseas capital inflows. For example, by 25 December 1993, 836 projects had been licenced with a total registered capital of USD 7.5 billion to operate in Vietnam. However in the first six months of 1994, 185 additional projects with a total registered capital of USD 2 billion were granted licences to operate.

In order to support a targeted annual growth rate of 10% however, Vietnam would need an amount of USD 50 billion in investment, especially in FDI, since Vietnam's domestic savings are still low by international or even ASEAN standards. The competitiveness of Vietnamese products is also low even in the domestic market, and the country is basically agricultural. Agriculture is still 36.6% of GDP, and 78% of the population are living in the rural regions of the country. This economic structure is incompatible with a high and sustainable growth rate.

A huge gap between the developments in Vietnam and those in other countries in the region exists. And this gap can only be reduced by higher but sustainable growth rates over many decades in the future.

The population growth rate of 2.2% per year in Vietnam is too high and would defeat the GDP growth rate of 10% per year, as targeted by economic planners in Vietnam. For twenty years, a reduction of the population growth rate to 1.7% per year has been the government policy, but it has not been achieved. Much more effort by the government to quickly attain this level has to be undertaken.

Unemployment and underemployment, either created by economic reforms or by the natural winding down of the armed forces during relative peace times, are serious issues and are also creating many problems with social implications.

Physical infrastructure which is necessary to promote economic development and increase production is in very poor condition and requires huge investment to upgrade it. Investment in human resources (for example, education and health care) is equally needed.

Domestic savings and investment are abnormally low and do not allow a high and sustainable growth rate. In order to reach a targeted annual growth rate of 10%, Vietnam needs to double its domestic savings and investment and to sustain it at 30% of GDP for decades. Preliminary calculations have indicated that, in fact, Vietnam would need USD 50 billion in investment into its economy by the year 2000 in order to achieve this annual growth rate of 10%. This requires that Vietnam build up an economy with more sophisticated technologies by then.

Macroeconomic imbalances also create many concerns. Government budget deficits are high, and potentially may lead to a recurrence of high inflation. By July 1995, it was estimated that the annual inflation rate in Vietnam would be about 19.5%. At this rate, Vietnam would have a negative real growth rate.

In terms of external debts, Vietnam still owes a lot to the former USSR and other countries. This will remain a real burden of debt repayments and will affect the balance of payments for Vietnam for many years in the future. A solution to this problem is growth in production and also in exports.

The market economy, while getting a boost from the supply of experts trained in laissez-faire economics by international foundations and agencies in the past few years, has not yet been fully established

(Le Dang Doanh, 1995). It must be admitted however that the steps taken to transform the economy by training officials in Western and market economics are correct, even if the benefits are longer-term.

The role and the function of the state are not yet reformed sufficiently to satisfy the needs of a market economy (Le Dang Doanh, 1995). Public administration has also to be quickly reformed and streamlined to respond efficiently to market economics management and practices. This is a more pressing problem in the reform agenda as the office of the Prime Minister in Vietnam and some of the recent cases reported in the media have indicated.

4.2 Vietnam's Growth and Development Strategies

In order to maintain the impetus of economic growth and developments achieved in the past few years, Vietnam has to continue economic reforms on a consistent basis and to overcome problems faced by the economy in the existing transitional stage of the reforms.

Some of the pertinent issues and their possible solutions are described below. First, a well functioning market mechanism with the appropriate legal framework must be created. This includes the establishment of a legal capital market (the currently proposed Stock Market Centre in Hanoi for Vietnam is a good example of this development), a securities market, the legalization of the real estate market, the reform of the banking system, the gradual creation of a convertible currency and the management of the exchange rate of the Vietnamese Dong (VND) in the interest of an export-oriented economy.

Further reforms of the taxation system and public finance must be implemented in order to reduce the overly high budget deficit and to keep inflation (which in the first six months of 1995 reached an annualized rate of 19.5%) under control. The inflation rate must be lower than the GDP growh rate and must be one digit. Serious and consistent efforts must be made for the implementation of a legal bill and receipt system, a sound book-keeping and accounting system, and independent auditing and transparency on annual financial sheets of all types of business, including the commercial state banks. These are elementary and obligatory preconditions for an efficient management system and for international cooperation (Le Dang Doanh, 1995).

Efficient coordination of the ODA projects within the framework of a national master plan of development must be ensured. The inflow of foreign capital in the different forms – ODA, FDI, commercial loans, etc. – requires a system of controls and guidance in order to avoid counter-productive effects.

State-owned enterprises (SOE) must be reformed according to a well-prepared programme. On the one hand, the main SOEs must be reorganized and upgraded in order to be competitive, and to enhance efficiency. On the other hand, small and medium-sized SOEs which are no longer relevant in a market economy have to be reformed within the framework of a programme for change.

Short of substantial financial assistance from international countries and organizations, the private sector needs more assistance and promotion from the state in order to make a greater contribution to development of the national economy. Domestic capital can be better mobilized for economic expansion and social development. Importantly, Vietnam has to establish and sustain a competitive investment environment protected by enforceable laws and international agreements and treaties in order to further attract FDI. This can be done through training, research and education, as well as through trade promotion and the introduction of suitable investment and taxation laws.

A master plan for industrialization and modernization of the national economy for different sectors and regions must be elaborated and coordinated. A similar plan in the form of a roadmap for economic reforms must also be elaborated and implemented. Equally Vietnam needs to coordinate the reforms in other social sectors such as education, health care and social insurance which are increasingly important for social and economic progress. Also, Vietnam must introduce immediately efficient measures to protect the environment by intensifying the monitoring of the exploitation of natural resources.

Reforms of public administration are under preparation. They must be combined with the economic reforms and focus on building a legal state of the people, by the people, and for the people, a competent and efficient public administration, and a reduction of smuggling and corruption to a minimum.

There is a dialectic relation between reforms, social and political stability and growth of the economy (Le Dang Doanh, 1995). In order to sustain stability, Vietnam needs to reach high economic growth and tangible social progress. But stability does not mean inertia and stagnation. High economic growth and reforms require a stable social and political environment as well as a competent and efficient and responsive-to-the public administration.

Finally, in the next few years Vietnam needs to overcome fairly and squarely the obstacles and the problems it currently is beset with in order to reach an economic take-off. For the long term, a bright future is facing the Vietnamese nation. This leads us to a summary of the prospects for Vietnam in the next ten or twenty years.

5 VIETNAM'S PROSPECTS TO 2010 AND BEYOND

5.1 General Prospects

Although Vietnam has the potential to be a major market and economy in the ASEAN in particular and in the Asia Pacific in general early in the twenty-first century or (as some have suggested) at the beginning of the twenty-first century, it must first face some significant challenges and obstacles. Some of these obstacles have been described earlier.

From the political standpoint, Vietnam is now a free and democratic country with freely elected members of the national congress. It has been claimed by some prominent senior Vietnamese government officials that Vietnam, for more than a century, is not only free from foreign occupation but also free from foreign predominance as well as foreign models.

The fact that Vietnam has been able to achieve remarkable economic results in the past few years, while other socialist countries, including the former USSR, have almost gone under, suggests that maybe Vietnam's economic progress and success are unique. It is perhaps based upon this perception of a unique path of economic development and its outcomes that the present government of Vietnam wishes to embark upon programmes to promote further progress for the country and for all aspects of it, be they social, political, or economic.

While it is proper for Vietnam to decide by itself its own way of development, it is interesting to note that its own way is dictated nevertheless by the universal principles of attainment of social progress and economic gain: to create a prosperous economy for all its people, to maintain an orderly state ruled by laws, to create a civilized and harmonious society, and to be a friend and trading country of all nations in the region and beyond.

Future prospects for Vietnam and its success depend largely upon these guiding principles, applied both on the international and domestic levels. On the international level, Vietnam has to find ways to integrate its economy into the regional and world economy, to narrow the economic and social gaps with the countries in the region, and as a result, to deal with competition from the countries in the ASEAN, the Asia Pacific, and beyond. Towards this end, Vietnam has signed a great number of international conventions, bilateral agreements (e.g., for the protection of mutual investments, avoidance of double taxation, and acceptance of international arbitrage for settlement of business disputes).

Vietnam is also a recipient of a large number of aids from private (such as the Ford Foundation, the Fulbright Foundation, the Sasakawa Foundation etc.) and international (such as the World Bank, the ADB, the IMF, the UNDP, SIDA, CIDA, AusAid, etc.) organizations to help it modernize the economy and complete the transition from a command economy to a free market one or a mixed economy.

On 28 July 1995, Vietnam became the seventh member of the ASEAN. It also has applied to be an associate member of the Asia Pacific Economic Cooperation (APEC) forum and of the WTO. Currently, Vietnam is receiving financial aid from Japan to familiarize its experts with the working of this international trading organization.

It is well known in economic theory that the tenet of free market economics worldwide is simply: competition promotes growth, quality of goods and services, and improves the living conditions of the people. In order to support this tenet, Vietnam has, on the domestic level, started to introduce a legal framework for a market economy in accordance with international standards where competition is the key of operation. The first right step in this direction was the Bankruptcy Law which was promulgated in December 1993. The Constitution of 1992 also has legalized the economic reforms of Doi Moi, including matters of private ownerships and market mechanisms. It is worth noting that since 1988, Vietnam has promulgated 38 laws and 50 decrees-laws. There are about 10,000 by-laws passed by the government. These include the Company Law, Private Business Law, and Bankruptcy Law.

The role of the National Assembly has been strengthened. Now, it has a more important function buttressed by the promulgation of laws and by expressing the voices of the voters in the formulation of government economic policies. Some of these notable examples are fights against smuggling and corruption.

Public administration has been streamlined. State agencies are now more interested in feedback information from the business community, and more ready to have dialogues with the people. Also more economic information has been made available to the local and international public through dissemination of reports and statistical bulletins and also through international collaboration between government ministries and foreign governments, institutions, corporations or individuals.

Foreign direct investment has been given a priority status by the government and large FDI projects have been recorded in recent years. In the past, Vietnam did not have sufficient capital to embark on significant economic developments, and economic policy was mainly directed at a reduction of inflation.

Today Vietnam can attract and has actively promoted to attract (via a number of current research, training, and consulting projects – of say the Ministry of Trade in Vietnam – to study and promote FDI) further FDI for its industrialization and modernization of the economy. There is a call now for an efficient economic policy to utilize this source of capital from FDI to repay debts and to sustain a competitive investment environment.

The prospects for Vietnam can be reflected by the fact that, in the past few years, its internal economic development had pushed ahead under the conditions of severe external unfavourable restrictions such as the decline of Soviet aids after 1989 and the US embargo to February 1994.

Economic development of Vietnam now has a more favourable environment to promoting growth and investment than in the past few years. This environment includes the cancellation of all direct subsidies through prices, the introduction of a market pricing system, the depreciation of the Vietnamese currency VND, the unification of different exchange rates by introducing an official floating managed exchange rate regime, a two-tiered banking system, positive real interest rates, and the liberalization of domestic trade and commercial and non-commercial trade.

Vietnam has also fundamentally changed its import and export markets to overcome the collapse of the former USSR which was its most important foreign trade customer and its largest credit provider until 1990. Foreign trade now has been deregulated, moving from the state monopoly of foreign trade to more open and diversified participation of the private sector. This has helped to increase exports more than ever before.

The entire taxation system has been successively overhauled, allowing a higher mobilization of domestic revenue to the budget. Rapidly rising government expenditures can now be covered in this way. The first modest government savings have even been reported and since 1992, the government has ended the use of credit from the Central Bank to cover even part of the budget deficit. The SNA-based system has been introduced in the national economic accounting system to be consistent with international practice. A new accounting system whereby the annual financial statements of all registered companies are to be compulsorily audited and transparent will be introduced in 1995.

From a general perspective then, the prospects of Vietnam in the next decade or so depend upon and will be moulded by these fast developments in many sectors and in many regions in Vietnam's economy. Surely, the prospects are there for those who now see the potentials of Vietnam and are prepared to participate or invest physically and financially in it.

One of the many countries that has taken the challenge in Vietnam and attempted to exploit the opportunities available there is Australia. The involvement of Australia in Vietnam has a long history going back over 40 years, and it includes both the government and private sectors.

Below, we give an account of what Australia is doing in Vietnam at the present time. This provides the foundation for future cooperation and development. In other words, the prospects in Vietnam for investment from the private and public, political and commercial, institutional and individual sectors in Australia depend largely on the current activities as well as the targets set by the government of Vietnam in its planning programmes.

Put in another way, the prospects for Australia in Vietnam follow the likely trends of the current operations and involvements by Australian agencies and corporations and individuals in the future to the year 2010 or beyond in tandem with Vietnam's official economic strategies. These prospects should also be looked at from the perspective of an international competitive environment since, in terms of investment in Vietnam at this stage, Australia is only ranked sixth among other nations with a commercial interest in Vietnam.

5.2 Prospects for Australia

From a general perspective, the prospects in terms of trade, business, and cooperation for Australia in Vietnam are good and are expected to grow at a rapid rate. This assessment is based on bilateral trade activity between the two countries, private investment activity and cooperation by Australian companies in Vietnam (ranked sixth – or even fifth – in terms of investment value in the list of all investing countries in Vietnam as at 1995), and also on increasing aids from the Australian government to assist Vietnam's economic development and modernization programmes to promote trade and investment between the two countries.

Aid from the Australian government (through DEET and DFAT) to Vietnam is expected to increase as a result of Australia's current general commitment on international aid, and its promotion of future trade and investment. It is also a favourable fact on the part of Australia that it has established long-term working relationships with Vietnam in many areas of commerce (and politics) in the past 35 years or so, from the time of the Commonwealth Bandung Conference establishing the Colombo Plan. These relationships have grown especially stronger since June 1990 when agreements on trade and cooperation were signed between the two countries. Since then regular meetings have taken place (March 1991, August 1992, and October 1993) in order to find ways to promote and expand cooperation, business, and trade.

Since 1990, the trade balance between Vietnam and Australia has increased more than ten times (from AUD 41.9 million to AUD 452.9 million). The areas of trade expansion include economics, sciences, technology, arts, education, and training. This trend is expected to continue in the next decade or so either on a bilateral basis or because of the presence or existence of regional economic association frameworks such as AFTA and APEC.

Up to July 1995, Australia was ranked number six in terms of FDI in Vietnam with 46 investment projects totalling USD 668 million in capital. Given the different cultures between Vietnam and Australia and the small size of the population of Australia, the ranking is especially significant, and it has some implications for future trade and business between Australia and Vietnam.

The following patterns of economic development and their likely resulting prospects for trade, business, and investment in the various sectors and regions in Vietnam have been prepared by official planning agencies. They will be used as the yardsticks in our report to provide the likely trends and directions in the future. These trends and directions will assist government agencies and the business community in Australia to formulate reliable policies for the purpose of business, trade, and investment between the two countries.

The discussions below cover the current and planned activities of the Australian public and private sectors in Vietnam and the implied prospects for Australian agencies, institutions and corporations. The opportunities for individual business people in Vietnam are also examined and are related to the planning policy of the government of Vietnam for the next decade or so. The plan of the discussions is divided into three parts:

1. Trade prospects
2. Investment and cooperation prospects
3. Official government development aid programmes

5.2.1 Trade

In 1993, trade between Australia and Vietnam totalled AUD 366.8 million and this consisted of AUD 251 million in exports and AUD 115.5 million in imports. The increase of this trade over 1990 is nine times. This is a remarkable achievement during the period of the US embargo on Vietnam. It seems reasonable on the grounds described above to predict that this trend will continue into the twenty-first century.

In 1994, trade rose by 23.5% to AUD 452.9 with AUD 289.4 million in exports (a rise of 15%) and AUD 163.5 million in imports (a rise of 41.5%). This rapid growth in trade between Australia and Vietnam was among the fastest growth in the world during this period. In the first six months of 1995, preliminary estimates indicate a trade of AUD 550 million of which exports accounted for AUD 340 and imports for AUD 210 (including trade through a third country).

The trade imbalance in favour of Vietnam at this stage indicates that greater efforts on the part of the private and government trade sectors in Australia can be made to expand its exports to Vietnam. This can be achieved through the promotion, niches-identifying, partners-identifying, capital raising, and contract-signing efforts of both Australian government agencies (such as Austrade) and the private business sectors.

In a recent report (see Tran Van Hoa, 1995), it is found that almost all Vietnamese companies covering about 12 sectors of the economy and interviewed in our survey in Hanoi during February–April 1995 indicate that they do not know anything about Australia and wish to make contact with Australian companies for business purposes.

Contact through trade associations or chambers of commerce and industry in both countries can be made in order to introduce likely business investment partners. This contact could help to avoid mismatched, misrepresented, or ill-suited connections with damaging results to both parties, as many overseas companies have reported.

With the introduction of a stock exchange centre in Hanoi soon, the capital market will have better facilities for attracting capital inflows and for the distribution of these into profitable industries in an efficient manner. An obstacle to this interesting development is an acute shortage of skilled manpower in the management of physical and financial commodities in Vietnam.

Specialist training in this area of human resources is a priority in the financial and banking systems in Vietnam, as identified recently by Vietnam's Ministry of Trade. It is in this type of activity that Australia could provide much needed expertise to Vietnam in the future. Some training support has already been given by the Australian government in this case through mainly AusAid and DEET programmes. At this stage the private sector in Australia plays a small role in this activity.

Another prominent feature of the growth in trade in Vietnam in recent years is a surplus in exports, especially in crude oil. In addition to crude oil, Vietnam also exported seafoods, coffee, footwear etc.. The volume of trade in these commodities was not large, due to strong competition from the countries in the region, especially China with its better quality products and cheaper prices.

Australia could provide help of mutual benefit to Vietnam here in the form of manufacturing and marketing technology transfer through joint venture activity or through training programmes. It also can provide funds for market research by Vietnamese or Australian experts to identify suitable areas of market penetration in Australia for Vietnamese goods and vice versa.

Imports from Australia include refined oil which accounted for one third of all trade in 1994, and electrical products, communications, medicine, mining, transport, cotton, wool, chemicals, and foodstuff. A promotion campaign to introduce other Australian products and expertise such as sugar, wheat, and cold storage technology, would certainly enhance trade flows from Australia to Vietnam.

Exports from Vietnam to Australia can also be re-exported to other countries. Products imported from Australia are of a better quality and in high demand even if they are more expensive. A difficult problem in this case is the long distance transport and costs between Vietnam and Australia which will render Australian products less competitive in relation to other countries trading with Vietnam. Increased efficiency and productivity through economies of scale and high-tech production and management and distribution may overcome these problems. Joint ventures are another standard solution adopted by many transnational companies in other parts of the world to similar problems.

Another solution here is to create suitable niches in trade (for example, Telstra in communications, BHP for oil and gas exploration) for the Australian goods and services that can be identified and have a comparative advantage in Vietnam.

As a by-product of a niche in Vietnam, Australia should also expect to have the flow-on effects of its experience and operation in Vietnam onto other countries in the region, notably Cambodia, Laos, and Myanmar (the so-called Greater Indochina).

As part of a niche creation programme, it is interesting to note that plans have been made between Vietnam and Australia to exchange trade information, enhance contact between businesses in the two countries, organize exhibitions of Vietnamese products in Sydney and Melbourne (April 1994), and to provide short training courses on market research, banking facilities etc.. These efforts have helped to improve trade between Australia and Vietnam but the level of activity is still low considering the possible links between Australia and Vietnam. More active promotion of Australian goods and services in Vietnam is required. This can be done via stronger investment commitments and wide-ranging cooperation between the two countries.

This action is more relevant when one takes note that in the next ten years or so, Vietnam has formulated plans to produce more import-substitution goods and at the same time to promote greater exports.

5.2.2 Investment, Business, and Cooperation

As its major development and modernization programmes to catch up with developing and developed countries in the region or in the global context, Vietnam places importance on:

1. High growth rates and long-term successes in industrialization
2. Exports-oriented and import-substitution manufacturing
3. Adoption of market economics and streamlining of public administration
4. Exploitation of domestic natural resources as a priority
5. Encouragement to higher domestic saving rate
6. Decentralization and establishment of satellite cities for big metropolises and small cities along main regional routes
7. Protection of industrialized and investment projects

These programmes require huge physical and human resources to support them in the short as well as long term. Vietnam as it is today is not able to meet the requirements of these programmes without assistance from outside countries.

The prospects for Australia are derived from the benefits of investment, cooperation, and business with Vietnam in tandem with these targets and, as has been discussed before, the long-standing relationship between Vietnam and Australia.

In terms of investment, until July 1995, Australian companies were granted 58 investment permits worth a total of USD 870.3 million, in which 49 projects are operating with an investment of USD 668 million, and in which nine projects (15.5% of all projects) worth USD 202.3 million (23% of all investment value) have been withdrawn.

These rates of withdrawing are higher than the national investment withdrawal rates which are 15% of all projects and 7% of investment value.

Australian investment in Vietnam is concentrated in the areas of major economic importance such as oil and gas exploration, coal, steel exports, telecommunications, pharmaceutical products and banking.

Investment outside these areas may be more beneficial to Australia, and also provide good prospects. Possible areas in which Australia has a comparative advantage in Vietnam are hydroelectricity, farming techniques, forest management, and electronics, to name a few.

5.2.2.1 Oil, Gas, and Mining

Exploration of oil and gas (the major national natural resource), manufacturing of oil-based products, the building of at least two oil refineries, and mining of precious stones etc. are four major objectives in the long-term development programmes of the government of Vietnam to at least the year 2020. In these respects, Australia has featured well in Vietnam and its prospects for further investment and cooperation are excellent. Current activity by Australia in oil, gas and mining are described below.

Large oil and gas projects by BHP are on stream (except Lots 120 and 121 off the central coast which are to close down due to non-economic prospects). Lot Dai Hung 05-1A has started producing oil and in the first six months of 1995 generated USD 20.7 million income. This is only a quarter of the predicted amount.

Current renegotiations on cooperation are being made. BHP is also working with a number of companies to develop and administer gas production offshore in Southern Con Son. Anzoil of Australia and New Zealand also is exploring the Red River basin near Tien Hai.

Collaboration between Vietnam and Telstra Australia has produced results, and in 1994, both parties had increased their investment in order to improve telecommunications facilities in Vietnam.

Other projects in the mining area which have received permits include those by Canada: gold mining in Bong Mieu, graphite extraction in Lao Cai (which due to a current lack of markets may cease), sand mining in Da Nang (which has not operated due to a lack of capital), and Vinausteel in Thai Nguyen (which will start production late in 1995 at about 180,000 tons per year).

The Ministry of Heavy Industry has issued five permits to Australian companies for mining exploration (copper in Sinh Quyen, Lao Cai, gold in Pi Toong, Son La, and Hinh River, Phu Yen, zinc in Cho Don, Na Tum, Bac Thai, gold in Tra Nang, Lam Dong, and gold in Luong Son, Hoa Binh). In addition, a number of Australian companies have asked for permits for gold exploration in Lai Chau, Da Lat, Ninh Thuan, Binh Thuan; Ma River, Thanh Hoa, Nghia Lo and Quang Ninh. These have to wait until the government ratifies its policy on primary (mining) product developments.

On chemicals, BHP is preparing a joint project to produce one million tons of urea from natural gas in Southern Con Son.

On oil, gas, and mining activity then, Australian companies seem to have good prospects in Vietnam. This is achieved through past cooperation and commitments and also through Australia's comparative advantage in this activity.

While other international companies (such as Samsung from South Korea) have started their investment on offshore oilfield exploration in Vietnam, this is however done against a background of a long-standing relationship between Vietnam and Australia. The competition is nevertheless there.

As Vietnam is also interested in plans for mining and extraction of precious stones etc. in the country, this area of investment and training would present another good prospect for Australian companies and they could, due to their expertise and experience, do well in the future in Vietnam in particular and in Indochina and Myanmar in general.

5.2.2.2 Energy

In its industrialization, Vietnam places importance on the energy sector, especially on the domestic capability to exploit further coal reserves, to manufacture petroleum, and to produce LPG.

Hydroelectricity is another target for development in Vietnam. This is particularly relevant since Vietnam has plans to utilize during the next 20 years or so its abundant water energy resources. It should also be noted that Vietnam has the world's sixth largest hydroelectric station in Hoa Binh.

The demand for energy in Vietnam continues to grow at a rapid pace. By 2000, Vietnam requires 25–27 billion kWh and by 2010 it has a projected need of 68–75 billion kWh. By 2010, Vietnam will consider a plan to build a nuclear power station. Some activity by Australia in these areas of energy is described below.

Coal washing ventures (in Cua Ong, Cam Pha) have produced good results. The construction of a coal washing station in Nam Cau Trang, Hon Gai, and a joint venture to build a factory to produce coal-based products are also under way.

Some Australian companies from Queensland are interested in developing further coal-based products for exports in the city of Quang Ninh.

As the coal reserves are enormous in this area with excellent sea export facilities, the prospects are there for suitable companies. A recent dispute between Westralian Sands and the local government in the area and the withdrawal of some companies from operation indicates that careful preparation should be made in this kind of activity.

On electricity, the Australian companies PPI and SECV have contributed to investment in technology in management, transmission, and protection to a high voltage (500KV) line between the North and the South. Also in the near future, Australia will provide technology to build a coal-based electricity station at Pha Lai II (600MW).

Other Vietnamese development programmes on energy between 1996 and 2000 include a gas turbine station to produce electricity at Phu My (600MW), a hydroelectric station at Ham Thuan – Da My (472MW), and hydroelectricity at Song Hinh (70MW). Further development plans for energy production exist for the twenty-first century. Vietnam's requirements for energy programmes are urgent and in the medium term (1997–98) the government has set the objective to electrify the whole of Vietnam and provide an adequate supply of energy to industries and residential areas.

5.2.2.3 Construction

As Vietnam has embarked upon a modernization process of the economy, construction plays an important part in this development. As a result, an adequate supply of building materials especially cement, glass, ceramics, glazed tiles and steel is high on the priority list for development in the country.

In terms of building glass, Vietnam would require a total of 20–25 million squared metres by the year 2000. Also, it has been estimated that, by 2000, Vietnam will need 15–16 million tons of cement per year, and by 2010 it will have a projected requirement of 30 million tons of cement per year. Particular requirements for construction materials are from the regional areas where special needs for bricks, tiles, crushed stones, sand and pebbles etc. are acute in some cases.

At present, there are four Australia–Vietnam joint ventures in the construction area: Mekong to produce concrete in Ho Chi Minh City, a joint venture to build and develop Ho Chi Minh City, a joint venture Hai Van-Thiess to produce concrete in the South, and a joint venture to build houses in Hanoi. All are operating profitably. The joint venture Vina-Thiess has closed down as a result of non-profitable operations.

Vietnam has also imported building materials from Australia (toilet ceramics, water pipes) and concrete pumps, concrete mixers, and concrete manufacturing accessories for the facilities in Ha Tien.

Negotiations are being made between officials and investors, lawyers, advisers, and contractors in the construction sector in order to expand specialist training in the area.

Currently, Thailand provides some construction materials to Vietnam. Since some building materials from Australia (such as textured bricks) are known to have a better quality than Thai products, Australia could benefit in trade in this area if research shows that their quality and prices are competitive.

Some other transnational corporations such as Samsung from South Korea have started their investment in cement production in Vietnam. International competition is therefore present in this case.

5.2.2.4 Agriculture and Foodstuffs

At present, Vietnam has a high proportion of its national production in agriculture, and foodstuff technology is not adequate to supply the needs of the nation.

Prospects for Australia in this case are investment in the areas of high productivity techniques in agriculture (for example, rice and cane sugar production, irrigation, tea and coffee plantations, cattle farming etc.) and advanced food processing and storage technologies.

Vietnam is endowed with fertile agricultural land in the South, and for many centuries this land has produced the majority of rice (and rubber etc.) exports to neighbouring countries. In some northern areas of Vietnam, the number of crops per year has increased as a result of crop adaptation and improved irrigation. Australia could assist in this further by providing expertise in crop selection and genetic engineering in primary produce. In the Da Lat area, vegetables are grown abundantly in seasons. It is a lack of cold storage and transport technology and facilities that means this produce is not available throughout the year and in all regions of Vietnam. The prospects for investment and profits for a suitable Australian company in this area are excellent.

It is worth noting that Vietnam and the Australian Council for International Agricultural Research (ACIAR) have signed nine projects to carry out research on cattle raising, animal medicine, plantation, animal protection etc.. Some preliminary results are promising. Also, as part of the Australian government aid programme, a number of Vietnamese scientists have been offered scholarships to study agriculture and food technology overseas. Other initiatives include Australian investment in two cattle stations for milk production in the North. In the South, preparations are being made to set up similar facilities. A joint venture to produce timber was started in 1990 and is operating with a turnover of AUD 1 million per year. Lack of capital has prevented this company from producing more.

5.2.2.5 Fisheries

Vietnam has plans for rapid development of sea and freshwater farming, and of offshore fishing. At present, there is no bilateral cooperation between Australia and Vietnam on fisheries. In practice however, Australia has helped to build (via the International Ad Hoc Committee on the Mekong River) a green prawn farm in Vung Tau (completed in 1988).

Australia also has expertise on the farming of king prawns, pearl-bearing oysters, synthetic boats, aluminium cladding for boats, sea management, environmental protection, and other sea products. This expertise could be exploited by Australian companies for business developments in Vietnam.

Training by Australian training organizations and institutions in these areas of expertise would also be profitable as far as investment in training is concerned.

5.2.2.6 Forestry

Being devastated during the war years, the forests of Vietnam have not recovered from the damages sustained during this period. This is aggravated further by unplanned usage of timber and forests in all regions of Vietnam. That is, the usage is not being compensated adequately by reforestation and other regreening programmes.

In the past, Australian non-government organizations have provided small grants (worth about AUD 300,000) to forestry associations and these have produced good results in terms of technology, forestry training, and improved forestry expertise of Vietnamese officials.

The Ministry of Forestry has supported four collaborative projects with Australia to improve technology, reforestation, the greening of bald hills, and the restoration of Tam Dao, Vinh Phu, and Dac Lac forests, and Ba Vi hills (National Park).

As a result of many years of war activity, Vietnam is currently short of timber products, and it also lacks the expertise in timber plantation. In view of Vietnam's economic development however, there is and will be a permanent shortage of timber. Investment in capital and expertise by Australia in (softwood) timber plantation (for paper and building products and for environment protection purposes) seems acutely required in this case.

The present programme of 'the return of the rubber industry' is being planned for 1995 to 2000 with the building of enough rubber processing factories to produce 40,000 tons of rubber per year.

Up to 600,000 to 700,000 hectares of rubber plantation will be available by the year 2020.

5.2.2.7 *Land Management*

Land management is important for Vietnam in its development process and in its preservation of national and historic landmarks and parks consistent and synchronized with sustainable industrial and rural environments.

From January 1993 to April 1994, the General Commission on Land Management completed the project 'Special Research on Land Management in Vietnam' funded by the UNDP and the government of Western Australia for three cities: Hanoi, Hue, and Ho Chi Minh City. This has helped to modernize land management procedures, to provide training to officials, and to widen development options.

Further investment and participation by Australia in town and urban planning activity as well as resort holiday development (for example, in Do Son, near Hai Phong, and in Sa Pa, near Lao Cai) and environment impact studies (such as the case of hotel construction in the Ho Hoan Kiem area in Hanoi) and other land use and management activity would provide valuable opportunities for Vietnam.

Real estate management is another area of activity and investment that Vietnam is acutely in need of. Prospects here are promising for the Australian Real Estate Institute and other property development and management companies.

5.2.2.8 *Communications, Transport and Civil Aviation*

On sea transport, Australia is looking for overseas partners for ship building in Vietnam.

On railways, Vietnam has bought 13 second-hand diesel locomotives,

11 of which are working well. Queensland Railways has sent experts to Vietnam to advise on a suitable gauze rail system and to train railway officials.

On his last visit to Australia, the Secretary General of the VCP, Do Muoi, signed an agreement to build a signal network between Hanoi and Lao Cai, and to build the railway bridge My Thuan on the Tien River.

Australia has provided 3,200 tons of steel during 1994/1995 to construct bridges over the rivers Gianh, Hien Luong, Lai Vu, and Duc Hue. Two Australian joint ventures on ready mix concrete and building materials are doing well.

As infrasructure is in bad shape after many years of war in Vietnam and, in addition, whatever is available now is far out of date with modern transport needs and technology, further cooperation between Australia and Vietnam is needed in this area of infrastructure improvement.

Vietnam has to study its marine needs and to sign agreements with Australia to develop necessary initiatives. Australia can provide its expertise in identifying some of these needs, and also provide investment to achieve the objectives so identified in Vietnam.

In accordance with their aviation agreements, the two countries, during 1994 and mid-1995, operated 113 flights by Qantas (15,765 passengers and 19.7 tons of cargo) and 113 flights by Vietnam Airlines (13,288 passengers and 158.4 tons of cargo). This air traffic flow will rise as income per head in Vietnam improves. High on the list of future development in air traffic between Vietnam and Australia would be tourists or tour groups to Vietnam from Australia and vice versa later. To upgrade its personnel, expertise and fleet, Vietnam Airlines has also started its programme to train pilots with funds provided by Australia. It has also leased two Boeing 767 from Ansett Airlines and has sent its staff to Australia for pilot training, technology upgrading, air hostessing, and learning English.

On 31 July 1995, new aviation agreements between Australia and Vietnam were signed in Australia.

5.2.2.9 Vietnam Post

Telecommunications in Vietnam are available, but their prices are expensive even by the income per head standard of developed and industrialized countries. As a result of this supply and pricing policy, there is a plan by Vietnam to rectify the situation and to bring more competition (and lower costs in telecommunications) into the country.

A second telecommunications provider in the country was announced by the government of Vietnam a few months ago. Vietnam Post has successfully signed cooperation agreements with Telstra to improve international communications in Vietnam and has started the setting up of telecommunications links between Vietnam, Thailand and Hong Kong.

A joint venture to provide paging services in Ho Chi Minh City expired in 1994, but the company has asked for an extension of the service permit due to its success so far.

Vietnam and Australia have also collaborated on a project to study laws on post and telecommunications. Phase 1 of the project has been completed. Phase 2 of the project will commence soon.

The rise of the Internet and other cyber-space worldwide will have a great impact on telecommunications in Vietnam. There will therefore be a high demand for experts and facilities in this area.

Considering the current state of information technology in Vietnam and its future needs, the prospects here for hi-tech institutions and software training companies in Australia are enormous. (See section 5.2.2.15 below.)

5.2.2.10 Education and Training

In the process of modernization of the country and the economy, there is a need for reforms of the present education system in Vietnam. This has been recognized by the government and supported by international organizations such as the World Bank (which a few months ago made a loan of USD 400 million to Vietnam to carry out the reforms).

As far as Australia is concerned, assistance in education and training in Vietnam have been the domain of operation of the Australian government (through DEET and AusAid) and other governments to date. The private sector has only had a minor role. This is rather unfortunate, as the private sector or educational institutions in Australia could play a more active part in Vietnam's education reforms, training, and education. The bad experience suffered by Australia's private enterprises when moving into the education market in Asia in the past few years appears to be the main reason for this present inertia.

Since 1992, the ATAS scholarship programme of Australia has provided between 150 and 200 scholarships to Vietnamese officials to study English in Australia. During 1995/1996, Australia will provide 54 ADCOS undergraduate and postgraduate scholarships to Vietnam. These are select scholarships offered on merit only to students of good ability to study in Australia. As at May 1995, more than 2,000 students had applied for these scholarships.

The Ministry of Education and Training (MOET) in Vietnam and the Department of Employment, Education, and Training (DEET) in Australia have signed agreements to provide Vietnam with a number of short-term scholarships, funds to organize two seminars on vocational training and a number of small scholarships for educational training. At present, there are more than 400 students and researchers funded under this programme in Australia.

In addition, Vietnam has a number of agreements in many areas of study with many Australian states, universities, and research institutes, to upgrade the level of education and training of its officials. Good results have been obtained under these schemes.

As mentioned above, the marketing of education by Australian institutions in Vietnam is on a small scale at this stage and is dominated by a few universities or colleges while nominally represented by some education foundations. This is inadequate as the potential of Vietnam as a large market of education exports either in the country (with a branch of the Australian institution operating there) or in Australia (where Vietnamese students come to Australia for their studies) for other competent and enterprising organizations in Australia is substantial.

This education export income could exceed AUD 600 million per year as a rough estimate by 2010, and surpass many countries in Asia in terms of education export income for Australia. The multiplier effect of this injection of income into the economy can be more precisely measured by standard econometric methods if there is a need for it.

The potential for successful educational ventures comes from a number of sources. These include Vietnam's population of 73 million as at 1995, the country's deep-rooted yearning and admiration for learning – especially high learning, a national need for human resource development to promote growth, the fast rising per head income of the people, and a healthy respect for Australia's education system.

5.2.2.11 Human Resources

In its modernization process, Vietnam, due in part to a lack of funds and not to a lack of awareness of the problem, has not been able to carry out a retraining of its labour force in general or its officials in particular. There is a programme by the government of Vietnam (as made known via the State Planning Committee) however to retrain 20,000 cadres at all levels of function and in all regions in the country, if sufficient funding is available.

As far as overseas assistance is concerned, Vietnam and Australia have signed, in Australia, an agreement to initiate human resources development for Vietnam. The two countries have also exchanged experience, and cooperated to improve standards in the services industry. Vietnam has proposed to send officials to Australia to study industry practices, forestry management, and seafood products developments.

Again here, the prospects for the private sector in Australia to develop business in human resource development in Vietnam are good. This could be done as a joint enterprise between the Australian or other international governments and a training company or institution.

A current initiative which is worth mentioning is that from Wollongong University and the International Consulting and Training Center, Ministry of Trade, in Hanoi to develop two training courses of four week duration each to train selected Vietnamese officials and businessmen in modern economic policy formulation and monitoring, and in commodity market operation to provide experts for the proposed Stock Exchange Center in Hanoi.

Further developments in this area are in high demand in Vietnam, and as a by-product of its relevancy, in the countries in the region. Some of these countries are Laos, Kampuchea, and Myanmar.

5.2.2.12 Science and Technology

On science and technology, Australia has made some headway in Vietnam as part of its international assistance and trade promotion programmes. Vietnam and Australia signed cooperation agreements on science and industry in September 1992. The National Centre for Natural Sciences and Industry in Vietnam and the CSIRO in Australia also signed an agreement of cooperation in May 1993.

Australia provided consulting and expertise on the technical problems experienced with the 500KV transmission line between the North and the South in Vietnam. Vietnam has also proposed to use funds from the ODA programme to investigate the environmental impact of the 500KV line and to construct relay stations along it.

A current project using advanced computerized econometric modelling methods to investigate and forecast foreign investment in Vietnam for trade and business developments is funded by the Australian and Vietnamese governments and undertaken jointly by Wollongong University and the Research Institute for Foreign Economic Relations, Ministry of Trade, in Vietnam.

The project also provides specialist training for Vietnamese officials on hi-tech analysis of contemporary economic policy formulation and analysis as used routinely by most Western governments in national economic management. The findings from the project will be presented at the end of the project in 1997.

5.2.2.13 Broadcasting

Collaboration between Australia and Vietnam in the area of broadcasting has already taken place and has produced some good results.

During 1994 and 1995, the committees on cooperation in the two countries have met many times and proposed to push for cooperation in technical training and radio programming for the central station in Vietnam, for improvement in regional broadcasting, and for English teaching on radio. Improvement in broadcasting sessions and programmes is also sought.

Prospects for learning on air and for distance education on air (which are currently popular in some states in Australia) are also good. The Australian government (through DEET and DFAT) has committed to provide Vietnam with funds to support development of this area.

The private sector and educational and training institutions in Australia could take note of this development in broadcasting and its possible educational and training uses in Vietnam, and provide suitable investment and training.

5.2.2.14 Tourism

The number of domestic and international tourists in and to Vietnam has increased enormously in the past few years after the open door policy was adopted by the government of Vietnam. While the majority of tourists to Vietnam nowadays are overseas Vietnamese, the predicted trend is that more international tourists will come to Vietnam as more information is known about touristic attractions in Vietnam and the infrastructure and facilities of the tourist industry there improve.

In 1993, international (including overseas Vietnamese) tourists to Vietnam, especially to the South, numbered about 400,000. It is expected that in 1995 and 1996, the number of these tourists will reach one million. In spite of this growth in tourism (both domestically and internationally) and the unspoilt nature of many scenic and historic locations in Vietnam, the infrastructure is not yet there to support this growth and to develop tourist or holiday resorts.

At the moment, roads and rails and touristic facilities are inadequate to many touristic attractions (such as Chua Huong, Tam Coc, Tam Dao, the beautiful Ha Long Bay, or the legendary Ṣa Pa in the North). Air transport (apart from privately organized helicopter services from Hanoi to Ha Long Bay) to these resorts is also non-existent. Hotels and rest and recreation facilities and services also leave much to be desired.

Since tourist spending accounts for a large proportion of GDP in many countries (for example, in Thailand, annual income from tourists exceeds annual income from the national rice exports), the economy of Vietnam would benefit a great deal from developing its tourist industry to a minimum of the international standard in infrastructure and services.

Here Australia could supply much of the know-how, technology and even capital raising for key developments in rest and recreation facilities, building, services, and other infrastructure of the tourist industry in Vietnam.

5.2.2.15 Information Technology (IT)

Vietnam considers IT to be vital for a dynamic process of modernization in the country and economy. The formation and development of an information technology industry in Vietnam would also keep the country in tune with international trends.

The need for an IT industry comes from its necessity and applications in other sectors of the economy (such as manufacturing, services, public administration, etc.), and also from IT being an important industry itself in the present global context.

From now to 2010, Vietnam has plans to:

1. Develop an IT industry for IT accessories and parts for domestic uses and also for exports.

2. Develop programmes for use of IT in communications, information science, medicine, and industries SKD, CDK, and IKD. By 2010, up to 60% or 70% of activity in all walks of life in Vietnam will be done via IT.

In view of its experience and expertise in IT in the past, Australia could play an important part in this industrialization development. The involvement could be in the form of software and hardware training as some Australian and British companies have been doing in Vietnam. Or, it could be in investment through joint ventures or subsidiaries.

5.2.2.16 FDI

As an important component of its economic development programmes, investment requirement looms large in the planning process of the government of Vietnam. This strategy has been bolstered by recent discussions and evidence in an empirical and practical context from developing economies in the past few years as well as in a theoretical context of FDI determination and causation in the sense of Helleiner (1990) and Dunning (1993).

More specifically in the context of actual statistics for development purposes, it has been calculated that, in order to achieve an average annual growth rate of 15% between 1996 and 2000, and similarly for 2001 and 2010, Vietnam would need an investment value of USD 15–16 billion (at 1994 prices), and in excess of USD 60 billion in the ten years after that.

This requirement is substantial when compared with the level of investment during 1991–95 which was about USD 6 billion. During 1991–95, the composition of national investment was:

1. State investment	54%
2. Business investment	3.5%
3. Private investment	11%
4. FDI	31%

In order to support the level of development as planned during 1996–2000, the proposed composition of investment in Vietnam would be:

1. State investment	20%
2. Business and private investment	20%
3. FDI	60%

To achieve this level of investment on the domestic level, the government of Vietnam plans to attract savings by offering higher saving interest rates (currently they are 1.7% per month for residents of Vietnam in VND accounts), creating viable and profitable businesses for investment, and facilitating banking transactions between Vietnam and overseas.

To achieve the targeted level of FDI, Vietnam plans:

1. To accelerate the building of industrial parks for manufacturing industries. It has been estimated that every hectare of industrial parks so built will create 250 jobs in the parks and 500 jobs in the supporting sectors outside the industrial parks. The value of wages for each job could be as high as USD 3,000–4,000 per year.

2. To speed up the commencement of approved FDI projects on exploration and production of oil, gas, electricity, steel, and cement.

3. To remove restrictions on FDI projects and to streamline FDI project application procedures which at present are cumbersome and counterproductive.

4. To organize accredited agencies to promote FDI.

Cooperation currently exists between Vietnam and Australia to find ways to promote FDI via the University of Wollongong and the Research Institute for Foreign Economic Relations, Ministry of Trade in Vietnam.

Further collaboration and support in this area by the Australian government or the Australian corporate and private sectors would be particularly appropriate.

The reasons for seeking a Vietnamese partner are obvious and include for example strategic locations, local market knowledge, cultural, political and social contacts, access to networks, past relationships, and a suitable on-going facility. One important aspect of FDI by Australian companies in Vietnam which needs rectification is the present attitude (from about 89% of the interviewed Australian companies in a recent survey) of these companies concerning their mistrust of their Vietnamese counterparts and partners during their negotiations on FDI based projects (Maitland, 1995).

5.3 The ODA Program

The purpose of an ODA programme can be discussed from an economic context in which international aid is given by international organizations (such as the UNDP, the World Bank, the Asian Development Bank) and NGOs to needy, stable, and developing economies with an objective of promoting economic growth or the standard of living in the recipient countries as well as facilitating international trade (for example lowering the tariff barriers) with the donor and recipient countries. This is often analysed from a static and short-term framework of classical economic theory with competition from the recipient countries and detached from a country's social and political policy (see for example Lahiri and Raimondos (1995)).

A long-term view of ODA's social and economic benefits is often adopted by donor countries especially in a bilateral context of trade and investment, say between Australia and Vietnam.

At present, Australia has two commitments to provide ODA aid to Vietnam to the value of AUD 62 million during 1991–94, and AUD 200 million during 1995. The components of this aid are as follows:

1. Training: Training for officials of the MOET, State Planning Committee, Civil Aviation, and the Ministry of Justice;

2. Infrastructure: The 500KV transmission line (Ministry of Energy), building codes (Ministry of Construction), study on Bac My Thuan bridge (Ministry of Communication and Transport), water supply for four provinces, Ha Tinh, Bac Giang, Bac Ninh, and Tra Vinh (Ministry of Construction), improvement of the Office of the Chief Architect and Planning Admnistration (People's Committee of Hanoi), water research in An Giang, town planning for Da Nang, and in the South.

3. Health: anti malaria office, health care, upgrading the hospitals in Dong Luong (Nghe An), Ha Nam (Nam Ha), community medicine programme on fever, and eye inspection programme.

In general, almost all projects supported and funded by Australia are currently operating well.

The chief expenditure in these projects is however on consulting, training and specialists which account for 80% of all value of the projects. Expenditure on other items is still as a result very low.

It has been argued that some of the ODA programmes have not been directed to the needy targets in Vietnam as perceived by Vietnamese experts. As a result, some misallocation of ODA funds has taken place. Prospects for more beneficial outcomes for both Australia and Vietnam could be achieved if more consultation is considered between the two countries in this regard.

References

Dunning, J. H., *Multinational Enterprises and the Global Economy*, Wokingham: Addison-Wesley, 1993.

Helleiner, G. K., *Direct Foreign Investment and Manufacturing for Export in Developing Countries: A Review of the Issues*, Aldershot, UK, 1990.

Lahiri, S. and Raimondos, P., 'The Welfare Effects of Aid under Quantitative Trade Restrictions', *Journal of International Economics*, Vol. 39, 1995, pp. 297–315.

Le Dang Doanh, *Vietnam's Economic Situation and Economic Reform*, CIEM, mimeographed, 1995.

McCarty, A., Paunlagui, M., and Vu Quoc Huy, *Vietnam Databank 1976–1991* (not dated), National Centre for Development Studies, Australian National University.

Maitland, E., 'Australian Companies in Vietnam', *Vietnam Economic and Political Update 1995*, Australian National University, Canberra, Australia, 1995.

Ministry of Trade, Hanoi, Vietnam, various publications.

Nguyen Thi Ngoc Lan, 'Investment Pattern, Trade and Economic Growth in ASEAN and AFTA: Implications for Vietnam', MCOM Thesis, Faculty of Commerce, Wollongong University, Australia, 1995.

Nguyen Thi Van Anh, 'Foreign Investment in Vietnam', MA Thesis, Faculty of Economics, Thammasat University, Bangkok, Thailand, 1995.

Nguyen Tien Hung, *Economic Development of Socialist Vietnam 1955–80*, New York: Praeger, 1987.

Quinlan, J. P., *Vietnam: Business Opportunities and Risks (A Guide to Success in Asia's Next Dragon)*, Singapore: Heinemann Asia, 1995.

Reidel, J., Comer, B., Le Dang Doanh, and Tran Du Lich, *Transition to Market Economy in Vietnam*, Asia Foundation Project, Hanoi, 1995.

Research Institute for Foreign Economic Relations, Ministry of Trade, Hanoi, Vietnam, various publications.

Statistical Yearbook of Vietnam, Statistical Publishing House, Hanoi, various issues.

Tan, J. L. H., 'Introductory Overview: AFTA in the Changing International Economy', in Tan (ed.), *AFTA in the Changing International Economy*, Singapore: Institute of Southeast Asian Studies, 1996.

Tran Hoang Kim, *Economy of Vietnam: Review and Statistics*, Hanoi, 1992.

Tran Van Hoa, 'Current Patterns and Future Trends of Trade and Foreign Investment in Vietnam: The 1995 Business Survey and an Econometric Analysis', mimeo.

UNDP, *Country Program Report*, Hanoi, various issues.

United Nations Statistical Yearbook, Washington DC, various issues, 1995.

World Bank, *Vietnam Transition to the Market: An Economic Report*, Report No. 11902–VN, 1983.

2 Foreign Investment and the Macroeconomy in Vietnam

Le Dang Doanh

1 INTRODUCTION

In 1977, two years after the country's reunification, the government of Vietnam issued a document regulation (or rules) on Foreign Investment in Vietnam. At that time, the regulation did not receive support from the former Soviet Union and Eastern Europe. Although some capitalist groups regarded this regulation as a considerable sign to be available before any foreign investment activities were carried out in Vietnam, the Cambodia event took place and was followed by the southern border war with China. As a result, the economic cooperation door with capitalist countries was shut. Under these circumstances, the regulation did not have any particular significance.

During the years 1976–86, Vietnam received aids from the former Soviet Union and other members of the Economic Assistance Committee, which were worth an average of one billion roubles annually. Most of these aids were used ineffectively. Apart from some projects such as the Hoa Binh hydroelectric station, the Bim Son cement factory, the Thang Long bridge, etc. which have produced positive effects especially since the end of the late 1980s, the vast majority were used for importing equipment which was either not used to its full capacity, or even not used at all. Part of the credit terms was used for importing consumer goods, compensating for a serious shortage of consumer goods in the country. All this has created a great debt problem until now.

Vietnam's economy continued to be troubled until the middle of the 1980s: production in the agriculture and industry sectors increasing slowly, a serious budget deficit, hyper-inflation, and credits and aids from the former Soviet Union declining sharply. Under these circumstances, the idea of thoroughly renovating the socio-economic life in Vietnam was conceived and officially approved at the Sixth National Party Congress. The main content of the renovation programme was to convert from a centrally planned mechanism to a market-oriented one under state management, and to transform the economy into a multi-sector economic structure.

In order to develop their economy rapidly, at that time, the Vietnamese people realized that the economy could not depend on only traditional capital sources. This meant that the domestic funds must be mobilized mainly from the agricultural production sector and the credit capital and aids from the SEV countries. Vietnam also saw the importance of diversifying its external economic relations because, first, there were signs of a reduction in the credit resources and aids from the former Soviet Union and Eastern Europe, and second, Vietnam had been left further and further behind in comparison with other countries in the region. Also in this period, Vietnam had witnessed the success of China, NICs and ASEAN countries in using foreign investment as a chief driving force to develop the economy.

The Foreign Investment Law issued in December 1987 was the result of the above assessment of the situation. It marked an important turning point in the foreign investment activities in Vietnam. In 1991, with the collapse of the Soviet Union, Eastern Europe and the SEV, the necessity of foreign investment was once more affirmed because there were dramatic changes in the real financial status in Vietnam.

Loans and aids from Russia and Eastern Europe, which had in some periods accounted for 38% of Vietnam's annual total budget, no longer existed and Vietnam had to negotiate to postpone the payment until after 1995. Vietnam had also begun to pay off the foreign debts of 10 billion roubles and 400 million USD. With a large payment of between 200 and 300 million USD annually, it meant that the increase in payment was from 0.2% of GDP during the years 1986–90 to about 2% of GDP from 1990 onwards. Budget deficit has always been at a high level of about 7% of GDP.

To reduce the budget deficit without causing high inflation, Vietnam had to limit its money supply to compensate for the budget deficit. As a result, the government had to borrow money from domestic as well as foreign sources. This method generated a burden of payment and of interest. Under this circumstance, Vietnam had to seek foreign investment as well as ODA as important measures to develop the economy. Furthermore, foreign investment was not simply considered to be the most important capital source to develop the economy but also the main factor to increase output and production, to change technology, to accumulate experience, and to transform the economic structure in Vietnam from being mainly dependent on agriculture to being dependent more on the industry sector.

This chapter consists of four parts. The first part surveys the international experience in attracting foreign direct investment (FDI). The second part presents the status of foreign investment in Vietnam during the past seven years (1988–95). The third part analyses the effects of foreign investment on Vietnam's economy and the predicted requirement for foreign investment during the period from 1996 to 2000. Finally, the fourth part explains the investment opportunities and the problems faced by Vietnam in order to attract more investment capital.

2 FDI AND ASIAN COUNTRIES' EXPERIENCE IN ATTRACTING IT

When a company decides to supply goods on the foreign market it often has to choose between the options of international trade or direct investment. The question is what are the factors that affect the company's decision to choose the direct investment format.

According to the macroeconomic theory on the movement of a company's capital, whether a company decides to invest abroad or not depends on three conditions. These are: the monopoly on special advantages, regional advantages, and the self-organizing ability to make the full use of special advantages.

According to the first condition, the company must have special advantages, otherwise it will not invest in foreign countries, and the benefits from these advantages must outweigh the costs of investment abroad. These advantages are derived from the company's product market advantages (marketing ability, product differentiation, etc.).

The second condition strongly affects the company's decision in choosing a location for investment in order to harness the special advantages through selling products in host countries or producing in host countries for exports. These advantages result from the country's rich natural resources, an abundant, skilled and cheap labour force and low transport and communication costs. In addition, special advantages are also manifested in the government's policies such as the regulations on trade, labour, environment control, and investment-encouraging policies.

Lastly, after acknowledging the special and regional advantages available, the company will need to decide whether to conduct business itself or to hand over the manufacturing to another party.

The theory mentioned above will help us to understand the three investment forms which have been taking place in developing countries: (1) Investment in the natural resource exploration sector; (2) Investment in goods production in order to supply the local country's market; (3) Investment in production for exports.

It is clear that in the form of investment in natural resource exploitation, the regional advantages are most manifest. The advantage of a foreign company is that they have the potential of capital as well as technology to implement the exploitation. This advantage often exists for a relatively long time, as it is shown by the data from the ASEAN countries.

In the early period of independence, the economic growth of most of the ASEAN countries depended on the exploitation of the abundant natural resources. These countries were important suppliers who provided basic materials such as kerosene, rubber, vegetable oil, tin, timber and many kinds of tropical agricultural products and sea products. The ratio of manufacturing goods to total product until the 1980s was still very modest: 5% in 1971 and 13% in 1981. The process mechanism of transformation from import-substitution production to export-orientation production took place later in the NICs because the abundance of natural resources delayed the difficulties facing those countries.

Foreign investment activities in the ASEAN countries were then mainly focused on the resource exploitation sectors. Until the late 1970s, the US was still the biggest investor in the ASEAN. The US invested mainly in exploitation industry, especially the oil producing and refining industries. In 1987, American investment in oil production in Indonesia was 80% of total investment, and in Malaysia it was 63.3%. In the Philippines, 80% of total foreign investment in the mining industry, metallurgy, and natural gas belonged to American companies while, in Singapore, 50% of the US investment was concentrated on oil refinement.

The FDI wave in developing countries appeared in the 1950s and 1960s when foreign investment was mainly used to tap into the local country's market. During their developments, East Asian countries carried out import-substitution production strategy and trade policy on domestic production protection. Foreign investment in this period was chiefly to avoid the tariff barriers, and it was considered to be the form that replaced commercial imports. However, this strategy faced its difficulties: the domestic limited market restricted production output (which caused the increase in domestic production costs); the import-substitution production industries often demanded a lot of capital, and required more skilled labour and high technology. That was contrary to the East Asian countries' situation then. Those difficulties themselves limited the countries' regional advantages.

Nowadays FDI intended to supply capital to the local country's market is often seen in the service sector. Regional advantages here are formed by the nature of this type of activity itself, that is, the demand for investing rights in the local area to supply its market.

The advantage of an abundant and cheap labour force is an important factor that attracts foreign investment in the East Asian countries, especially the NICs, in their early development. However, this advantage is gradually reduced along with the development, and it is an essential determinant that helps to explain the movements of FDI-based capital sources in the region.

The NICs in their early development had an abundant, untrained and relatively cheap labour force in comparision with the industrial countries such as Japan, the US and West European nations. These were both the challenge of solving unemployment and the advantage of NICs: hence, NICs often paid attention to the industries that employed a lot of labour. At the same time, foreign investors were also interested in investing in those countries with the intention of making use of the advantage of a cheap labour force to produce goods that were consumed right in the local country, or exported to other countries, even back to the investing countries. When the redundant labour force problem declined, there were wage increases, and a trained and skilled labour shortage. Consequently, the NICs began to lose their labour advantages in comparision with their neighbouring ASEAN countries.

The ASEAN countries, except Singapore, started developing their production industry later than the NICs. However, they also faced similar problems to the NICs in labour issues. That is a reason why industries that employ a lot of labour must be focused on. The labour advantage of the ASEAN countries attracts the attention of investors not only from the US, Japan, and Western Europe but also from the NICs.

Nowadays, labour advantage can be found in China, India and Vietnam, and this advantage is still attractive to foreign investors. The low labour cost in those countries becomes an advantage in competing with the ASEAN countries to attract foreign investment; even the companies from the ASEAN also invest in those countries. These countries carried out the strategy of export-orientation production together with free-trade policy.

When Vietnam carried out this strategy it gradually eliminated trade restrictions, especially on commercial imports, by reducing tariff barriers, and step by step wiped out non-tariff barriers. Moreover, those countries created export-encouraging measures such as diversifying export markets, applying market exchange rates, reducing domestic currency supply, and establishing export processing zones. In fact, foreign-invested companies, especially the 100% foreign-owned ones, often tend to export more than the local ones, and account for a high ratio in the export turnover of invested countries. This happens because foreign companies have the advantage in accessing export markets, and the ability to provide the parent company or the subsidiary ones with goods in the same global production network. Statistical data show that foreign investment activities strongly increased after this strategy and policy were applied.

In the long term, free-trade policy is often combined with agricultural policy reforms. The East Asian countries, in the process of liberating importation and applying market exchange rates, carried out many policies such as upgrading industrial environment, chiefly through strengthening competition; improving production capacity and effectiveness; eliminating interference that deforms the market such as price controls; and fully providing services (infrastructure, for example).

In general, in most countries, while the loosening of restrictions to domestic as well as foreign investment quickly takes place, other industrial reforms do not catch up with it sufficiently, especially the administrative and law regimes.

In order to resume the competition on the international market and the regional advantages, the countries which are losing labour advantages have to undertake mechanism transformations: shifting from the industries that employ a lot of labour and have low added value, to the ones that consume a great amount of capital, demand high technology, skilled labour, and have higher added value. Moreover, together with the declining labour advantages, many NICs have a surplus in their current account and their currencies' appreciation may at the same time negatively affect export-production industries and make the manufacture abroad cheaper. All those things force the companies to move manufacturing bases which employ a lot of labour to other regional countries to reduce the labour costs.

However, this changing process takes place with different contents and levels among the East Asian countries. Hong Kong and Singapore with their domestic market restrictions and increasing labour costs and joint management are concentrating on mechanism transformation from production to service. Hong Kong is actively moving its manufacturing bases to South China, while Singapore moves its bases to Indonesia,

Malaysia and Vietnam. At the same time, those countries also create measures to encourage foreign investment by multi-national companies under the form of establishing local headquarters. However, both countries are facing difficulties in manpower that can meet the requirements of high added value service industries such as banking, accounting, advertising, education and consumption activities.

In the medium term, the production sector still plays the principal role in Taiwan and South Korea. However, their industrial structures have changed their direction to manufacturing industries that have higher added value, demand more capital, higher technology and more skilled labour. Both countries are now moving the industries that employ much labour and low or average technology to the countries that have lower labour costs in East Asia and China. They at the same time continue to eliminate restrictions and to encourage foreign investment, especially the investment in high technological industries. Furthermore, they also invest in high industrial countries to improve technology.

The ASEAN countries are in the process of improving and expanding production as well as strengthening investment in the industries that have high added value, improving domestic manufacturing capacity through unrestricted import of heavy-industrial products and consumer goods.

Although the East Asian countries have high economic growth, the financial market and financial institutions have not been fully developed yet. Formerly, the financial market and financial institutions were limited by strict regulations. Foreign securities were restricted in controlling and possessing domestic securities' stakes. Since the late 1980s, the restrictions to the financial market have been notably eliminated and a more dynamic market in financial activities has been formed. Limitations on foreign companies' properties have been loosened. In the early years, FDI was the main form of foreign capital invested in the East Asian countries, investment capital has now remarkably increased.

The growth of the minor financial market has created a new financial source and reduced the dependence on commercial loans which were used for compensating for developing expenditure. The more dynamic activities of the financial market have partly reduced the interest rate differential between mobilized funds and lending funds, through which financial expenditure was reduced. Financial sources flowing into the East Asian stock markets not only provide the minor financial market with more capital but also increase investment sources through issuing new shares so that they can have capital to expand production capacity and import new technology.

Table 2.1 The Ranking of Reasons for FDI

Countries	Ranking
NIC	1. The increasing labour cost 2. The appreciating currency 3. Developing countries' competition 4. Low cost manufacturing bases 5. New market
ASEAN	1. Domestic market scale 2. Technology 3. Shortage of trained labour 4. Risk reduction 5. Emerging markets

In recent years, multi-national companies have been big investment partners (accounting for about 70% of total direct investment capital in East Asia). Table 2.1 shows us the order of importance of the reasons that explain the growth of the multi-national companies in investing abroad. Multi-national companies of the NICs put the increasing labour costs and their appreciating currency as their first reasons. However, there are differences in ranking the other causes among the NICs. South Korean multi-national companies pay special attention to the trade barriers and transport costs to European and Northern American markets. Hong Kong's multi-national companies want to find the area that has lower rent and lower land prices to invest in as well as to reduce risks. Multi-national companies of Singapore consider limited domestic labour and consumer markets as the chief reasons for finding external investment opportunities.

On the other hand, ASEAN countries' multi-national companies recognize the restrictions and disadvantages of domestic markets and the necessity of adopting technology as the first-rank reasons that promote investment abroad. Many ASEAN countries' leaders consider investment abroad to be the way of adopting technology and skilled labour so as to expand manufacturing right into their countries. In fact, these leaders are seeking foreign partners to establish subsidiary companies and this way they can have access to high technology and skilled labour. We know that the above mentioned changes in business environment have reflected the changes in the labour division of East Asian economies.

The investment process itself is the process of labour division inside multi-national companies to set up a global production network.

Between the parent company and its subsidiaries, between subsidiaries themselves, trade relations are established to serve production lines making complete products. As a result, investment activities of multinational companies have promoted trade relations in the region and formed close relationships between trade and international investment. On the other hand, the investment activities also show that the increase of foreign capital sources resulted from not only traditional comparative advantages but also other important factors. For example, the invested countries must have an attractive investment environment, gradually reduce uncertain elements, and move towards free trade policy, especially liberalizing export activities.

All of the things which have already been discussed can explain one of the most important points in foreign investment activities in East Asia, namely that the investment in the region has increased surprisingly. The investment from Japan and the NICs has surged considerably, making them the biggest investment partners in the region. The investment activities themselves create a process which develops the industrial production structure on a large scale that is also appropriate to regional trends. The activities are also the means to work out a distinctively Asian industrial development model. That means the transformation of the basic factors that determine comparable advantages.

3 THE EFFECT OF FOREIGN DIRECT INVESTMENT (FDI)

One of the distinguishable points in the world economy in the middle of the 1980s was the high economic growth and the stability of East Asian countries. The growth could be explained by regional reasons as well as by the specific characters of each country.

There are fundamental factors that explain the high growth. The countries have a plentiful and skilful labour force, economic competitiveness in international markets and investment efficiency. Except for South Korea, the NICs have relied mainly on the FDI to develop production for exports. Even South Korea has now begun to appreciate FDI more than overseas loans. All the NICs have been rich in capital but they have continued further promoting foreign investment activities, having access to technology, managerial skills and marketing techniques from foreign countries. The investment has been focused on high technological industries and services with high added value, cre-
hese countries new comparable advantages which will con-
the maintenance of high growth.

In addition, FDI also creates domestic demands by increasing commodities of local companies, creating jobs for the native people and strengthening trade relations in the region. Considering carefully the importance of foreign investment, East Asian countries have recently applied various measures to encourage investment activities: the high rate of savings and the stability of the macroeconomy. Moreover, FDI has played an important role, mainly since the middle of the 1980s.

To achieve the targeted rate of FDI, East Asian countries have maintained a very high ratio of investment (about 30–35% of GDP, as compared with the average rate in the world of 20%). It is known that, for developing countries, if domestic investment is more than domestic savings for a long time, these countries will face financial deficits because it is difficult for them to approach the international financial market. This will curb the speed of growth. Meanwhile, the NICs generally have high domestic savings, so the surplus is bigger than the current accounts and they have become capital-export countries. ASEAN countries have difficulties in capital raising and they have to rely on the foreign investment capital sources to maintain economic growth.

The NICs' success in their economy is often supported with external development strategies, not only in trade but also in investment. For example, in June 1994, South Korea took measures to open more widely its market to attract more foreign investment. At the same time, Indonesia had a review on Foreign Investment Law to promote further foreign investment. In November 1993, Thailand loosened the restrictions on foreign companies' properties in the automobile industry and permitted foreign companies to own 100% of capital instead of 49% as before.

The above mentioned measures are very important in attracting foreign investment. However, they are not radical enough. These countries need to improve further the status of investment, in which the most important problems to be solved are to reform the financing sector, to strengthen the infrastructure investment, and to manage the macroeconomy.

4 FDI IN VIETNAM FROM 1987 UP TO THE PRESENT

Over past years, together with efforts to perfect the system of legal documents on investment, Vietnam has continuously reinforced diplomatic relations with other countries as well as improved the domestic investment environment to attract increasingly more FDI capital. The efforts have had positive effects and have brought about initially encouraging results.

By the end of 1994, there were 1,200 projects licensed with the total registered investment capital of USD 11,964 million, as shown in Table 2.2. The average growth was about 50% per year, a rather high rate in comparison with that of other countries in the region (about 27% per year from 1987 to 1992). The total number of projects licensed in the first six months of 1995 was 206 with the total capital of USD 3,589 million. As compared with that of this time in 1994, the number of projects has increased 35% and the investment capital has increased 225%. Among the above mentioned projects, there are 225 whose licence was withdrawn or the operating duration expired (accounting for 16% of the number of projects), with the total investment capital of USD 1,125 million (accounting for 7% of the investment capital). Therefore, there are now 1,191 projects operating with the capital of USD 14,432 million.

However, to know exactly the net resources of foreign investment capital flowing into Vietnam over the past years, it is necessary to take into consideration the following factors.

Firstly, up to now there have been 203 projects whose licence was withdrawn, with the investment capital of USD 949.5 million, accounting for 15% of the projects and 6% of the total registered capital. This percentage is similar to that of many neighbouring countries. Secondly, the investment capital consists of legal and borrowing capital. The proportion of legal capital is estimated to be about 50%. Thirdly, the Vietnamese side also contributes to the legal capital, mostly in the form of land and workshops, estimated to be about 25% to 30% of the legal capital. Finally, in practice, the Vietnamese and foreign sides often appreciate their contribution higher than the real legal capital.

If compared with the total capital invested in other countries in the region, that invested in Vietnam is still low, about 1.5% to 3% and 0.6% to 2.2% of investment and working capital respectively (see Tables 2.3 and 2.4)

Most of the licence-withdrawn projects were small scale and were those which were granted licences in the early years of implementing the Foreign Investment Law, and they belong to the fields of the consumer goods industry, sea products, hotels and tourism.

These projects' licences were withdrawn due to a number of reasons. These were:

Table 2.2 Foreign Direct Investment in Vietnam Per Year

Year	Registration: Number of projects	Registration: Capital (million USD)	Working capital (million USD)	Working rate (%)
1988	37	366	60	16
1989	70	539	100	19
1990	111	596	200	34
1991	155	1,388	260	19
1992	193	2,117	535	25
1993	272	2,887	1,001	35
1994	362	4,071	1,520	37
6/1995	206	3,593	1,140	32
TOTAL	1,406	15,557	4,816	31

Figure 2.1 Investment and Working Capital, 1988–95 (million USD)

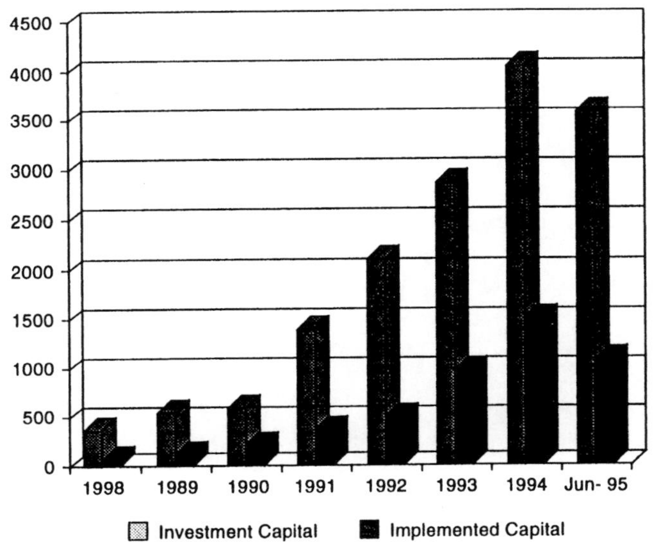

Source: The State Committee for Cooperation and Investment (SCCI)

- Many companies were brokers, dealing in contracts.
- The foreign or Vietnamese side was not capable of financing the project.
- There was a disagreement inside the Managing Board itself.
- Changes in the market and prices were not foreseen.
- The legal system was not stable or clear, causing many disputes in the implementing process of projects.
- The state management was not strict enough, causing such serious mistakes to happen that the licence was withdrawn.

The average ratio of working foreign capital invested in Vietnam over the past years is on the average level as compared with that of the region. However, it is necessary to understand that besides the fact that each project must pass certain years to use up the registered investment capital, there are other reasons for the slow process of project implementation such as the difficulties facing investors from the time they receive the investment licence until they begin to carry out the projects.

Formerly, many investors thought that after they had received the licence, every procedure was considered to be finished and they could start contributing capital and the project could go into operation. However, besides the administrative procedures such as operating registration, seal engraving, and account opening, the joint venture enterprises had to apply for land grants and construction permits. It took many projects six months or a whole year to receive these permits after the licence was granted. Then the investors had to deal with the difficult problems of population removal and site clearance. This is shown more clearly when we analyse in more detail the working ratio in each field.

The oil and gas field, accounting for nearly one third of the total working capital, has a fairly high working ratio of 57%. The banking and finance field, accounting for 5% of the working capital, has the working ratio of 70%. The hotel trade and industrial production are the areas which use most land and have the legal rates of 10% and 25% respectively.

On 28 December 1994, the government issued Decree 191/CP to confirm continually its determination to improve the investment environment. Under this decree, state agencies connected to investment activities are supposed to provide particular guidance and time for finishing each aspect of activities to simplify the administrative procedures for planning, approving, and implementing FDI projects.

Many things which formerly needed application for permission will only need registering from now on. The waiting time of the projects'

Table 2.3 Foreign Direct Investment Capital in Countries in the Region (million USD)

	1990	1991	1992	1993	1994
Vietnam	596	1,388	2,117	2,887	4,071
Total ASEAN	31,581	22,373	29,563	17,306	39,048
Indonesia	8,751	8,778	10,323	8,144	23,724
Philippines	961	778	285	528	2,339
Malaysia	6,517	6,139	6,445	2,443	4,277
Thailand	14,128	4,988	10,848	4,216	5,881
Singapore	1,224	1,690	1,662	1,975	2,827
China	6,596	11,977	58,124	111,345	81,400
India	73	235	1,500	2,905	2,855
TOTAL	38,846	35,973	91,304	134,443	127,374
The proportion of investment in Vietnam compared with other countries (%)	1.5	3.8	2.3	2.2	3.2

Source: Normura Asia Focus, 5 April 1995

Figure 2.2 Sources of Foreign Investment Capital in Countries in the Region (million USD)

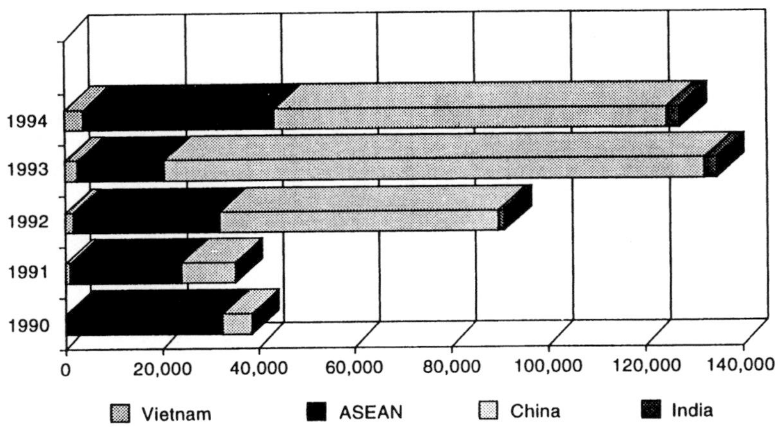

Table 2.4 The Net Investment Capital of Countries in the Region (million USD)

	1988	1989	1990	1991	1992	1993
Vietnam	60	100	200	260	535	1.001
ASEAN	6,911	7,575	11,974	12,926	16,034	16,517
Indonesia	576	682	1,093	1,482	1,777	2,004
Philippines	936	563	530	544	228	763
Malaysia	719	1,668	2,332	3,998	5,183	5,206
Thailand	1,105	1,775	2,444	2,014	2,116	1,751
Singapore	3,655	2,887	5,575	4,888	6,730	6,829
China	3,194	3,393	3,487	4,366	11,156	27,515
India	287	350	112	200	390	
The proportion of investment in Vietnam compared with other countries (%)	0.6	0.8	1.2	1.5	1.9	2.2

Source: Pacific Economic Outlook 1995–96

Figure 2.3 The Net Investment Capital of Countries in the Region (million USD)

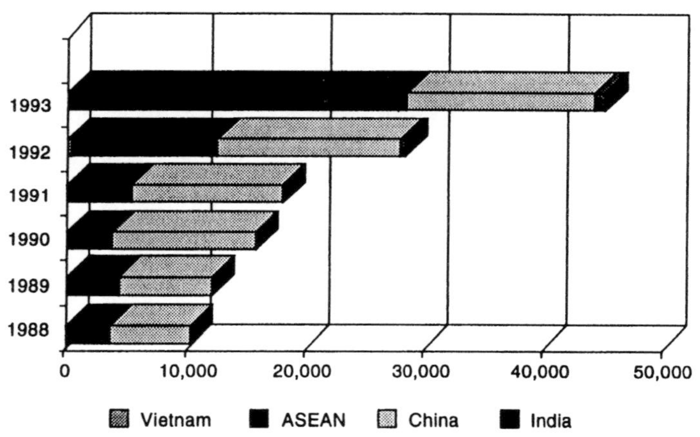

owners will be shortened, especially for granting construction permits.

The government also decided to divide projects into two types (formerly there were three types): A and B. And now there are only two levels of authorized administration: the Prime Minister is in charge of projects of type A, and the Chairman of the State Committee for Co-operation and Investment (SCCI) for type B projects. The management of local areas is the responsibility of the local authority. The activities in the first six months of 1995 show that the time for the projects' implementation is shortened considerably. Many construction projects have started to be built only six months after the licence has been granted.

The structure of foreign investment falling into the various sectors has two notable changes: the investment in agriculture has declined sharply whereas that in oil and gas has increased rapidly (see Table 2.5).

The investment in agriculture, forestry and fishery has declined sharply to 6% in 1994 from 21.9% in the period 1988–89. In total, for the period 1988–94, it accounts for 2.4% of the investment capital and nearly 5% of the projects.

The investment proportion for these sectors is still small due to the impact of outside factors and Vietnamese agriculture itself. It is possible to point out here important outside factors.

First, there are always changes in the labour division in Asia and agriculture only plays a modest part in these countries. Second, on the international market there is serious competitiveness of agricultural products, causing temporary changes and reduction in the agricultural prices over the past years. Meanwhile, Vietnamese agriculture itself has not been very attractive to foreign investors because of some difficulties such as the low labour efficiency, the low living standard of the rural population, a very limited international market for Vietnam's main agricultural products, and the poor infrastructure of the country. Therefore, investors understand that investing in the agricultural sector will take a long time to get back the capital, and they would suffer many risks and a low proportion of returns, whereas there are many other fields which have higher profit-earning ratios and are more suitable for investors' strategies.

During the early years after the Foreign Investment Law was issued, the major foreign investment was mostly from powerful oil companies whose projects were offshore. This was to reduce the economic and political risks in Vietnam's oil and gas industry which has considerable reserves and has been exploited very little. Next came the foreign capital invested in hotels and tourism, a field which has great

Table 2.5 The Structure of FDI Divided into Sectors in Vietnam (% of registered capital)

Fields	1988–90	1992	1994	1988–94
Petrol	31.9	26.2	2	8.8
Industry	13.2	40.0	30	39.0
Agriculture, Forestry, Fishery	21.9	6.2	7	2.4
Tourism, Hotel	23.7	16.5	17	
Services	*	4.1	28	
Telecommunications	9.0	4.0	3	7.2
Construction			11	0.5
Bank and Finance		2.6	1	1.2
Other fields	0.3	0.4	1	

* Included in Tourism, Hotel

Sources: The General Department for Statistics, and SCCI

opportunities for profits owing to the development of relations with foreign countries and could avoid the exchange rate fluctuation risk. In the years 1988–90, the investment proportion of the oil and gas industry to total investment was 31.9%, and of the hotel and tourism industry 23.7%.

From 1992 onwards, however, the investment in industries (mostly in consumer goods production, food processing, electronics, chemicals and exploration) has gained the leading position. The increase in the investment in the production industry is a signal showing that investors have changed from concentrating on the exploitation of Vietnam's natural resources, especially oil and gas, into making use of a plentiful and cheap labour force and the current economic advantages of Vietnam. In the coming years, it is expected that foreign investment in Vietnam's infrastructure will increase rapidly with the presence of industrial and export processing zones.

Up to now, most of the provinces and cities over the country (except Tuyen Quang, Cao Bang, Lai Chau and Kon Tum) have had foreign investment projects. However, the distribution of foreign investment capital is not equal among the localities and areas.

In terms of foreign investment, ten leading provinces and cities have received up to 80% of the projects with 90% of the registered capital and 89% of the working capital. The projects are mainly concentrated in three major national economic areas. They are:

1. Ho Chi Minh City – Dong Nai – Ba Ria – Vung Tau which account for 53% of the investment capital and 54% of the projects;

2. Hanoi – Hai Phong – Quang Ninh accounting for 31% of the investment capital and 23% of the projects;

3. Quang Nam – Da Nang making up 4% of the investment capital and 3% of the projects.

Over the past year, although the capital invested in the North has increased at a higher rate, the main part of FDI in general has been focused on the South (see Figures 2.5 and 2.6).

The unequal distribution of investment among the localities and areas is difficult to assess because the decision over which localities to invest in depends much on the foreign investors.

A study of the structure of the invested sector shows that investment areas with high profit earnings over the past years have been in localities and cities which have specific conditions and advantages of social and economic infrastructure. Nevertheless, it also points out that although Vietnam has many abundant and plentiful natural resources, especially in the North, the country has not been able to attract foreign investment capital yet due to such obstacles as the poor traffic system, untrained labour force and capital shortage. The unequal distribution originates not only from the advantages of infrastructure but also from other important factors such as the different attractiveness of the investment environment among the different areas.

As compared with the Northern provinces, Ho Chi Minh City and its surrounding provinces have a more dynamic business atmosphere, coping more quickly with the market economy and having wider relationships with foreign investors. Moreover, the state has not had appropriate and encouraging policy to attract investment in the provinces of the Northern and Central parts and Tay Nguyen.

There have now been more than 700 companies from 50 nations and territories who have invested in Vietnam.

The NICs rank in the highest positions among the business partners who have invested in Vietnam. The fact that the NICs easily have these positions is possibly because the investment of industrial countries has still been small and has not entered into a surging stage. On the other hand, the NICs themselves have regarded Vietnam as one of the first-ranking invested countries in their investment strategies.

The NICs have been moving their enterprises overseas because their standardized and traditional products which have used intensive labour have become too costly. This is due to the lack of untrained workers, the increase in wages and the appreciation of these countries' currencies, which have caused the domestic producers to earn low profits. Moreover, these countries are not allowed to enjoy favourable trade status. They have begun to have difficulties in further penetrating prosperous markets where they have tried to become established. So this situation has urged them to look for investment opportunities in countries which will have enjoyed favourable trade status.

Moreover, the NICs have learned the experience and marketing techniques of labour-intensive products, so that they could make use of the advantages when investing in production for exports to countries which have low labour costs. Meanwhile, Vietnam is a country of regional advantages in terms of its low labour costs and was allowed to enjoy the favourable trade status when it became a member of GATT and to enjoy the most favoured nation status after there is normalization of relations with the United States. Furthermore, Vietnam has favourable conditions for making products to sell in regional and international markets, particularly in the markets of Indochina and Southern China.

As a result, we find it easy to understand the presence of the NICs, mainly in the manufacturing industry, of the standardized and primarily processed products in Vietnam such as food, garments, textiles, the assembly of simple electronic products, and wood processing. These countries have begun to invest in high profit-earning industries such as manufacturing, cement, steel, assembling automobiles and motorbikes and producing accessories and parts.

Japan also has established bases for large investment in Vietnam. In addition to the advantage of having cheap labour, Vietnam has been able to attract Japanese investment because of the conformity of Vietnam's conditions with Japan's investment strategies.

First, it is a strategy that Japanese investors look for countries to invest in, then to make the right products for selling in the local markets or for exporting to other countries or even to Japan. Second, they want to have investment projects in the areas near Japan. Third, they focus their investment on small and medium-sized businesses.

Japan thinks that Vietnam, as a place of low labour costs, has favourable conditions for the production of labour-intensive products which can be sold in Vietnam and other countries. Yet, due to many reasons such as the poor infrastructure and an incomplete legal environment, while Japanese companies implement their investment

Table 2.6 Countries and Territories Investing in Vietnam

Countries and territories	1994			6/1995			1988–6/1995		
	Projects	Investment capital	Legal capital	Projects	Investment capital	Legal capital	Projects	Investment capital	Legal capital
Japan	8	9	10	15	21	15	8	10	
NICs	54	48	49	46	40	30	51	53	
Taiwan	19	10	12	15	17	13	17	18	
Hong Kong	14	15	14	5	1	2	15	15	
South Korea	12	7	6	13	11	8	8	8	n.d.
Singapore	9	16	17	13	11	7	11	12	
ASEAN	9	8	8	6	3	2	9	4	
EEC	10	17	16	10	12	12	13	14	
The US	6	6	5	5	8	7	3	4	
Other countries	13	12	12	18	16	24	16	15	

Figure 2.4 The Regions with Investment in Vietnam from 1988 to June 1995

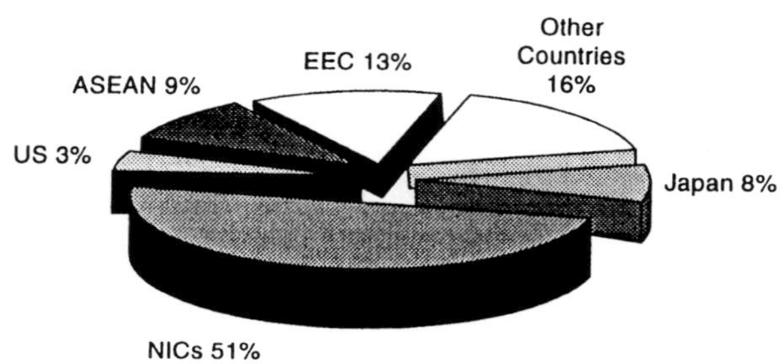

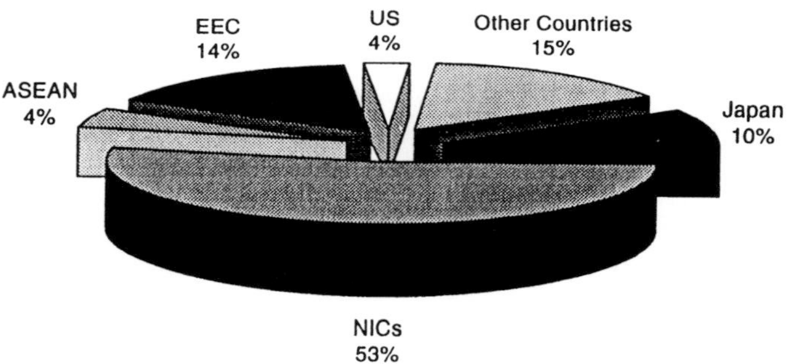

projects in Vietnam, the Japanese government has also given considerable financial support for Vietnam as other official development aid worth USD 500 million (the country has given the largest official development aid to Vietnam). Japan has also lent Vietnam a commercial loan worth USD 479 million to construct its infrastructure and plans to build in the South a seaport with the investment capital worth USD 900 million. So it is possible to conclude that Japanese companies have actively invested in the infrastructure construction, and in the coming years they will identify Vietnam, which is considered a market to sell their products, as a country to manufacture (products).

The average size or scale of a project has increased considerably, from USD 9.9 million in 1988 to USD 17.4 million per project. This rate could be higher if we eliminated those projects whose licence has been withdrawn or operating duration has expired (see Table 2.7). During the period from 1988 to 1993, the number of projects of under USD 5 million investment capital was 73% and those of above USD 5 million was 27%, among which the projects from USD 5 million to USD 20 million accounted for 16% whereas those of USD 20 million upwards accounted for 11%. If we take into consideration small projects whose licence was withdrawn, those whose operating duration has expired and those of increased investment capital, the average rate could be much higher.

In recent years, many projects with large investment capital have increasingly appeared in the country. Before 1993, there were only two projects with capital of more than USD 170 million but during the period 1993–94, there were eight projects of USD 170 million and above. Over the first six months of 1995, the registered investment capital has increased strongly due to the presence of large-scale projects, particularly certain projects which have investment capital of 'up to USD 524.5 million. To the end of 1994, the ten biggest invested projects held up to 20% of the total invested capital.

Almost all projects were of small size or scale when the Investment Law was newly issued and implemented; the investing climate in Vietnam was also very young. As a result, foreign investors forming small companies with a small amount of capital were at an exploring stage (approaching state), looking for projects with only a small chance of failure and likely to get the projected returns. Moreover, potential companies were influenced by the US trade embargo, except petroleum companies.

After the embargo was relaxed, and then lifted, foreign investors have been better aware of Vietnam's investment environment, and have had some experience in dealing in Vietnam's market. Investors now take part in embarking on larger projects for a longer period of time.

As a matter of fact, most foreign investments in Vietnam are direct and are comparatively higher than financial investment.

The Foreign Investment Law issued in 1987 defined three kinds of FDI: joint venture, 100% foreign-owned capital, and cooperation contract.

In 1992, there were changes to this law with some new kinds of investment: Build, Operate and Transfer (BOT). Joint venture has so far been very popular in Vietnam. Up to 1994, it accounted for up to 64% of submitted projects with 70% of the total investment capital. Projects with 100% of foreign capital were 28.7% and 16.2% respectively, and with cooperation contract, 7.5% and 13.8% respectively.

As is the case with foreign investors in other regional countries, foreign investors in Vietnam are always interested in joint ventures as they are not aware of the customs of the localities they are in;

Table 2.7 The Scale of an Annual Average Project (million USD)

1988	1989	1990	1991	1992	1993	1994	6/1995	1988/6.1995
9.9	7.7	5.4	9	11	10.6	11.3	17.4	11.1

Table 2.8 Classification of Projects According to their Size

	1988	1989	1991	1992	1993
Below 5M USD	78	76	82	73	68
Over 5M USD	22	24	18	27	32

Source: *Foreign Investment into Vietnam*, World Publishing House, 1994

Table 2.9 Ten Biggest Investment Capital Projects to 1994

Name	Location of Investment	Capital (million USD)
Chingfong Haiphong joint venture	HaiPhong	288.3
Intelsa cooperation	HaNoi	287.0
Hualon Vietnam Company	DongNai	242.7
Phu my hung joint venture	Baria-Vung Tau	242.0
Red River Town	HaNoi	240.0
Vedan Vietnam	DongNai	216.1
Noga Saigon	Ho Chi Minh City	216.7
Hiep Phuoc electrification	Ho Chi Minh City	205.5
Sao Mai Cement joint venture	KienGiang	181.8
Orion Hanel	HaNoi	170.6

Source: Vietnam Economic Times, 1994–95

consequently, they choose joint ventures to get a better knowledge of these localities, people and customs, and to share difficulties and failures with the local people. Moreover, in Vietnam, joint venture is the most preferred form of investment as investors have great difficulties in land-use-right to operate on their own. It has been noted that 98% of Vietnamese partners have been state-run companies. However, this kind of investment has been rapidly decreasing and accounted for only 64% in 1994. There had not been one 100% foreign capital project up to then, but this tends to be increasing and one can obviously note the trend in the last few years.

All this shows that foreign investors now want to be independent of local partners' decisions in running and operating their companies. What

Table 2.10 Types of Investment

Year	100% foreign capital (%)		Joint venture (%)		Cooperation contract (%)	
	Projects	Capital	Projects	Capital	Projects	Capital
1988	3	–	83	49	14	51
1989	9	2	72	61	19	37
1990	5	1	80	66	15	33
1991	8	17	89	78	3	5
1992	20	14	70	62	10	24
1993	28	23	67	71	5	6
1994			n.d.			
1988–94	28	16	64	70	8	14

Source: *SCCI*

Figure 2.5 Types of Investment

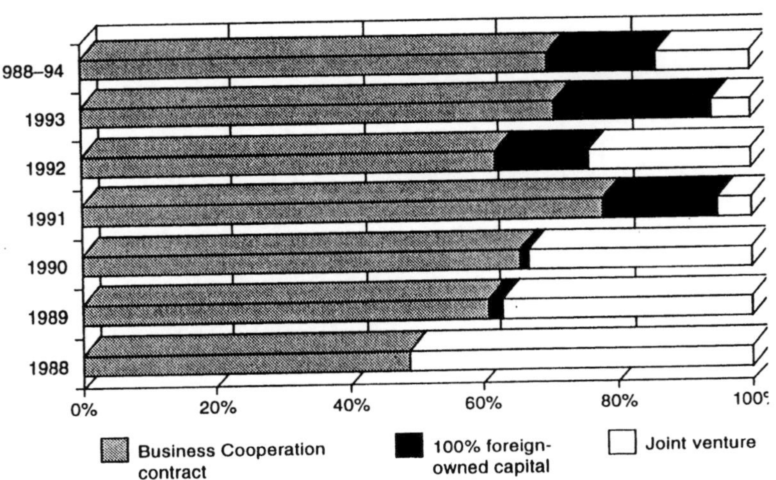

is more, quite a number of Vietnamese people taking part in joint ventures are inexperienced and badly prepared in this new kind of task; this also shows the limitation of Vietnam's capital.

Also, the changes in the Foreign Investment Law in December 1992 and other regulations issued later have helped a lot in changing the assessment of the joint venture and 100% foreign capital investments.

The joint venture investment is carried out mostly for the sharing of the product in exploring and exploiting petroleum. In fact, this is the only means that foreign investors can choose when they get involved in this sector. There also are joint ventures in other sectors, but these are small projects only with total investment capital of under USD 1 million and have a working life of less than two years.

BOT is applied to infrastructure construction projects and there has been only one project carried out in the BOT form which is a water-supplying project for Ho Chi Minh City with a total capital investment of USD 30 million since the official regulations in Foreign Investment Law were changed and amended.

There currently are six export processing zones (EPZ) that have been given operating licences. These include five EPZs that are managed by enterprises with foreign investment capital and the Can Tho EPZ which was built by Vietnam. These EPZs can accommodate more than 700 factories. In addition, the Tan Thuan EPZ has already built its infrastructure, there have been some other EPZs in operation and some others are being built or going to be built.

The Vietnamese government has issued an Industrial Zone (IZ) Regulation so as to attract foreign and domestic investment capital for IZ infrastructure construction and to set up industrial factories in these zones. The arrival of the industrial zones helps to overcome the EPZ's difficulties as the industrial zones can process both export and domestic consumer goods.

Foreign companies seem to have a great interest in IZ development-investment. So far Vat Cach and Dong Nai industrial zones have been granted licences. There have been many other foreign companies who have asked for establishment licences of IZs. These include Daewoo in Hanoi IZ, Ha Tinh IZ, Song Be IZ and Ba Ria–Vung Tau IZ.

In fact, Vietnam's foreign investment activities have shown that there has been an increasing FDI in the country. However, the density of FDI in Vietnam still stands in a modest position compared to that of other regional countries. FDI has expanded to other industrial areas to exploit Vietnam's cheap and abundant labour force and this also reflects the strong movements of investment current in the region.

5 FDI'S IMPACT AND PROSPECTS IN VIETNAM

5.1 FDI's Positive Effect on Economic Growth

Since 1989, Vietnam's economy has consistently reached a remarkably high growing rate: 5–6%, 8–9% in 1990–91 and 1992–94 respectively.

Table 2.11 EPZs with Licence in Vietnam

EPZ	Location	Total capital investment for infrastructure construction (million USD)
Noi Bai EPZ	Hanoi	30
Hai Phong EPZ	Hai Phong	150
Da Nang EPZ	Da Nang	24
Tan Thuan EPZ	Ho Chi Minh City	89
Linh Trung EPZ	Ho Chi Minh City	14
Can Tho EPZ	Can Tho	8

Source: SCCI

However, due to the low economic base of Vietnam, the country has a very low rate of GDP despite high growing rates (see Table 2.12). On the other hand, the low GDP rate is also due to the low income of the whole country. This results from the frequent budget deficit problem that Vietnam has long experienced. Consequently, there is the need for capital flow from outside countries to make up for this deficit problem. Besides ODA and other loaning lines, FDI has played an important role in these changes in the past few years. FDI's capital has, up to now, amounted to over USD 4 billion which accounts for 50% foreign capital, 27% of total investment capital and 6% of GDP. In order to double the country's GDP in a decade (1991–2000) which means reaching a growing rate of 8–8.5% in the years 1996–2000, Vietnam needs a total investment capital of USD 40 billion, 50% of which is foreign capital. ODA holds USD 7–8 billion and the rest is in FDI capital of USD 12–13 billion.

Therefore, it can be seen that, as in many other ASEAN countries in the first stage of their high economic growth, foreign capital, especially foreign investment capital, plays an important role in helping to achieve a high economic growth. For Vietnam, success and effectiveness of FDI activities in the coming years will significantly affect the overall result.

Until 1990, Vietnam's economy was still mostly subordinate to agriculture, and the growth rate of this sector contributed largely to the economic growth in general. In the period 1991–94, the attainment of a vigorous economic growth rate was due to the high growth rate in the fields of gas, oil, construction and industry. The economic framework has therefore changed considerably, and that has led to an increase in the industrial sector and a corresponding decrease in the agricultural

Table 2.12 Economic Growth (1990–94) (Unit: % GDP)

	1990	1991	1992	1993	1994
Growth rate	5.1	6.0	8.6	8.1	8.7
Investment rate	11.7	15.1	17.0	19.4	19.9
Domestic economic rate	7.4	13.1	16.3	11.2	15.0
Surplus in current account	4.2	1.9	0.7	8.3	4.9

sector (see Table 2.13). As long as that process of change continues, the process of shifting from mainly an exploitation of natural resources to an exploitation of the abundant labour resources will also take place.

Reviewing the FDI framework in terms of the line of production during the past few years, we can find that FDI during that time has played an active role in the shifting of the economic framework, particularly, the framework of more concentration on the sectors of industry, service, exploitation, and the tendency of shifting from the exploitation of natural resources, mainly in the oil field, to the exploitation of the advantages of the labour force.

In order to determine the causes of industrialization and modernization in the coming years, FDI is to be considered as an important source to invest in the spearhead industries like gas, oil, steel, cement, electronics, etc. (see Table 2.14) and to have a long-lasting influence on Vietnam's economy in the fields of supplying advanced technology, and modern methods of management. Nevertheless, we have seen that FDI activities over the past years and in the coming years play a significant role in ensuring a stable economic development.

5.2 FDI's Help in Expanding Domestic Demand

Increases in FDI help to create new opportunities for local entrepreneurs due to the fact that entrepreneurs often act as suppliers of materials for newly founded enterprises. To meet that ever-increasing demand, entrepreneurs should take all the initiative to expand domestic investment by themselves. Furthermore, the increase of FDI parallel to the increase of domestic investment would contribute to rising individual earnings and household consumption through job-creating programmes. So, FDI can be expected to contribute to increasing economic growth via encouraging domestic demand development.

What has been done in practice during the past years shows that FDI activities are a significant element to help to increase domestic demand. This is partly indicated in a relatively high rate of working

Table 2.13 Economic Framework (Unit: %GDP)

	1990	1993	2000
Agriculture	40.3	36.4	31.3
Industry	18.7	24.7	26.6
Service	40.9	38.9	42.1

foreign capital out of total investment capital (approximately one-third), and more clearly in the vigorous growth rate of service, hotel, construction, and industry. These also considerably contributed to economic growth during the past period.

FDI projects have created jobs for about 65,000 direct and regular workers and thousands of indirect labourers. In general, labourers in companies or enterprises with FDI capital can be seen to have much higher levels of salary than others.

Up to the year 2000, it is estimated that FDI will bring jobs to approximately one million labourers.

5.3 Influence of FDI Activities on International Economic Relations

The contribution of foreign entrepreneurs to expanding Vietnam's export activities was still limited in 1994, accounting for only 8.3% of total export turnover and 20% of industrial exports. It is easily understandable, due to the fact that these enterprises are on the way to implementation, especially the implementation of big projects for exports. In the first half of 1995, a range of important projects in the industry, hotel and service sectors that were put into operation, will considerably contribute to increasing of foreign currency income and exports. Table 2.15 shows that half of the income of enterprises with FDI during the past years is in terms of foreign currency. However, one fact that should be noted is that more than a half of that foreign currency income is from domestic sources. For exports, low increases in value are mainly caused by processed products.

East Asian countries, especially the NICs, are not only the main partners for investment but also the principal commercial clients of Vietnam. In 1993, these countries took up to 86% of Vietnam's total export value in which 85% was exports and 84% was imports. However if we consider the framework of exports and imports between Vietnam and these countries we find that the increase in trading activities

Table 2.14 Estimated FDI Framework (1991–2000)

Line of production	Working capital (million USD)	Rate (%)
Petrol	7,500	35
Heavy industry	1,500	7
Cement industry	1,500	7
Light industry	2,000	9
Industrial zones	5,000	23
Two high-tech zones	600	3
Fishery, forestry, agricultural sectors	800	3.5
Infrastructure	1,000	5
Hotel, office for rent, residence	1,500	7
Service	300	0.5
TOTAL	21,700	100

Figure 2.6 Sectoral Investment Structure

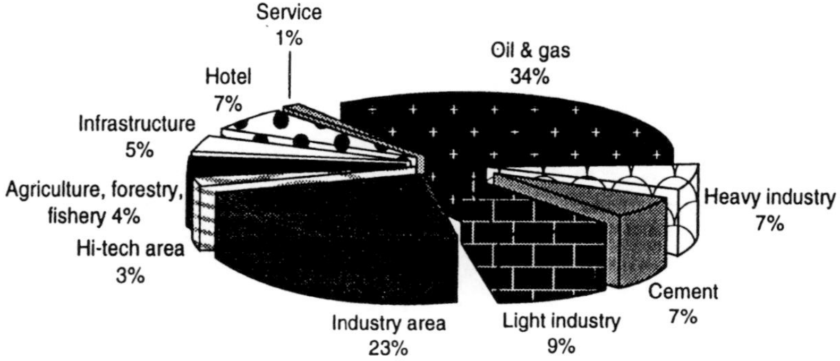

between Vietnam and the countries in the region over the past few years is not a result of investment activities made by these countries in Vietnam, but is merely due to commercial activities separate from investment activity. It seems too early to have a deep understanding of the inter-relationship between commercial and investment activities in Vietnam.

In the period 1993–94, the trade balance deficit regained its high level because of an increase in imports. One of the important factors leading to that increase was the import activities of the enterprises with FDI capital to join capital for founding enterprises in Vietnam.

Table 2.15 Export Earnings of Enterprises with FDI Capital (1988–94)

	1988–91	1992	1993	1994	1988–94
Working FDI capital (million USD)	620	535	1,001	1,520	3,676
Turnover (million USD)	192	230	358	776	1,446
Export, services for foreign currency (million USD)	82	160	169	355	766
Export, services for foreign currency/turnover (%)	43	70	47	46	50

Source: SCCI

Therefore, it can be said that FDI activities have had a positive influence on the economy in these years as import activities served for trading and production activities. To some extent, the import level of the enterprises with FDI capital is dependent on the amount of FDI capital actually brought into Vietnam during that period. These levels are increasing with every passing day and estimated in the neighbourhood of USD 4 billion up to now.

In recent years, Vietnam's trade balance always posted a deficit, and that created pressure to decrease the value of Vietnam's currency, the VND. But also in that period that pressure has partly diminished thanks to the flowing of hard foreign currencies into Vietnam mostly through FDI and international development aids. In fact, for the same period, the Vietnamese government has bought foreign currency to stabilize the VND exchange rate. So, besides exports, FDI activities during the past years have become an important source of supplying foreign currency and have had an influence on the Vietnamese government's exchange rate management activities. In the coming years, when FDI reaches high levels, the relationship between trading and investment activities will become closer. When many enterprises with FDI capital are put into operation and begin making profits, the FDI activities will have a stronger effect on the flow of foreign currency in and out of the country.

Due to the fact that most FDI projects are now in the first stage of implementation, it is difficult to make any recommendations on the relationship between international trade and investment in Vietnam. However, lessons about this kind of relationship can be drawn from other countries' experiences, especially East Asian countries. During the period of implementing the policy of production to substitute importation, FDI activity mainly occurred to elude the tax barrier and it

Figure 2.7 Earnings of Enterprises with FDI Capital

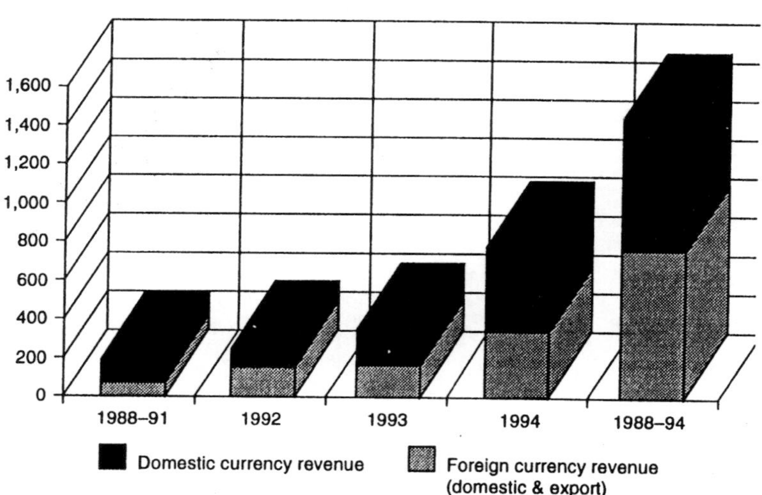

was considered a form of replacing imports. However, this kind of investment was not vigorously developed – one of the important reasons causing this circumstance being the limitations of the domestic market. Only when countries carry out the policy of production to serve exports can FDI activities be increasing rapidly at the same time.

One thing which should be noted is that foreign companies often export more than domestic companies do. One of the reasons here is that foreign companies have more advantages than domestic companies with a view to approaching international markets. Today when transnational companies are leading in international investment activities, the globalization of the production network has led to the necessities to exchange products between subsidiaries or officiates belonging to a certain group, and that has led to the increase of trade between countries, especially countries in the same region, and a more closely cultivated attachment in relationships between international trade and investment.

Less developed countries often wish that their enterprises with FDI capital operating in their territory could establish business relations directly with local companies under the form of collecting local materials used for production or indirectly under the form of creating demand for local suppliers. These countries also hope FDI activities will help to reduce tensions in trade balance through a policy of production for exports or production for replacing imports. However, it is often the case that transnational companies' commercial strategies do not always satisfy these hopes. On the contrary, host countries may face difficulties in exploiting the advantages of the FDI activities because of these strategies.

Multi-national companies with their anti-competition nature may carry out activities with a view to limiting competition which can be listed here with two typical forms having a negative influence on commercial activities of the host countries.

First, in order to minimize taxes on transferring profits abroad, affiliated companies try to import from their parent companies at high prices, while exporting to the parent companies at very low prices. As a result, expenditures on imports of the host countries (especially the less developing countries) rise and incomes from exports fall and this affects negatively the trade balance. Second, multi-national companies may make deals with one another with the purpose of fixing prices and dividing market segments or rights in owning a company itself. Parent companies may ask affiliates to import materials rather than buying them locally and limit the importing amount of the affiliates. For these reasons, the import and export values of transnational companies cannot meet the requirement from the host countries.

The host countries have devised a number of ways to cope with the above mentioned activities. In order to force foreign manufacturers to use domestic materials and to reduce imports to save foreign currency, the following methods are often applied: asking foreign manufacturers to use a certain amount of domestic materials; using import and foreign exchange restrictions; prohibiting the import of every kind of material that can be made domestically. The above methods can help to strengthen the inter-relationships between foreign and local manufacturers, and to reduce the trade balance deficit. However they also have negative effects, in particular, foreign manufacturers have to face the danger of using less developed materials and one of the important reasons is their limitation from domestic market.

According to the forecasts, to the year 2000, the world needs an annual USD 300 billion for investment, whereas there will be only USD 200 billion available and this will lead to the increasing investment pressure in the invested countries. As two Eastern–Southern Asian countries, China and India will have to face frequent budget deficits in the coming future, and they will have to strengthen the FDI flow and financial investment attraction to keep their economic growth increasing. In order to get the 10–11% annual growth rate in the five coming

Figure 2.8 Sectoral Structure

1988–90

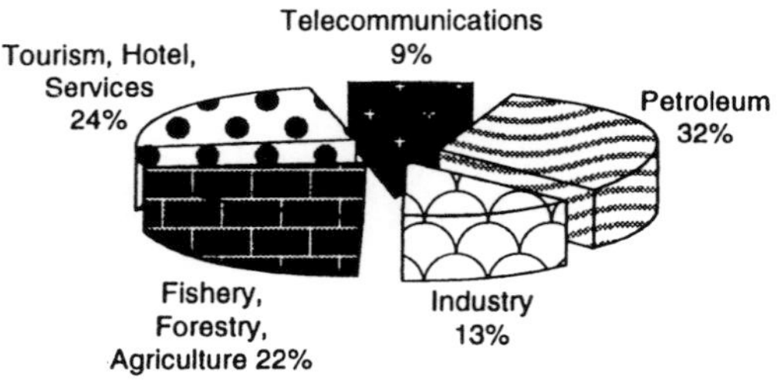
Telecommunications
9%
Tourism, Hotel,
Services
24%
Petroleum
32%
Fishery,
Forestry,
Agriculture 22%
Industry
13%

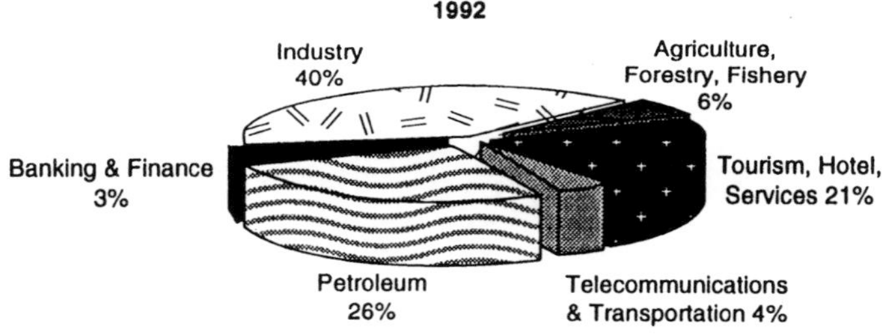
1992
Industry
40%
Agriculture,
Forestry, Fishery
6%
Banking & Finance
3%
Tourism, Hotel,
Services 21%
Petroleum
26%
Telecommunications
& Transportation 4%

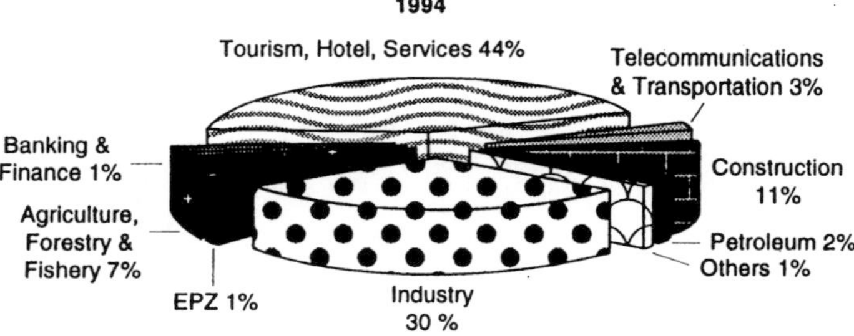
1994
Tourism, Hotel, Services 44%
Telecommunications
& Transportation 3%
Banking &
Finance 1%
Construction
11%
Agriculture,
Forestry &
Fishery 7%
Petroleum 2%
Others 1%
EPZ 1%
Industry
30 %

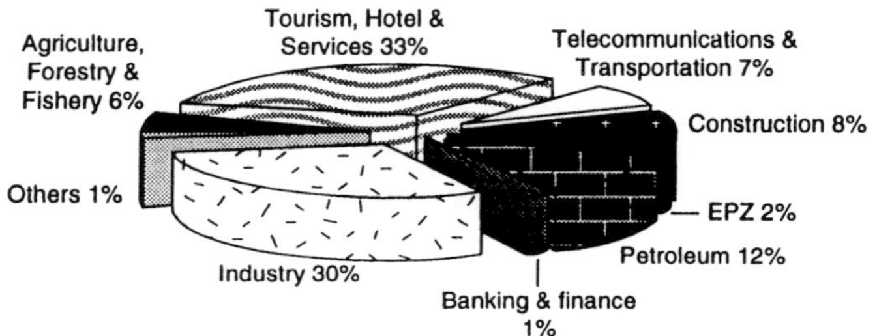
1988–94
Tourism, Hotel &
Services 33%
Agriculture,
Forestry &
Fishery 6%
Telecommunications &
Transportation 7%
Construction 8%
Others 1%
EPZ 2%
Petroleum 12%
Industry 30%
Banking & finance
1%

years, according to modestly estimated figures, Vietnam needs an amount of investment of USD 40–42 billion of which Vietnam hopes to attract an amount of USD 7 billion invested annually within five years, and USD 35 billion will be invested which accounts for up to 80% of total invested capital. Although this is a rate which is difficult to achieve, Vietnam hopes to develop the country's domestic capital flows so as to decrease its relative density, meanwhile keeping the attracted capital flows increasing.

Compared with the annual capital of USD 120–30 billion invested into ASEAN countries, China and India, the desired level of capital mentioned above for Vietnam is very modest and possible to be mobilized.

The crucial factor is that Vietnam has to maintain a competitive and aggressive investment environment to compete with other regional investment environments. A comparison between Vietnam's investment environment and that of other regional countries is useful.

It is well-known that there has been rapid increasing investment capital flow in Asia which holds a remarkable density of total direct capital investment into developing countries. However, there is a limitation on the capital directly invested into Vietnam when it is compared to that into other regional countries.

Being a major country in this area, Vietnam also enjoys some advantages in investment attraction. However, after Vietnam has attracted strong foreign investment activities, especially into hi-tech and increasingly valuable sectors, it has to cope with countries that have many more advantages.

The following observations are about Vietnam's investment environment compared to that of India, China, Indonesia, Malaysia, Thailand and the Philippines.

Human Resources

The ratio of population with a good education to total population in Vietnam is relatively higher than that in other regional countries. However, Vietnam lacks a skilful work force with expertise and knowledge to master complex technologies in the near future.

Although the salary paid to public servants in Vietnam is lower than that in other regional countries, the cost of labour that entrepreneurs have to pay for in these countries is usually double that salary. So it is acceptable to say the labour cost in Vietnam is not lower than that in the regional countries. It is a fact that business people having foreign investment capital cannot hire a labour force directly through the mass media but must hire through a state organization in charge of labour force management.

Infrastructure

This is the remarkable difference between Vietnam and other regional countries. Although a lot of regional countries now have to face infrastructural difficulties, their infrastructure is still much better than Vietnam's. The infrastructural weaknesses have been considered one of the main obstacles to direct investment activities in Vietnam. The upgrade of infrastructure based upon the state's budget, development aid and private investment will gradually eliminate this difference.

FDI's Preferences

There are not many investment preferences for entrepreneurs that own foreign capital to enjoy investment priorities unless they meet sectoral or invested zone requirements. Areas that enjoy investment priorities include export processing, production instead of imports, applications of advanced techniques and technologies, infrastructural and public services, those areas that promote the invested country's development and areas that are considered necessary by the host country. Regions enjoying investment priorities are undeveloped EPZs or free economic regions. Moreover, domestic and foreign investors, in Indonesia and Thailand, enjoy the same priorities whereas all entrepreneurs owning foreign investment capital in Vietnam can enjoy investment priorities.

In every country, the 100% ownership of foreign investment capital is always limited by rules such as foreign partners are not entitled to own 100% of invested capital in certain sectors or are entitled to it in other sectors. The 100% ownership of invested capital is usually considered through a number of requirements including production instead of imports, hi-tech, huge amount of capital, attraction of many employees, and investment into a certain region. However, the most important condition is export abilities and factories that export all of their products can easily be allowed to own 100% of foreign invested capital.

In Indonesia, foreign enterprises are often allowed to process a maximum proportion of 80% of their products, and after 20 years, this proportion must be reduced to 49% at the most. The projects with 100% foreign capital are also required to reduce the proportion of foreign processing. Vietnam does not impose limitations on the pro-

Table 2.16 Comparison of Tax Priorities

	India	Indonesia	Malaysia	China	Philippines	Thailand	Vietnam
Free duty or reduced taxes							
Free duty on increased capital	√		√				
Free duty on company's income							
Duration & condition of free duty	√		√	√	√	√	√
Reduce income tax & preferential duty	√		√	√		√	√
Applicability of other incomes	√		√			√	
Free duty or reduced taxes for imported-capital goods	√	√	√	√	√	√	√
Free duty or reduced taxes for imported materials	√	√	√	√	√	√	√
Free duty or inventions		√	√	√	√	√	√
Free duty or reduced taxes for loans given by foreign partners or organizations	√	√	√	√	√	√	√
Free of duties and other fees	√	√		√	√		√
Reduce income taxes							
Allowance of fast consumption	√	√		√	√		
Replace capital taxes in shift period			√				
Replace losses	√	√	√	√		√	√
Reduce export taxes	√		√			√	
Organizing and preparation fees	√	√	√	√	√	√	
Re-investment profit			√	√	√		√
Reduce taxes due to being invested			√		√		
Others	√	√	√	√	√	√	√

Table 2.16 Continued

	India	Indonesia	Malaysia	China	Philippines	Thailand	Vietnam
Reduce company's income							
Investment capital credit			√				
Capital credit of domestically purchased machinery & equipment					√		
Other tax credits	√	√	√	√	√		
Expand free duty & reduced duty duration	√		√		√		
Other special preferences on taxes							
Multi-national companies	√		√		√		
Exporters	√	√	√	√	√	√	√
Foreign banks			√		√	√	
Other legal rules profiting foreign investors						√	

portion of foreign processing, but it just regulates that the foreign sides' contribution must be no less than 30% of the main rights and guarantee for investment.

The Ownership of Foreign Investors in Business

All countries have their own regulations on the guarantee for investment by which no enterprises with FDI capital are compulsorily purchased unless in the very urgent cases for national security and social benefits, and they will be compensated according to market prices. However, in many countries (except Malaysia and Thailand), there is no regulation on the guarantee for the risks of being nationalized. And no country has regulations on the guarantee for risks caused by war or for risks caused by currency non-conversion. In these countries, besides the regulations specified by law, investment activities are also guaranteed by agreement for bilateral investment. Indonesia has a form of guarantee for multilateral investment due to its membership in the Multilateral Investment Guarantee Agency (MIGA) that has been supported by the World Bank.

Vietnam's constitution has affirmed that no nationalization is allowed except for very urgent cases relating to national defence, security and social benefits and the nationalization is done on the basis of compensation. However, Vietnam has not yet had regulations on the guarantee for war and non-convertible currency risks. Vietnam has already had some agreements of guarantee for multilateral investment, but many limitations still exist in comparison with other countries in the region.

Transferring of Money Abroad

In all countries, foreign investors are allowed to

1. transfer their incomes and legal dividends abroad
2. carry out settlements for both foreign loans and interest generated by those loans
3. transfer investment capital abroad
4. do other payments such as wages for foreigners working for the enterprises, money for indentations, money earned by selling processing quota, compensation, etc.

However, due to the fact that these countries are imposing a foreign exchange control system, all activities relating to the transfer of money abroad are being tightly controlled. They are often required to have approval from the responsible organizations and to fulfil all financial obligations, especially taxes, and they are allowed to transfer their incomes from dividends abroad.

Borrowing foreign capital requires the approval of the central bank. The transferring of money abroad must often be accepted by a bank or organization in charge of approving an establishment of the enterprises with foreign investment capital.

In Vietnam (according to the regulations on the law of transfer of foreign exchanges), the transferring of both principal and interest of foreign loans must be presented in detail in a techno-economic study that is to be submitted to the SCCI (now the Ministry for Planning and Investment) for protection and for priority designation to foreigners. Most countries enact a law that includes regulations on the pattern and trademark protection for a certain period of time.

Many countries have already signed bilateral and multilateral agreements to explain contents and scope of protection. Vietnam has promulgated an ordinance on copyrights, technical designs, and trademark protection. Vietnam however has not yet attended to the bilateral or multilateral agreement. Copyrights are protected for 15 years, and trade-marks are protected for 10 years. These timeframes are relatively short compared to those in other countries. In such countries as Malaysia, the Philippines and Thailand, foreign investors often receive financial support or assistance from the government through the organizations at both the central and local levels when they invest in such priority fields as production for exports, using high technology and infrastructure.

As in other countries, Vietnam has worked out methods to protect domestic production industries. The enterprises with foreign investment capital also get the same protection. However, nearly every country still maintains a certain discrimination of behaviour between the state-owned enterprises and the private ones. These countries also have a certain restriction on the presence of enterprises with FDI capital in some domestic production industries. In Vietnam, the state sector still plays a key role in production activities (accounting for 70% of the output produced and 43% of GDP) and the discrimination of behaviour between the state and private sectors still exists. The government has also introduced restrictions to prevent enterprises with FDI capital from engaging in such industries as automobile, soft drink, milk, beer production etc..

Such countries as Thailand, India and Malaysia have recognized the enterprises' right of processing. However, to reach this understanding, the enterprises have to satisfy a number of specific conditions. Other countries consider land as property belonging to the government and only use it for allocating or leasing. Enterprises with FDI capital are entitled to rent land for using as a production plant or a business place. However, in practice the statistics show that the foreign sides often face difficulties in renting land and have to set up joint ventures with the Vietnamese sides who use land-use rights as capital contribution.

Tax Incentives

Though all countries have their own policies of tax incentives towards the projects with FDI capital, their extent and the conditions of the incentives give us some ideas on the the forms of preference used by the countries involved. Vietnam, therefore still lacks some important preferences of tax that are often applied in the market economies.

The comparison of tax incentives described in Table 2.16 is applied to FDI by the countries in the region. If we only look at a comparison of low level regulations, we can see that Vietnam has introduced many incentives to attract foreign investors. However, due to the fact that the execution and enforcement of laws in Vietnam are not yet adequate, the most recent regulations on investment incentives still expose many limitations in practice.

Key Elements Affecting FDI in Vietnam in the Coming Years

FDI activities during the past years have demonstrated that the investment projects whose licences have been applied for or which are in operation are only focused on a number of specific fields. These fields cover oil exploration and exploitation, consumer goods processing and food processing, and accommodation in some provinces.

When we look at Vietnam's potential, we note that many fields and economic sectors have not yet been exploited, even though these fields would promise high profits for the investors. From an analysis of the international situation and the trend of actual FDI activities in Vietnam over the past few years, we have noted that the forthcoming FDI activity in Vietnam will be strongly influenced by a group of key elements. These are the prospect of investment of transnational corporations in the world by an integration of the regional and world economies, the ability to improve the domestic investment environment, as well as the economic, legal, and social environment.

As has been mentioned above, transnational corporations' investment strategy is more committed to keeping an important role in international investment in Vietnam in a region that has seen the on-going process of labour division and composition change in the multi-national corporations. Maybe Vietnam will become a rallying point where transnational corporations will set up a production base in a production network, particularly for the stages of investment that need labourers with low or average skills.

The participation of Vietnam in GATT (or WTO) and the ASEAN has helped to enhance Vietnam's position in the international arena, to avoid a discrimination of behaviour and to gain a preference for less developed countries. In order to get a more favourable condition to expand the market, Vietnam has to work to make investors more at ease and more assured when investing in Vietnam.

Although the investment environment in Vietnam has improved step by step, this environment is still less attractive than that in other countries in the region. This is due mainly to a weak or out-of-date infrastructure, a lack of freely convertible currency, a narrow market purchasing power, a synchronous policy system, a redundant bureaucracy, and cumbersome administrative procedures. And corruption is still a social evil that has not yet been abolished.

The existing infrastructure system can be seen as the biggest obstacle for development of FDI activities during the past years. This obstacle has existed for many decades and more of its nature has been exposed because Vietnam's economy is on the move and expanding its relations with the outside world. The backwardness of Vietnam's infrastructure is reflected by the overloading of some sea-ports, airports, roads, railways, an insufficient supply of water and electricity, and communications that have not yet kept pace with the market demand.

In the coming years, Vietnam will mainly depend upon development aids and budgetary funds to concentrate on upgrading and preparing the socio-technical infrastructure. Furthermore, the government encourages the private sector to invest in infrastructure constructions under many formulas, i.e., implementing the BOT projects, construction of centrally industrial zones, and investment for construction of EPZs. With the progress made in infrastructure construction, Vietnam will have more favourable conditions to overcome the previous imbalance in investment. The country will then be able to make the most out of its potential to become a more and more attractive place to FDI.

The financial system in Vietnam is still under tight control. These very controls are creating difficulties for foreign investors, since foreign exchange restrictions have the effect of increasing their working capital that is based on foreign funding to service the business activities.

Another difficulty is the absence of a stock market, and this forces the enterprises with FDI capital to rely on either their own capital or on borrowing with high interest bearing loans from the banks. The investment environment in less developed countries often contains many uncertainties that may cause dangers for foreign investors. In order to attract foreign investment, less developed countries must always try their best to reduce uncertainties in the investment environment.

Vietnam has made a certain amount of progress in macroeconomic stabilization that has considerably helped to create a stable investment environment. However, there still exist many uncertainties in that environment which mostly are caused by laws and regulations, administrative procedures and the practice of laws.

There still exist some inappropriate points and unsuitable aspects to a market mechanism. For example, there are many governmental organizations at all levels which are involved in the process of examining, approving, and implementing projects, and a great deal of information is required to meet many standards. Such examining procedures are still heavily affected by the traces of a centrally planning economy, and they replace the position of the entrepreneurs in some works, limit the choice for the investors, and slow down the process of investment implementation.

These procedures may not yet have exposed all of their defects or flaws given that there are not many submitted projects in the first period. But when the number of projects begins to increase as expected, the big projects will become obstacles for the growth rate tempo of FDI.

Many foreign investors have remarked that a rather open and expansive investment environment has been achieved in Vietnam. However, in practice, from the various steps which a project has to take in order to process its implementation and the undergoing of many complicated procedures, we have drawn quite contrary results. It can therefore be said that the improvement of the law environment and the strengthening of the execution ability of FDI play a very important role in attracting FDI.

During the past years, together with a high economic growth rate, macroeconomic stability and an open economy, the investment environment in Vietnam has been considerably improved, making it easier to attract more and more FDI. The very FDI activities themselves have contributed a not-small part to economic growth and created preconditions for maintaining sustainable development, expanding foreign economic relations, and integrating in the world and the regional economies. In the coming years, in order to implement industrialization and modernization, the role of FDI should be stressed more.

However, the FI activities, as we have seen during the past years, still face many obstacles due to the limitations of technical infrastructure, legal systems, and economic policies. They are the limitations that are very difficult to avoid for developing countries that are undergoing the process of shifting from a centrally planning mechanism to a free market one. These limitations also are challenges to Vietnam to overcome in the coming years in order to make the most out of investment opportunities that are on a spectacular rise in a severely competitive and dynamic economic region.

References

Asian Development Bank, *Asian Development Outlook*, Oxford University Press, Oxford 1991, 1992 and 1994.

Gates, Carolyn L. and David H. D. Truong *Foreign Direct Investment and Economic Change in Vietnam: Trends, Causes and Effects*, NIAS Report Series no. 20, Copenhagen, 1994.

Le Dang Doanh *Vietnam Country Report*. Presented at the International Conference on Asian Transitional Economies Project, Osaka, 30–31, October 1994.

Le Dang Doanh and Adam McCarthy, *Economic Reform in Vietnam – Achievements and Prospects*, in Seiji J. Naya and Joseph L. H. Tan (eds) *Asian Transitional Economies, Challenges and Prospects for Reform and Transformation*. ISEAS-ICEG, Singapore, 1995.

Pacific Economic Cooperation Council (PECC), *Pacific Economic Outlook*, PECC Secretariat and The Asia Foundation, Singapore, San Francisco 1995, 1996.

Tran Dinh Thien, 'Foreign Direct Investment in Vietnam'. *Vietnam's Socio-Economic Development Bulletin*. No. 4, 1995 pp. 29–34.

Dang Duc Dam, *Vietnam's Economy 1986–1995*. The Gioi Publishers, Hanoi, 1995.

World Bank *Vietnam Public Sector Management and Private Sector Incentives*. Report No. 13143-VN. Washington, D.C. 1994.

3 Foreign Investment Law in Vietnam: Legal and Economic Aspects and Comparative Analysis

Luu Van Dat

1 GENESIS OF VIETNAM'S FOREIGN INVESTMENT LAW (29 DECEMBER 1987)

Historical Background

1. The Vietnamese people's resistance against the French expeditionary force and other foreign occupiers or invaders in Vietnam immediately after the cessation of hostilities of World War II ended victoriously in 1954. However Vietnam's independence as a whole country was short-lived and it was divided by the Geneva Convention also in 1954 into two regions with two different political systems.

Almost 20 years on, the whole country was finally reunified in 1975. It is particularly important since 1975 that the leaders of Vietnam have tried to develop their country's economic, scientific and technical ties with countries all over the world in order to exploit effectively Vietnam's potentials to reconstruct and develop its economy.

It is true that Vietnam could only possibly develop the above mentioned ties after the South's liberation and the reunification of the country. Supported initially for a long time by the full cooperation, assistance and aid from the socialist countries, in a traditional way, Vietnam now plans to diversify its forms and partners of cooperation, and to make use of foreign direct investment in its economic development plan, at the same time using the principle of mutual interest and benefit.

2. On the 19 April 1977, the Socialist Republic of Vietnam (SRV) issued the Foreign Investment Rules in Vietnam, including Decision Number 115/CP (also known as Investment Rules of 1977).

The 1977 Investment Rules and other documents guiding the Rules' execution and implementation had made the earliest legal base for foreign investors, without any distinction of a socio-economic system, to directly invest and carry out business in Vietnam.

The 1977 Investment Rules have seven Chapters, and 27 Articles, and include the principles of investment areas, investment procedures, solutions for disputes, and the foreign investor's legal status.

Comments on the 1977 Investment Rules:

In May 1977, the National City Bank commented that: 'The Vietnamese have shown to be fairly practical when issuing the Foreign Investment Rules which seem unusual to be issued by a socialist government'.

After having analysed the difficulties that foreign investors had to face in their business dealings in Vietnam then, the Bank concluded, 'Despite of the above mentioned difficulties, Vietnam will possibly be successful in attracting investment in the coming years, as this country is always longing to expand its trading ties to other Western countries. What is more, Vietnamese leaders have decided key issues in this field already.' This forecast became true ten years later.

3. During the period between the late 1970s and early 1980s, due to the unfavourable international conditions for the development and expansion of foreign economic relations in Vietnam, the 1977 Foreign Investment Rules failed to bring about expected results.

During this period, the country's investment projects were mainly focused on exploring petroleum in the continental shelf of the southern part of Vietnam, and were undertaken by German, Italian and Canadian petroleum companies.

In 1980, a Vietnam-Russia Petroleum cooperation project was established and it is known to be based upon an Agreement signed by the Vietnamese government and the former Russian government. This project was in the framework of the two countries' policy of full cooperation for the purpose of exploration and exploitation of petroleum offshore in Vietnam. This cooperation started the early period of effective foreign direct investment into Vietnam.

Although the project had been signed and put in operation long before the 1987 Foreign Investment Law of Vietnam was issued, this important and potential project was basically using the elements of the principles and rules of the 1987 Foreign Investment Law, and was, what is more, getting encouraging results.

4. On 29 December 1987, at the second session of the 8th Legislature, the Vietnamese National Assembly approved the Law of Foreign Investment in Vietnam. On 9 January 1988, the President of Vietnam's State Council signed to approve the announcement of Vietnam's Foreign Investment Law.

The 1987 Foreign Investment Law succeeded and developed further the 1977 Investment Rules, and at the same time, started off from a new national and international context. It included important corrections and amendments appropriate for Vietnam's open economy policy in the Renovation or Doi Moi period as well as suitable to the well known principles in international investment laws.

The 1987 Foreign Investment Law was initiated from the country's economic and scientific-technical development standards and for an economy during the transitional period from a centralized planning management mechanism to a free marketing one.

This Law contains the government's guidelines, the socialist orientations, with the purposes of strengthening national interests and meeting the need and interests of foreign investors.

5. A study and comparison of the 1987 Foreign Investment Law and the 1977 Investment Rules would help us to get a useful understanding of the Vietnamese government's guidelines on the renovation process, economic policies, foreign economic relation management mechanism in the foreign investment areas, and the making of the trading laws in Vietnam.

The 1987 Foreign Investment Law and Vietnam's Legal System in the Renovation Period

1 Legal Systems in the World

According to the conditions of every nation's history, there have been many different legal systems which have been constituted in the world.

Looking at every nation's legal characteristics, legal experts hold that there have been the following legal systems formed:

(a) The continental legal system or civil law, derived from the ancient Roman law, is applied and prevails in most of the continental European countries and the countries affected by this continental legal system.

(b) The Anglo–American legal system or common law
(c) Socialist countries' law
(d) Religious law

In fact, all of these legal systems (except the religious law) tend to get close to one another not only in terms of their content but also in the ways of making law in different contexts, especially in the area of trading laws. However, each still maintains its characteristic and typical features.

2 *Characteristics of Vietnam's Legal System*

2.1 The main characteristics of Vietnam's legal system were regulated in the 1992 Constitution of the SRV.

(a) Article 12 states that: 'The state uses laws to run its society'.

(b) Article 31 states that: 'The state teaches its citizens how to live and work under its laws and constitution'.

Article 91 states that: 'The Standing Committee has the following rights and duties:

1/ . . . . (not reproduced here)
2/ . . . . (not reproduced here)
3/ . . . . To explain the country's laws, constitutions, and decrees'.

(c) Article 130 states that: 'Judges and jurors have to give judgements independently and in accordance to the country's laws'.

2.2 Based upon the 1992 Constitution of the SRV and the above mentioned quotations, we have the following comments:

(a) The Vietnamese state is a jurisdictional state in which social and daily relations have to be adjudicated by laws.

(b) Being a socialist-jurisdictional state of the people and for the people, the Vietnamese state actively and persistently strives to gain the targets of a wealthy people, a powerful country, social justice and a civilized society.

(c) Vietnamese law is the written law. Positive law is very important.

(d) Vietnamese law courses are mainly law documents that include:

- Documents approved by Vietnam's National Assembly and Vietnam's Standing Committee of the National Assembly (laws, decrees . . .)

- Documents issued and promulgated by the country's President (orders, decisions . . .)
- Documents issued in accordance to Articles 112, 116, 117 of the 1992 Constitution of Vietnam by the government (resolutions, enactments), by the Prime Minister (decisions, instructions), by ministers and government's members (decisions, instructions, circulations).

Besides, international treaties (bilateral and multi-lateral treaties) signed or participated in by the Vietnamese government contribute an important source to Vietnam's laws.

(In the case where there are differences between Vietnam's national law provisions and international treaties that Vietnam has signed or participated in over a certain issue, international treaties will be applied.)

(e) Courts and judges have to give judgements and settlements on dispute cases according to the law's regulations and provisions without a responsibility for explaining the law.

Vietnam's National Assembly Standing Committee is the only one state body to be competent to explain law, constitution, and decrees of Vietnam.

(f) Jurisprudence, legal customs, and legal theory are not considered to be laws in Vietnam.

2.3 Remarks:

(a) Based on what has been mentioned above, the legal system in Vietnam has similar characteristics to the continental legal systems, especially in the way of making laws.

However, regarding the content of the law, the Vietnamese law has typical characteristics that make it different from the laws of other countries: Vietnamese law is initiated from Vietnam's conditions and contexts in the 1987 Renovation period and in accordance with the consideration of the country's good morals and good customs.

At the same time, the Vietnamese law attaches much importance to the essence of foreign laws which belong to the continental and Anglo legal systems, particularly in trading and international relations and other well known international principles.

(b) In dealing with Vietnam's laws, we come to realize that we cannot study only each particular document but we have to study every and all related documents comprehensively and systematically. That is, we have to study not only the meaning and content of a certain provision of a term but also to analyse political, economic and social features in Vietnam.

On that basis, we can go more deeply into the spirit of the law, the ideology of the legislators and the law expert drafters.

2 THE FOREIGN INVESTMENT LAW OF 1987

The Foreign Investment Law of 1987 in Vietnam's Laws

1. Going into the Renovation period, the Foreign Investment Law of 1987 is the first act related to business activities between Vietnam and foreign countries that has been approved by Vietnam's National Assembly.

The Foreign Investment Law of 1987, therefore, has a special significance and plays an important role in Vietnam's legal system in general, in law on business, and international private laws in particular.

2. Different from the investment law of some other countries, the objective of the Foreign Investment Law of 1987 does not include investment in general and is limited to foreign direct investment activities in Vietnam.

According to the Foreign Investment Law of 1987, foreign investment could be understood to be activities by which foreign individuals and juridical persons bring into Vietnam capital in foreign currency or any kind of properties allowed by the Vietnamese government to conduct their business in Vietnam's territories, conforming to the formulas specified by law (Article 2 of Vietnam's Foreign Investment Law).

The Foreign Investment Law of 1987, therefore, neither has the function of regulating other forms of foreign investment in Vietnam such as granting loans, official development aids (ODA), nor of regulating investment by Vietnamese citizens abroad.

The Foreign Investment Law of 1987 does not have the function of regulating domestic investment activities conducted by Vietnamese citizens (individuals and juridical persons) in their own country.

Foreign indirect investment activities, both outside investment and inside investment, are the object of many legal documents and other written texts specified by law.

Among the legal documents already promulgated, there have been laws on encouraging domestic investment that have been approved by Vietnam's National Assembly at the Fifth Meeting of the National Assembly, Session IX, dated 22 June 1994.

At the current stage, Vietnam's investment laws consists of foreign investment law in Vietnam and domestic investment law. Each of the above laws aims at different goals (but having the same final goal) and all have different objectives and scope of implementation.

Regardless of its significance and the degree of importance, the Foreign Investment Law of 1987 only holds a certain position in Vietnam's investment law and business legal system.

3. The Action of the 1987 Foreign Investment Law – The law on encouraging foreign direct investment in Vietnam encourages all foreign investors, regardless of their nationality to invest capital, techniques, and technology in Vietnam.

To achieve the above mentioned purpose, the 1987 Foreign Investment Law has created a legal framework for foreign direct investment activities in Vietnam, a legal background, standards and conditions:

(a) To bring business opportunities in Vietnam to foreign investors.

(b) To help them to seek and to choose between investment projects suggested by the Vietnamese sides or proposed and decided by the foreign investors on an effective form of investment and trade, in accordance with their capabilities and meeting the investors' interest on the principle of 'free to do business' in the market economy.

When seeking investment opportunities or choosing an investment project, investors should pay due attention to the goals of the investment law, and the ideology of Vietnam's law makers. These are:

(a) Expanding scientific and economic cooperation between Vietnam and foreign countries on the basis of equality and mutual benefits;

(b) Export promotion;

(c) Developing Vietnam's national economy in the direction of industrialization and modernization on the basis of effectively exploiting natural resources, labour, and other potential of the country.

4. With the above mentioned objectives and goals, the Foreign Investment Law of 1987 mainly regulates such relations as follows:

(a) Relationship between foreign investors and the state and state bodies in Vietnam;

(b) Relationship between foreign investors and Vietnamese partners under the form of business cooperation (business cooperation on contract, joint venture, building-operating and transferring [BOT]);

(c) Relationship between enterprises with foreign investment capital (as a Vietnamese juridical body) and Vietnam's state organizations, domestic and foreign clients.

5. The Foreign Investment Law of 1987 is applied in the whole territory of the SRV including 'inland, offshore islands, sea territories, and air space' (Article 1 – the Constitution of 1992), as affected from laws being approved by Vietnam's National Assembly.

Progress of the Foreign Investment Law of 1987

1. The Foreign Investment Law of 1987 has 6 chapters and 41 articles. There are many similarities with the investment laws of some developing countries. It is a 'frame act'. The Foreign Investment Law of 1987 contains the fundamental rules, and legal standards in the field of investment. Some of the main topics are:

(a) Form of investment
(b) Legal position of companies, and enterprises with foreign investment capital
(c) The rights and obligations of the foreign investors
(d) The way by which the Vietnamese government controls the investment activities of enterprises with foreign investment capital. This requires the Vietnamese government to enact written texts to set in concrete the rules introduced in the investment law and to provide guidance on the implementation.

At the current stage, the objective and subjective conditions have not yet enabled Vietnam to compile complete acts as other countries do, especially in the fields that are covered under the Renovation period. Furthermore, Vietnam still lacks the experience and practices in the fields of economics and finance, to name only two.

Pursuant to Article 42 of the Foreign Investment Law, the Ministerial Council or Council of Ministers (the government) has enacted Decree No. 139/HDBT, dated 5 September 1988, providing detailed regulations on the implementation of the Foreign Investment Law 1987.

The Foreign Investment Law of 1987 and Decree No. 139/HDBT are the first important legal documents to create a legal framework for foreign investment in Vietnam, and inaugurate an era of renovation of business law in Vietnam.

Besides Decree No. 139/HDBT, Ministries and related state organizations (Ministry of Foreign Affairs, Ministry of Finance, Ministry of Labour, War Invalid and Social Affairs, Ministry of the Interior, Ministry of Foreign Economic Relations, General Department of Customs, etc.), in their turns, have enacted written texts, providing guidance on the implementation of the Foreign Investment Law and Decree No. 139/HDBT in accordance with their functions and jurisdictions.

The above documents together make up Vietnam's set of investment laws, a special legal system being applied to foreign investment activities, to foreign investors, to Vietnamese partners acting in the investment field, and to enterprises and companies with foreign investment capital, but not applied to internal business organizations.

The legal status of the companies owning foreign capital is different from that of the domestic trading companies. Rights and duties of the foreign investing companies are of a broader sense and also of a limited sense when they are compared with those of the domestic companies.

The foreign investing companies, once trading in Vietnam, are Vietnamese legal entities and they have to observe Vietnam's laws in general as well as trading laws in Vietnam.

There are, however, laws applied to the special cases of investment activities or economic sectors. In such cases, the investment law is applicable.

2. The Foreign Investment Law of 1987 and Vietnam's investment laws are on the move to completion.

The Foreign Investment Law of 1987 has been amended twice, in 1990 and 1992, by the law of corrections and amendments for foreign investment law in Vietnam. (At the Seventh Session of the Eighth Legislature 6/1990 and the Second Session of the Ninth Legislature 12/1992 of Vietnam's National Party Congress).

In order to be suitable to the corrections and amendments to the Foreign Investment Law of 1987, law implementation instruction documents must have corresponding adjustments.

In 1991, Vietnam's Council of Ministers (presently the government) issued Decree No. 28 HDBT, dated 6/2/1991, to replace Decree No. 139-HDBT.

In 1993, the Vietnamese government issued Decree No. 18/CP dated 16/4/1993 to replace Decree No. 28-HDBT.

The Foreign Investment Law of 1987 and two laws of regulations and amendments for foreign investment law in Vietnam issued in 1990 and 1992, Decree No. 18/CP, and documents instructing the implementation for Decree No. 18/CP issued by related Ministries and agencies (SCCI, State Planning Committee, Ministry of Trade, Ministry of Finance, Ministry of Labour, War Invalid and Social Affairs, Ministry of Science, Technology and Environment, Ministry of Transportation, Ministry of Interior Affairs, State Bank, General Department of Land Management, Customs Department, etc.) are all legal documents and are to be observed in the investment activities in Vietnam.

3. The above mentioned improvements to the Foreign Investment Law 1987 are aimed at meeting the necessity of the process of renovation in Vietnam, policies and management mechanism in Vietnam, as well as at improving the legal environment in the foreign investment area.

When comparing the Foreign Investment Law of 1987 with the corrections and amendments issued in 1990 and 1992, Decree No. 139/HDBT issued in 1988 with Decree No. 28/HDBT issued in 1991, Decree No. 18/CP issued in 1993, and documents instructing the implementation of investment law, we have some following comments:

(a) The Foreign Investment Law of 1987 was developed in line with the 'open' tendency and suitable to a theory on an open economic system, Vietnam's international integration policies, a development of a multi-commodity and multi-sector economy, marketing mechanism, state management, and plans to create a favourable legal climate for foreigners to invest in Vietnam.

The above mentioned tendency is positive, stable and united.

The 1990 Law and the 1992 Law have broadened the rights of Vietnamese business to cooperate with foreign partners, and allowed Vietnamese business of different economic compositions, including private economic compositions, to cooperate with foreign partners.

The 1992 Law has provided a diversifying form of investment, completed BOT contracts, EPZ organizations, and has expanded the life of the investment projects from 20 to between 50 and 70 years.

Enactment No. 191/CP dated 28/12/1994 issued by the government of SRV concerning the regulations to form, to improve, and to implement investment projects, and Enactment No. 192/CP dated 28/12/1994 promulgating the Regulations of Industrial Zones have had important corrections and amendments on the procedures and ways of simplification to reduce some difficulties for investors and to create favourable conditions for foreign investors to invest in Vietnam.

(b) Based upon realities, earlier issued regulations and instructions were overhauled, and corrected specifically, fully and more strictly.

As a result, these regulations and instructions on the requirement of direct investment activities are getting more and more complex and diversified.

Moreover, these factors not only meet the acceptable requirements of the foreign investors and Vietnamese partners but also are compatible with the general international law in the investment area.

As a result, the corrections and amendments to the legal investment documents that have been carried out in Vietnam cannot be regarded as unstable factors of the investment law of this country.

This phenomenon is similar to the general evolutionary rules happening in the countries that are developing their foreign investment activities.

4. Despite the fact that there are still weak points and deficiencies which need to be studied and corrected, the Foreign Investment Law of 1987 is developing favourably and in the right direction.

Vietnam's investment law has brought into full play its attraction to foreign investment in Vietnam.

4 Priority Areas to Attract Foreign Investment Capital to Vietnam: Present Conditions and Prospects

Nguyen Quang Thai

GENERAL VIEWPOINT

It is recognized that in order to expand national economic development, its production must be increased, saving or thrift strictly practised, and accumulation of physical and financial resources rapidly increased from the inside of the economy itself. For poor countries at an early development stage such as Vietnam, Laos, Cambodia, and Myanmar, it is necessary to mobilize further part of the accumulation of capital from foreign countries.

Capital from outside the country is of great significance, as can be seen from the following points:

1. Foreign capital contributes additional *financial resources to investment*, thus complementing domestic capital resources. This is of importance especially to developing as well as developed countries. In the case of the former, domestic capital resources are particularly limited while the need for investment funds is large.

2. Foreign capital may be used to generate a process of *technological transfer*, even if such a transfer may not be in the highest category. Usually, foreign countries in their programmes involving investment and technological transfer have certain restrictions on their 'hardware' transfer (machineries, equipment) and 'software' transfer (technical secret, managing technology), just to avoid possible competition with other countries having their capital invested abroad.

This means that these countries often transfer to the invested countries only 'second rate technology' that may not be acceptable or competitive in the home country. This may include the sort of technology that may create pollution, or that has been or will be of reduced efficiency. Thus, it is fair to suggest that a caution is required on the part of the host country in the case of its receiving foreign capital.

3. As has been mentioned above, the arrival of foreign capital is often accompanied by technological transfer, more or less. Therefore, if the most could be made of this technology transfer, it could contribute to a training of a contingent of leading cadres, engineers, foremen and skilled workers. And more could be learned for increasing productivity and product quality, and for reducing environment pollution.

4. Foreign investment is often seen by overseas investors as a measure of 'capital exportation', creating goods as 'substitutes for imported goods' mainly for the host country.

At the same time, this does not exclude either the possibility of *finding outlets* through negotiations, consuming part of the products and of the goods gradually approaching the international market. Thus, foreign investment (be it direct or indirect) is always capable of boosting exports.

In the case of foreign capital resources, the part that belongs to foreign private investment is of important interest.

This has been known as foreign direct investment (FDI).

A characteristic of FDI capital is that it does not lead necessarily to loans and debts except for a number of cases when the host country is short of capital and it has to borrow both capital and 'corresponding capital'. Anyway, FDI capital basically does not pose difficulties such as debts and payments.

However, since most of the capital invested in a host country belongs to foreign capital investors, in spite of the fact that domestic production also increases as a result, foreign investors are, in the view of many, likely to collect their profits as quickly as possible and to transfer their capital abroad out of their greed for profits or for a good return rate to the investors' capital.

There are also those foreign capitalists who do not bring in capital as planned but mobilize capital from the customers or use this as the mode of reinvestment. Thus, there is a certain gap between a practical and nominal mobilization of foreign capital.

In the process of Doi Moi (or Renovation) in Vietnam which was announced by the government of Vietnam in 1987, the state has paid good attention to the form of FDI in order to attract more FDI.

It should be noted that, in fact, by the end of 1977 and long before the Renovation announcement in 1987, Vietnam's National Assembly had already adopted the rules on foreign investment.

So far, with a few amendments, this Foreign Investment Law of 1987 has been considered relatively effective and sufficient, having over 50 legal documents attached to it as guidelines to its application and implementation.

Foreign direct investment is having its growing effect on changing the economic situation in Vietnam. FDI capital is being increased. The period of five years from 1991 to 1995 saw the implementation of some 26% of the total national investment at a value amounting to nearly USD 4 billion.

For the period ending in late 1995, licences had been issued to more than 1,500 projects with a total investment capital of more than USD 19 billion in which over USD 5 billion had been implemented.

These projects had contributed an important part during this period to the growth of Vietnam's economy, with the creation of more jobs (over 70,000 people are directly involved and 150,000 people are indirectly involved in the concerned areas of foreign investment) and by increasing the value of export goods. In fact, exports in the two years 1993–94 increased to a value of USD 500 million, and USD 248 million of taxes had been collected by the government in this same period.

With an aim to attract more foreign investment capital, the government of Vietnam has had an official policy of investment in the priority areas in order to orient FDI projects into those directions where the state wants them to be more concentrated and more rapidly effective for the sake of a general national planning strategy to promote economic and social growth.

FDI PROJECTS IN THE PERIOD 1988–95

General

In the initial stage of Vietnam's recent economic development, especially in the first three or four years of the Doi Moi period, 1988–91, the attraction of FDI capital was relatively 'easy' (see below) because of the difficulties the economy was experiencing, namely, the conditions of high inflation and a socio-economic crisis.

The Vietnamese government agencies could allow FDI investment to be directed to those fields of operation that domestic investment capital could in fact support but, because of a lack of capital, found it difficult to mobilize. So in the first three years, 1988–90, the structure of licence issuance and implementation of FDI projects had the following characteristics:

1. *In skills and branches*: FDI projects used to focus on 'easy gain' branches like restaurants, hotels, and tourism. In some cases, investment went to oil and gas exploration and tapping.

2. *In the territory of operation*: The allocation of FDI capital was used to be focused in the southern provinces, especially the provinces belonging to key economic development areas (such as Ho Chi Minh City, Dong Nai, Song Be, and Ba Ria – Vung Tau).

3. *In value*: FDI projects were of relatively small scale: each was valued at about USD 8.4 million. There were 213 projects with a total investment capital of USD 1.794 billion.

4. *In the form of investment*: FDI projects were mainly joint ventures or business cooperation contracts. These two forms were accepted by the Investment Law of 1987. The time limit for joint business and its implementation was also relatively short.

5. *In counterpart*: The range of investment counterparts (that is by foreign investing capitalist countries or companies) was relatively narrow.

Readjustment Period

In the period of five years, 1991–95, there have been certain readjustments in investment priorities by the government. These readjustments have had the effects of bringing about practical positive changes to the mobilization of capital, issuance of licences and their implementation.

1. In Terms of Branch Structure

In addition to those branches especially in the hi-tech industry (such as electronics and metallurgy), the distribution of FDI into the different sectors of Vietnam's economy as at 1995 is given in Table 4.1.

2. In Terms of Localities

The distribution of FDI capital in terms of localities in Vietnam as at 1995 is given in Table 4.2.

Table 4.1 Foreign Direct Investment (in terms of branches)

No.	Branch	Projects	Total investment in million USD
1	Industry	784	8,056.7
2	Oil and gas	21	1,125.4
3	Agriculture	34	305.3
4	Fishery	23	61.7
5	Communication, transport, post	45	1,066.0
6	Hotel, office, apartments, tourism, travelling	238	6,330.9
7	Services	63	16
8	Finance, banking	18	250.0
9	Construction	27	86.6
10	Education, training, public health, culture, sport	23	206.0
11	Export-processing enterprises	60	202.7
12	Infrastructure construction of industrial zone	7	335.4
	TOTAL	1343	18,128.4

* Not including projects invested abroad, licence revoked and overdue projects.

Source: Ministry of Planning and Investment, 12/1995

Table 4.2 Ten Leading Localities for FDI

No.	Locality	Projects	Total investment (in million USD)
1	Ho Chi Minh City	506	5,820.8
2	Hanoi	222	3,674.0
3	Dong Nai	145	2,379.6
4	Hai Phong	45	788.3
5	Ba Ria-Vung Tau	46	761.2
6	Quang Nam-Da Nang	36	496.8
7	Thanh Hoa	6	420.1
8	Song Be	58	419.1
9	Kien Giang	4	337.6
10	Hai Hung	17	206.8

* Not including oil and gas projects, total investment capital USD 1125 million

Source: Ministry of Planning and Investment, 12/1995

Table 4.3 Scope of FDI

Year	Project	Total capital (million USD)	Average (million USD/project)
1991	151	1,323	8.8
1992	197	2,168	11.0
1993	267	3,170	11.9
1994	342	3,765	11.0

In total, we have the following statistics

- 48 provinces and cities
- Total projects: 1322
- Total investment capital: USD 17,003 million.

3. *In Terms of FDI Value*

The scale (or value) of the investment projects was getting larger and larger, some of them amounted to several hundred millions in USD. The trend of the scope in FDI between 1991 and 1994 is given in Table 4.3.

4. *In Terms of Investment Form*

Besides the existing forms of foreign investment as permitted by the Investment Law of 1987, this stage of development has seen the additional appearance of new investment forms. Some of these forms are discussed below:

– Building of concentrated zones, and export-processing zones (EPZ). The Tan Thuan EPZ in Ho Chi Minh City was the very first to be approved, and it is now in operation with some 100 businesses.

– The 100% foreign invested capital projects account for a rather large proportion because of the preference given to their tax concession on the revenue (only 10% a year) and the longest tax exemption time (four years from their profitable business and four subsequent years with 50% of the tax only being paid).

– BOT 'Building – Operation – Transfer'. Foreign investors are greatly interested in this new area of investment, which is investment into infrastructure projects like roads, seaports, power stations, etc.

5. In Counterpart Structure

The volume of participating counterparts (investing countries) is getting larger and larger, involving over 50 countries and territories. Some of the leading investing countries in Vietnam's economy in 1995 are given in Table 4.4.

In total, we have the following statistics

- 52 countries and territories.
- 1,343 projects under operation (1,587 licensed projects).
- Total capital: USD 18,128.4 million (1,961 million USD).
- Projects: 228 with a capital of USD 1,251.9 million.
- Projects with licences revoked: 16 with a capital of USD 310.7 million.

The above results have been obtained as a result of the issuance by the government of Vietnam of a series of encouraging and guiding measures. These measures are namely:

1. The government has clearly pointed out its priorities for the attraction of foreign investment and these are conforming to its plan in general.

The highest priority in recent times has been with projects in the field of building infrastructure in the mountainous and difficult regions, afforestation, and other particularly important projects for the national economy.

Apart from the preferential policies mentioned in Decree 18/CP of 16 April 1993, the state again allowed localities to have additional preferential policies like a reduction of 50% of tax for the projects' deployment location, worker selection, and supply of electricity and water service.

However, these priority projects have attracted only a few foreign investors, and most of them are related to afforestation along the coast.

2. The FDI projects of the second priority are in the areas like infrastructure, resource exploitation (except oil and gas and rare minerals), heavy industry, (metallurgy, chemicals, engineering, cement), perennial industrial crops and investment in the mountainous and difficult regions.

For these projects, tax on the revenue was fixed only at 15%, exempted for the first two years after their profitable business began and

Table 4.4 Ten Largest Investing Countries (in 1995)

No.	Country/territory	Projects	Total investment capital
1	Taiwan	60	1209.5
2	Japan	56	1136.4
3	USA	25	830.4
4	Korea	47	556.3
5	B.V. Islands	22	413.3
6	Singapore	37	374.5
7	Sweden	2	341.7
8	Bahamas	1	264.0
9	Australia	9	189.0
10	Hong Kong	25	152.8

* Not including projects invested abroad

Source: Ministry of Planning and Investment, 12/1995

Table 4.5 Ten Largest Investing Countries
(Counted until the end of 1995, including projects in operation)

No.	Country/territory	Projects	Total investment capital
1	Taiwan	236	3315.8
2	Hong Kong	185	2154.0
3	Japan	126	2030.2
4	Singapore	113	1511.3
5	Korea	137	1506.5
6	USA	54	1141.7
7	Malaysia	42	846.7
8	Australia	47	703.2
9	France	70	638.6
10	Switzerland	15	584.8

* Not including projects invested abroad

Source: Ministry of Planning and Investment, 12/1995

reduced by 50% in the four subsequent years.

Moreover, after having finished their term, the properties are not to be transferred to the Vietnamese side (not including the BOT form of investment). For this reason, there has been a proliferation of this kind of project. Until October 1995, 11 project licences had been issued with a total FDI capital amounting to USD 1,225 million.

The attractiveness of these projects to foreign investors is also due to the fact that Vietnam has a rather good advantage in its ready contingent of skilled workers and a large domestic market with over 73 million people (in 1995), with a growing purchasing power as income per capita rises, and an export possibility to the neighbouring markets.

Foreign investors could be able to find strong enough partners inside the country especially now that Vietnam has recently set up a series of corporations as embryos of eventual powerful economic groups that could integrate with foreign countries and deal with them more efficiently.

For instance, the Cement Corporation is being integrated with several foreign cement groups to deploy large scale projects in all three zones of the country, the North, the Central and the South. The four recent projects alone have been able to attract USD 900 million, and six others are being prepared to have their licences issued with an FDI capital amounting to USD 1.4 billion.

The Hanel and Daewoo joint venture in Hanoi, in its development of an electronics industry in Vietnam, has obtained a rapid success with a high level of technology transfer that provides the possibility of exports and a capability to face international competition. Other projects for the plantation of sugarcane and its processing, and for the plantation and processing of coffee and tea, have also attracted the attention of foreign investors.

3. The BOT projects have begun to proliferate in large number. There have been 31 projects with 100% foreign capital with a total capital of USD 1.3 billion and 50% of them have been implemented. These statistics show the attractiveness of these projects.

Among the projects issued with licences, the Nha Be-Binh Chanh highway project was meant to disentangle the southern part of Ho Chi Minh City and to link the ports of the Saigon area to the 1A national highway system which is being restored and upgraded.

Ho Chi Minh City alone has seven BOT projects which have been established with a total capital of USD 810 million. The projects of the Ben Dinh-Sao Mai port also called for the same attention from the BOT investors with a total capital of USD 600 million.

The BOT projects normally obtain from the government a number of preferential conditions like an exemption of land rent tax, an enjoyment of a low tax rate on the revenue, a capital loan from the state bank, and the use of valued properties as mortgage in capital loan negotiations.

4. In the process of deployment of FDI projects, a problem is raised, and that is *of capital contribution rate from the Vietnamese side*, by making it higher than the present rate of 30%. This demands that the Vietnamese parties strengthen their integration into a partnership strong enough to deal with the foreign side.

For instance, in the Nghi Son cement projects, the Vietnamese side contributes 35% of capital with 15% coming from the Cement General Corporation, and 10% from each of the two provinces, Nghe An and Thanh Hoa. In this way, the interest of the Vietnamese side can be assured.

In the future, it will be necessary to study the possibility of gradual share repurchase to increase the capital of the host country.

Projects like restaurants, hotels and commercial centres obtain more benefits but the capital contribution rate from the Vietnamese side tends to be low. This has the undesirable result of greatly affecting national economic interest. The problem is being considered for a readjustment to a minimum level of 30%, just like other regulations that demand hotels to reach their three or more star standards.

5. For those non-encouraged projects like restaurants and hotels, there is no preferential treatment. However, once these projects have been transferred to the Vietnamese side after their operation, tax preference could be obtained (for example, an exemption of tax for the first two years after the business becomes profitable and a reduction of 50% of tax in the four subsequent years).

Projects that could enjoy priority are those reaching two among the following four indexes (except for the projects pertaining to the fields of banking, finance, insurance, accountancy service, audit and trade).

(a) Having more than 500 workers
(b) Using advanced technology
(c) Exportation of over 80 products
(d) Having a legal capital of over USD 100 million

In fact, using these criteria, a number of joint ventures in garment making could be considered for priority.

ORIENTATION OF PRIORITY FOR THE PERIOD 1996–2000

In the period 1996–2000, a five year plan is being established, and the Vietnamese government will pay due respect to the attraction of FDI capital to the country.

From the estimates of the investment plan, to ensure a GDP growth rate of 9–10% per year on average and over the entire country, it is expected to require an investment of USD 40–42 billion, and this is to be mobilized from FDI capital. This is a large amount of FDI capital. However the plan is of a high feasibility level as most of its capital has been under necessary consideration.

Tha main issues of the plan are:

1. *To raise the effectiveness of licensed projects, to ensure the interests of both Vietnam and the foreign parties.* In relation to the already licensed FDI projects, a number of them have been implemented while others have had their licences withdrawn, due to the inefficiency in business or to a lack of bright prospects. This situation should be considered a good natural survival process to push up the most efficient projects, and to ensure the benefits of the Vietnamese side and other partners.

There should be also a further consideration of the following points:

(a) We should pay greater attention to the *environment protection aspect* in the FDI projects in Vietnam as there are cases that licences have already been issued while a number of projects have not submitted any paper and documents on the pollution impact on the environment to be dealt with. These projects should finalize those reports with detailed measures for environment protection in place.

An example can be used to illustrate the issue. Due to a lack of environment protection concerns before its operation, the glutamate factory Vedan in Dong Nai has caused a great pollution problem with serious consequences. The Vietnamese party has therefore taken strict and rigorous measures to deal with it.

(b) The *technological transfer aspect* should also get more consideration. Many joint ventures in operation in Vietnam have in fact imported the material and do not need much processing / manufacture to be done locally in the host country and their work has been therefore rather simple.

For instance, iron sheet shaping techniques are very simple and the main work is to import iron sheets from abroad. The import of taxis by joint ventures is also in a similar situation which should be considered in the future.

(c) We should further promote the *export capacity* of the enterprises provided with FDI funds, to consider it as an important priority not only for new projects but also for already licensed projects.

(d) As to the *capital contribution in the joint venture* as mentioned above, the government of Vietnam should take further measures to push up the contribution of funds from the Vietnamese side.

(e) As to the *use of the local work force*, the state should continue to devise and consider carefully comprehensive policies on salary, insurance, training and control in this field to protect the benefits of the working labour force in the joint ventures.

2. *To attract new projects in line with the state's economic policies in the areas where national industrialization and modernization are under way*. The state should have to pay special attention to the following points in this area:

(a) To design a plan to attract foreign investment in line with the national general strategy and planning. A list of priority projects can then be made, with reference to investment sources from the Official Development Assistance (ODA), FDI or/and domestic funds. There should be a careful calculation or consideration of the priority fields and a combination of the various financial sources.

The state should define clearly its policies in invention ownership (intellectual property rights) protection, environment protection, technological transfer, tax and capital contribution.

(b) As to a *better evaluation of investment projects*, the government has recommended and the National Assembly has approved the nomination of a Minister responsible for the evaluation of the projects and the evaluation work shall be well coordinated and managed in the new system.

There will be an evaluation board to take care of state-controlled investment projects, and it will be in the form of an inter-ministerial board to consider big projects for approval, to safeguard all related fields such as economic, social and environment impact, technology, national security and defence.

(c) There should be a greater attention paid to *exports of products manufactured in the FDI projects*. As to the projects involved in the import of goods to be used as substitutes, it is recommended that more favourable conditions should be created in the exchange into foreign currency to import material and to repatriate part of the profits as prescribed by the state regulations.

(d) The state should overhaul and create all necessary legal framework and administrative reforms to promote FDI.

(e) The state should within its legal framework create the necessary conditions to undertake administrative reforms of the one-door system.

One example is the merging of the State Planning Committee (SPC) and State Committee for Cooperation and Investment (SCCI) into the Ministry of Planning and Investment (MPI) so as to create an integrated and unified unit responsible for the matter.

At local level, there will be the merging into the provincial or municipal Planning Service and Investment of the existing local Planning Committee and Foreign Economic Services – chiefly to improve the technical infrastructure situations (such as in transportation, telecommunications, water supply and sewerage, electric supply, land planning) so as to convince all FDI projects in the sectors that quick profit making is feasible in all of the FDI projects.

In the coming years, the list of FDI priorities will be as follows:

1. Infrastructure

In addition to the ODA and state-funded projects, authorization shall be granted to foreign investors who are able to make use of the permitted FDI forms such as joint venture and BOT, and to invest in infrastructure such as electric generators, transportation network, airfield, seaports, telecommunications etc..

2. Industrial development

The oil area still gets the attention of the government of Vietnam for further development. FDI funds can be concentrated on the development of oil exploitation industries, including gas (of which the expected output in the year 2000 shall be equivalent to 20 million tons of oil), oil refinery (in the immediate future, there will be the establishment of a 6-million ton per year refinery in Dung Quat (Quang Ngai province), an electrical generating plant in Phu Mi (Dong Nai), and the gas-conducting pipeline etc.

Such other areas as the production of cement, steel and iron, and heavy mechanics, are still classified in the FDI priority list for consideration.

Electronics, information and telecommunications in general are the areas which receive special treatment by the government in the multi-use of funds to quicken the production cycle and promote the use of high technology and of development in scale.

3. Construction of concentrated industrial zones, of export-processing zones and high technology zones

In the general direction in the immediate future, there will be the construction of a number of concentrated industrial zones in three key economic areas and in a number of cities or provinces endowed with favourable or good economic development conditions.

The state will encourage local investors to contribute their funds to the development of infrastructure. A good example can be drawn from the Song Be province's (Song Than area) experience where the government let the FDI projects and the local enterprises share its use, so as to avoid the abuse of the land and housing business in disguise, as is the case of a number of previously licensed joint ventures that enjoyed too many preferences.

There will be the construction of high technology zones, including those in Hanoi and Ho Chi Minh City.

4. Processing and light industry projects

Attention will be paid to the use of FDI to develop agricultural, forestry and aquatic or seafood processing, thus increasing the value of agricultural, forestry and aquatic products and meeting the local consumption demand and increasing the value of exported products.

Attention will be also paid to light, medium or small industries to attract the work force, and to create export-oriented satellite zones. The products from these industries include garments, textiles, leather goods and other domestic products.

5. Hotels, apartments for rent and tourist services

Permits will only be granted to those projects that are in agreement with the general planning of the government of Vietnam and their quality will be assured. There will be explanations to foreign investors of Vietnamese comparative advantages in construction costs, and diversified tourist potentials etc.

The state will reconsider the land (rental) costs and bring them within the appropriate limits in the new environment as well as in the land planning.

6. Finance, banking, securities and consulting

The state will encourage the use of FDI in joint ventures so as to increase the funds and types of cooperation.

5 Current Patterns and Future Trends in Trade and Foreign Investment in Vietnam: The 1995 Business Survey and an Econometric Analysis

Tran Van Hoa and Pham Quang Thao

This chapter describes the first survey of Vietnamese business information and expectations of foreign investment and other related trade developments in Vietnam vis a vis Australia and its other trading countries in the 1990s.

The survey was designed by the authors and carried out early in 1995 by ICTC staff of the Ministry of Trade in Hanoi and within the activity of the Australian Research Council and RIFER-funded research project 'Foreign Investment in Vietnam'.

Some preliminary findings based on a simple SPSSPC cross-tabulation method on major pertinent issues as assessed by a very wide spectrum of businesses in Vietnam in our survey are analysed and reported. Implications of these findings that are relevant to foreign investment opportunities in Vietnam, to trade development prospects, and to business promotion with Australia and other trading countries are also discussed.

1 INTRODUCTION

The importance of foreign investment (FI) on the activity, growth, and trade of an economy can be looked at from a number of perspectives.

First, the standardized national accounts (SNA) framework of the United Nations which has been adopted by most countries in the world to summarize their macroeconomic activity includes FI as a major component in the identity of gross domestic product (GDP). It can be said that the SNA matrix (and its related flows of funds currently used by the International Monetary Fund [IMF]) is essentially based on the Keynesian income accounting structure, and expanded further by the work by Kuznets and others over time. Within this framework, FI therefore affects the movements of GDP with a nonstochastic unitary impact parameter. FI here includes both inward and outward investment.

Second, from the theories of microeconomics and economic statistics, net investment cumulatively generates capital stock of an economy over time, and as such, FI, being part of total (that is, domestic and foreign) net investment, also plays an important part in the two or three-factor neo-classical production sector of a country.

In the current literature on the developing economies, many stages have been identified as the chronology of development progresses from the beginning over time. Thus in the early stage of development of a country at least, FI has been regarded as the principal ingredient for development and technology transfer (Tsai, 1989). This ingredient is furthermore capable of generating the subsequent effect of structural change in a country (Ramstetter, 1991) or promoting exports in the manufacturing industry (Helleiner, 1990). The role played by direct FI in the East Asian economic development in particular has been discussed by Hill (1990).

A dynamic macroeconomic theory of direct FI has also been suggested dealing with direct FI, structural adjustment, and international division of labour (Lee, 1990). The last aspect seems to be of particular importance at the moment with the rising Japanese yen in the world financial market and the relative high cost of labour in some developed and industrialized countries such as Japan. The role played by FI appears to have no political boundary. In fact, Lee (1993) has argued that in the new East Asian development environment, capitalism and socialism can interact successfully to promote the standard of living of a country's people.

A natural extension of this concept to such a newly developing country as Vietnam is obvious and defines its need more acutely. Vietnam, at least since the major reforms commencing in 1986 or thereabout, has been actively engaged in its current well known economic modernization and transition process, with the support, financially and otherwise, from official development aid (ODA) programmes, other international organizations, non-government organizations (NGO), private institutions, and other countries in the region and beyond. These reforms come about after Vietnam's many years of warring turmoil and relatively stagnant economic activity and subsequent low standard of living relative to its many neighbouring authoritarian, democratic or market-oriented Asian countries. In addition, Vietnam constitutes a big market with 72 million people (as at 1994) in the Asia Pacific region, and has huge natural and human resources which are at present untapped for production for local consumption or for international trade. Within this context, the need for FI and more of it to accelerate the growth rate in Vietnam is more pronounced than in any other LDCs in the region.

While FI is a necessity or a driving force for economic development and with it transnational technology transfer, many contemporary studies on the subject (see for example Lucas, 1993, and a recent survey of the literature in Tran Van Hoa [1995]) have discovered that the taxonomy of the real determinants of FI generally or specifically is not that easy and universally agreed upon. Even if the real determinants can be conceptually classified, the problem of how to reliably identify them in empirical studies looking at investment activity or economic development and growth using aggregate or broadly defined time series data has not been that simple.

The problem is more compounded in the case of microeconomic studies using either time series or cross section data. This arises from the fact that the significant direction of microeconomic impact or the transmission mechanism of the transactions of FI on the production or valued-added generating process at the firm's level can be generated or take place in many different ways in a Marshallian manner. For example, it can take place via either financial, human resource or management corporate activity. This multi-faceted and multi-directional causality can be elusive to reliable location.

In this chapter, we attempt to provide some useful information on the need to know more about the current state of foreign investment and its important related issues in the particular case of Vietnam from a Vietnamese perspective, and also to provide a simple analysis of this information for possible development of business and trade opportunities between companies and firms or even individual investors in both Vietnam and Australia. Naturally, our findings can also be used to assist any other country that wants to do business with Vietnam in the future, be it in the ASEAN, the Asia Pacific, or beyond.

Further studies on trade, investment, and business in Vietnam from a non-Vietnamese and transnational corporate perspective have been done on a small scale by research economists in Asia (for example, Nguyen Thi Van Anh, 1995) or in Australia (Maitland, 1995). A survey, on a larger scale, of international companies operating in Vietnam has also been carried out by the research project 'Foreign Direct Investment in Vietnam' being undertaken by the author and the Ministry of Trade in Vietnam. The results from this survey will be presented in due course.

The approach adopted in the present chapter is experimental or survey-based and this implies that meta-research (that is, gathering data when nothing is known about an issue) is used whenever no other type of information is available, and the analysis is carried out by an application of a simple cross-tabulation method which allows for a simultaneous interaction of many attributes among the subjects under study.

The outline of the chapter is as follows:

First, we describe the chronological process of our survey from the beginning of the design to the final interviews, pointing out on the way special features of our approach.

Second, we select the combinations of our multi-choice answers which are particularly relevant to the need to know of foreign investment problems in our research project or in a more general commercial policy application to business opportunities and trade development between companies in Vietnam and their counterparts overseas.

Third, the findings are then summarized in a standard statistical cross-tabulation form for ease of analysis and interpretation.

Finally, some preliminary findings that we believe are useful to our current and future research activity and also to significant practical commercial applications will be discussed in detail and policy recommendations will be made for consideration by business and trade authorities both in Vietnam and Australia.

Some of these findings will also be used to build scenarios of business and trade development so that the prospects from these perspectives will be properly evaluated by anyone who is interested in business opportunities and trade developments between Vietnam and other countries in the Asia Pacific region or beyond.

2 THE 1995 BUSINESS SURVEY IN VIETNAM

2.1 Brief History

The idea of a pilot survey of Vietnamese business information and expectations for use in a study of foreign investment in Vietnam and for assistance in business and trade development between Vietnam and Australia was first considered in Ho Chi Minh City, early in 1995, by the principal investigator, Professor Tran Van Hoa, of the research project 'Foreign Investment in Vietnam'. The project was funded by the Australian Research Council for the triennium 1995–97, and was jointly undertaken by the Department of Economics, University of Wollongong in Australia and the Research Institute for Foreign Economic Relations, Ministry of Trade in Vietnam.

The idea was a product of the knowledge that, at this stage, not much is known about Vietnamese companies and their interest and expectations in relation to foreign investment from Australia, and also that most Australian companies still do not know much about Vietnam's need for foreign investment and its final destination or allocation in businesses and industries as well as its possible rate of returns. Since a knowledge about business information and expectations is crucial in an analysis and development of foreign investment strategy and planning for corporations, government agencies, and individual investors alike, the survey was considered a timely, useful and important first step to more detailed and formal studies of foreign investment in Vietnam in the future.

The intended target of the survey was initially a group of 485 business and government registrants from all over the south-central and southern parts of Vietnam attending a one-day conference on 'Foreign Investment in Vietnam' in Ho Chi Minh City in January 1995. The academic programme of the conference was presented by Professor Tran Van Hoa, and the conference took place at Ho Chi Minh City's College of Foreign Trade, a branch of the University of Foreign Trade in Hanoi.

As the questionnaire was designed for quick, on the spot, responses from the target group, there were only ten questions on the questionnaire dealing with businesses' present activity and knowledge of and expectations for cooperation in foreign investment with Australia and other overseas companies. All questions involve a multiple choice type of answer.

Copies of the questionnaire were distributed to all 485 people at the conference and explanations were also carefully and repeatedly given to all of them on how to fill in the questionnaires. The registrants were encouraged to complete the questionnaires on the grounds that the feed-back information from the business community present at the conference would be important not only to their organizations and companies but also to further meaningful studies and realistic policy formulation on foreign investment and international trade in Vietnam.

However, at the end of the day, only 17 filled-in copies of the questionnaire were returned to the organizers.

2.2 The Final 1995 Business Survey and Data Collecting Approach

The idea of a survey of Vietnamese business information and expectations was brought to Hanoi in January 1995 and taken up later on at the International Consulting and Training Centre (ICTC) of the Research Institute for Foreign Economic Relations (RIFER), the Ministry of Trade in Hanoi, during February and March 1995.

In the new survey to be done in Hanoi in the spring of 1995, some of the questions on the original questionnaire used earlier in Ho Chi Minh City were improved upon, and some new ones were added to the list of the original ten questions. In the end, there are 14 questions on the questionnaire dealing, in addition to those described earlier, with the location and the size of the interviewed companies in terms of both the number of employees employed and also the amount of annual revenue obtained. A copy of this revised questionnaire (translated into English) and the data codes employed to describe the various responses is given in Appendix 5.1.

A sample of the companies to be interviewed was then selected randomly across all sectors of the economy. The source for the selection of the companies is from the official Vietnam Business Directory 1993–94, published by the Chamber of Commerce and Industry of Vietnam (VCCI) in Hanoi.

From our previous experience with the targeted business and government audience who were asked to fill in their questionnaires in South Vietnam earlier in the year however, we decided to abandon the mail/distribution/return technique and, instead, adopt the interviewing approach this time. A sample of 200 of the companies from the Vietnam Business Directory and their executives were then selected for the interviews.

Initially, staff from the ICTC were engaged in the international standard technique of telephone interviews in order to fill in the questions on the questionnaire. This proved however to be unsuccessful, as many interviewees contacted by telephone were either reluctant or unable to answer all questions on the questionnaire.

The next stage in our survey was then the use of the approach of personal visits from ICTC interviewers to the selected executives in these executives' offices in order to complete the questions in the survey. This approach proved to be highly successful with the result of returns of 100% of all companies visited by ICTC staff.

A bonus with this visiting approach is that some ambiguities in the responses were quickly solved or clarified on the spot by the ICTC interviewers in collaboration with the corporate executives. This clarification was done in strict consistency with the design and purpose of the questionnaire.

The final number of the questionnaires completed and acceptable is 81. All information from the returned questionnaires has been coded to an SPSS format on a Word for Windows textfile, and it is ready to be processed by the SPSS software package.

2.3 An Overview of Survey Results

Below we report some processed preliminary findings on business information and expectations of Vietnamese companies from our business survey dataset. The findings can be classified into two groups which are of relevance to our project: current business activity and planned future business, trade and investment expansion and expectations.

The first group provides information on the current patterns of foreign investment and business cooperation between the sampled Vietnamese companies and their overseas trading partners. Details of the analysis include the types of business and the types of business cooperation and all findings consider size and other information.

The second group provides some information on the possible future trend of foreign investment and business cooperation between the Vietnamese companies and other overseas companies. This information is broken down into details of types of business and business cooperation. Again, all details relate to the size of businesses and other information.

3 CURRENT PATTERNS OF BUSINESS AND INVESTMENT

3.1 The Size of Vietnamese Companies in the Survey

Objective and Definition

The size of a firm or company has always interested economists of all schools of thought and has generated fewer controversies than some other areas of political science. The size of a firm here can be defined in terms of its physical assets, the range of its operation, the amount of its financial assets or transactions, its controlling interests, or the number of employees employed by it.

The concept of size is important not only because the size of a firm reflects the relative role of the firm in relation to its industry or in the economy, but because, when the firm is big enough, it invokes the benevolent operation of economies of scale. It has been argued that in this case it also can influence government policy or the government itself. One of the drawbacks of the size of a firm is that when it is very big it would choke off all competition and become a monopoly with all the associated bad or non-optimal or non-Paretian effects on both the consumer and producer sectors of the market.

In order to have some idea about the size of the Vietnamese companies in our survey, we asked these companies about the number of employees they currently employed and also the amount of annual revenue they currently received.

These questions appeared to have posed many problems for the interviewees, especially on the labour supply issue. First, many companies use contractors or even subcontractors. Does our question cover all of them? Second, many companies use part-time or occasional workers. Do we include all of them in our question? And so on.

In the survey, there are altogether six classes of companies the size of which is defined by the number of their full-time employees: 0–30 persons, 31–50 persons, 51–100 persons, 101–200 persons, 201–500 persons, and 501–1,000 persons.

There are also six groups of companies the size of which is defined by the size of their annual income or revenue. These six groups of companies are: 0 billion–1 billion VND, 1 billion–10 billion VND, 11 billion–50 billion VND, 51 billion–100 billion VND, 101 billion– 500 billion VND, and 501 billion–1,000 billion VND.

Below, these six classes of companies as defined by their labour force are cross-tabulated against the six groups of companies as defined by their annual income or revenue.

Some Results (see Table 5.1)

There were four companies (4.9% of all companies interviewed) who could not answer our question on the size of their labour force. There were also eight companies (9.9% of all companies interviewed) who could not provide information on their annual revenue.

For the companies that employ up to 30 persons in their labour force (3.7% of all companies interviewed), two of them (66.7%) have an annual revenue of between 1 billion and 10 billion VND. The other company has no information about its annual income.

For the companies that employ between 31 and 50 persons (12.3% of all companies interviewed), 20% have no information about their annual income, 10% have an annual revenue of up to 1 billion VND. Both the 1 billion–10 billion VND and 11 billion–50 billion VND companies in this group each have a 30% share. Again, 10% of the companies in this group have an annual income of between 51 billion and 100 billion VND. No company in our survey has an annual income over the 100 billion VND per year range.

For the companies that employ between 51 and 100 persons (13.6% of all companies interviewed), both companies in the income groups of 0–1 billion VND and 1 billion–10 billion VND each have a 18.2% share. The largest group is for the companies in the 11 billion–50 billion VND per year range that post a 63.6% share. No company has an annual income of over 50 billion VND per year in this group.

The companies that employ between 101 and 200 persons account for 19.8% of all companies interviewed. Among these companies, 6.3% could not provide any information about their yearly revenue, 43.8% receive a revenue of between 1 billion and 10 billion VND per year, 25% post an income of between 11 billion and 50 billion VND per year, and 12.5% record a receipt of between 51 billion and 100 billion VND per year. 12.5% achieve an annual revenue of between 101 billion and 500 billion VND.

For the companies that employ between 201 and 500 persons (totalling 30.9% of all companies interviewed), 8% could not provide information on their income, and none of them earns less than 1 billion VND per year.

Also in this group, 20% receive an income of between 1 billion and 10 billion VND per year, 60% post a revenue of between 11 billion and 50 billion VND per year, and 4% make between 51 billion and 100 billion VND per year. Also, 8% of the companies in this group record an annual revenue of between 101 billion and 500 billion VND.

Table 5.1 Vietnamese Business Distribution Annual Company Income by Employed Labour (1995)
Annual Company Income (Row) by Labour Size (Column)

	0	1	2	3	4	5	6	Row Total
0	1	1	2	0	1	2	1	8
(not available)								
% row	12.5	12.5	25.0	0	12.5	25.0	12.5	9.9
% column	25.0	33.3	20.0	0	6.3	8.0	8.3	
% total	1.2	1.2	2.5	0	1.2	2.5	1.2	
1	0	0	1	2	0	0	0	3
(0–1b VND)								
% row	0	0	33.3	66.7	0	0	0	3.7
% column	0	0	10.0	18.2	0	0	0	
% total	0	0	1.2	2.5	0	0	0	
2	1	2	3	2	7	5	2	22
(1–10b VND)								
% row	4.5	9.1	13.6	9.1	31.8	22.7	9.1	27.2
% column	25.0	66.7	30.0	18.2	43.8	20.0	16.7	
% total	1.2	2.5	3.7	2.5	8.6	6.2	2.5	
3	1	0	3	7	4	15	5	35
(11–50b VND)								
% row	2.9	0	8.6	20.0	11.4	42.9	14.3	43.2
% column	25.0	0	30.0	63.6	25.0	60.0	41.7	
% total	1.2	0	3.7	2.5	8.6	18.5	6.2	
4	1	0	1	0	2	1	3	8
(51–100b VND)								
% row	12.5	0	12.5	0	25.0	12.5	37.5	9.9
% column	25.0	0	10.0	0	12.5	4.0	25.0	
% total	1.2	0	1.2	0	2.5	1.2	3.7	
5	0	0	0	0	2	2	1	5
(101–500b VND)								
% row	0	0	0	0	40.0	40.0	20.0	6.2
% column	0	0	0	0	12.5	8.0	8.3	
% total	0	0	0	0	2.5	2.5	1.2	
Column Total	4	3	10	11	16	25	12	81
%	4.9	3.7	12.3	13.6	19.8	30.9	14.8	100.0

Notes: Data from Vietnam's first business survey, ICTC, Hanoi, 1995. In all tables here and below, rows refer to 'No Answer' and five levels of Company Annual Income in billion VND. Columns refer to 'No Answer' and six levels of Labour Size. See Appendix 5.1 for the questions asked and the code numbers used. The results of cross-tabulation are obtained by SPSS PC.

For the companies that employ between 500 and 1000 persons (14.8% of all companies interviewed), one company could not provide any information about its income, and no company makes less than 1 billion VND per year. In this group, 16.7% record a yearly revenue of between 1 billion and 10 billion VND, 41.7% of between 11 billion and 50 billion VND, 25% of between 51 billion and 100 billion VND, and 8.3% of between 101 billion and 500 billion VND.

For all companies of all labour groups, 3.7% make only up to 1 billion VND per year, and 27.2% get between 1 billion and 10 billion VND per year. The largest group of companies here (43.2% of all companies interviewed) receive an annual revenue of between 11 billion and 50 billion VND, while 9.9% post between 51 billion and 100 billion VND, and finally 6.2% record between 101 billion and 500 billion VND.

Of all of our companies in the survey, more than 65% report a revenue of over 51 billion VND per year, and 79% make over 11 billion VND per year.

Of all of our companies in the survey, close to 66% report having a labour force of more than 100 persons, and 80% employ more than 50 persons.

3.2 Overseas Countries with Business in Vietnam

Objective and Definition

The extent of international business activity in Vietnam can be assessed to some extent by the number of countries currently involved in business with companies in Vietnam. A knowledge of this activity also can provide some information on the national focus of commercial activity by overseas companies in Vietnam.

The Vietnamese companies we interviewed in our survey are currently having business dealings with a total of 18 countries, including the European Union. Most of these countries are located in Asia (including Australia), Europe, and North America.

No country from the Sub-Continent, the Middle East, Africa, South America or the South Pacific is represented in the sample.

The distribution of these countries over the Vietnamese companies interviewed would give some useful information on the range, intensity, and penetration of the overseas countries in business and trade in Vietnam.

These countries are cross-tabulated against the six groups of companies. The six groups are defined in terms of the size of their annual revenue. The six groups identified are: 0 billion–1 billion VND, 1 billion–10 billion VND, 11 billion–50 billion VND, 51 billion–100 billion VND, 101 billion–500 billion VND, and 501 billion–1,000 billion VND.

Some Results (see Table 5.2)

Of the total of 81 companies interviewed, 13 companies have no international trade connections. This accounts for 16.0% of the total.

Two of all the companies interviewed (2.5%) indicate that they are having business dealings with Australia. This is the same level of business dealings as with Canada, China, and the former USSR or CIS.

Italy and Switzerland equally rank lowest in the group in terms of business dealings with Vietnam with only one company in the class (1.2%).

Next in the ascending ranking level of business dealings are France, Germany, Hong Kong, the European Union, and other countries (4.9%). Recorded as having slightly more business dealings with Vietnam is Singapore (6.2%), followed by the USA (7.4%), and Taiwan (8.6%). The finding that Vietnam trades more with the US than Singapore in our sample of companies is interesting.

Next in the ascending order of business dealings are Korea (12.3%) and Japan (13.6%). Japan occupies the top spot in terms of business dealings with the interviewed companies in Vietnam.

The findings above point out two interesting results with important implications for business expansion:

First, Europe and the former USSR states appear to have less business and therefore less trade importance with companies in Vietnam. The main commercial concern of Vietnamese companies currently is with countries in the Asia Pacific region including Australia.

Second, while Australia is known to be number six country in the ranking order by the amount of international investment in Vietnam according to the recent official information, most of this investment is outside the sphere of interviewed companies or is heavily concentrated on a small number of companies. In fact, in terms of annual company revenue, the Vietnamese companies involving business dealings with Australia include one 1 billion–10 billion VND company and one 51 billion–100 billion VND company.

Table 5.2 Vietnamese Business Distribution Annual Company Income by Trading Country (1995)
Annual Company Income (Row) by Trading Country (Column)

	1	2	3	5	6	7	8	9	10	11	12	13	14	16	17	18	19	RT
0	0	0	1	0	0	0	0	0	1	0	0	0	1	2	0	1	2	8
na																		
%R	0	0	1.2	0	0	0	0	0	12.5	0	0	0	12.5	25	0	12.5	25	9.9
%C	0	0	50	0	0	0	0	0	20	0	0	0	14.3	33.3	0	25	15.4	
%T	0	0	1.2	0	0	0	0	0	1.2	0	0	0	1.2	2.5	0	1.2	2.5	
1	0	0	0	0	2	0	0	1	0	0	0	0	0	0	0	0	0	3
0–1b																		
%R	0	0	0	0	66.7	0	0	33.3	0	0	0	0	0	0	0	0	0	3.7
%C	0	0	0	0	50	0	0	9.1	0	0	0	0	0	0	0	0	0	
%T	0	0	0	0	1.2	0	0	1.2	0	0	0	0	0	0	0	0	0	
2	1	1	0	1	1	1	0	3	0	0	2	0	2	0	1	2	7	22
1–10b																		
%R	4.5	45	0	4.5	4.5	4.5	0	13.6	0	0	9.1	0	9.1	0	4.5	9.1	31.8	27.2
%C	50	50	0	25	25	33.3	0	27.3	0	0	20	0	28.6	0	25	50	53.8	
%T	1.2	1.2	0	1.2	1.2	1.2	0	3.7	0	0	2.5	0	2.5	0	1.2	2.5	8.6	
3	1	1	1	3	0	1	1	3	3	1	5	1	4	3	2	1	4	35
11–50b																		
%R	2.9	2.9	2.9	8.6	0	2.9	2.9	8.6	8.6	2.9	14.3	2.9	11.4	8.6	5.7	2.9	11.4	43.2
%C	50	50	50	75	0	33.3	100	27.3	60	50	50	100	57.1	50	50	25	30.8	
%T	1.2	1.2	1.2	3.7	0	1.2	1.2	3.7	3.7	1.2	6.2	1.2	4.9	3.7	2.5	1.2	4.9	

Table 5.2 Continued

	1	2	3	5	6	7	8	9	10	11	12	13	14	16	17	18	19	RT
4 51–100b	0	0	0	0	1	0	0	4	1	0	1	0	0	0	1	0	0	8
%R	0	0	0	0	12.5	0	0	50	12.5	0	12.5	0	0	0	12.5	0	0	9.9
%C	0	0	0	0	25	0	0	36.4	20	0	10	0	0	0	25	0	0	
%T	0	0	0	0	1.2	0	0	4.9	1.2	0	1.2	0	0	0	1.2	0	0	
5 101–500b	0	0	0	0	0	1	0	0	0	1	2	0	0	1	0	0	0	5
%R	0	0	0	0	0	20	0	0	0	20	40	0	0	20	0	0	0	6.2
%C	0	0	0	0	0	33.3	0	0	0	50	20	0	0	16.7	0	0	0	
%T	0	0	0	0	0	1.2	0	0	0	1.2	2.5	0	0	1.2	0	0	0	
CT	2	2	2	4	4	3	1	11	5	2	10	1	7	6	4	4	13	81
%	2.5	2.5	2	4.9	4.9	3.7	1.2	13.6	6.2	2.5	12.3	1.2	8.6	7.4	4.9	4.9	16	100

Notes: Columns refer to 19 countries trading with Vietnamese businesses. See also footnotes to Tables 5.1 and 5.3.

The implication is therefore that there exists a need for more Australian investment in Vietnam or for existing Australian investment to be spread more to other areas of economic activity in Vietnam.

3.3 Classification of Current Business

Objective and Definition

The range of international business activity in Vietnam can be obtained from the number of sectors the overseas companies are currently involved in business with companies in Vietnam. A knowledge of this activity also can provide some information on the sectoral focus of activity by overseas companies in Vietnam.

The types of business currently engaged in by the Vietnamese companies we interviewed total 16. These types of business cover most sectors of the economy and are:

1. Electronics
2. Consumer goods
3. Hotels
4. Communications
5. Transport
6. Tourism
7. Manufacturing
8. Textiles
9. Agriculture
10. Mining
11. Forestry
12. Electrics
13. Construction
14. Chemical goods
15. Other goods
16. Non-specified industry

These 16 types of business are cross-tabulated against the six groups of companies. These groups are defined in terms of the size of their annual revenue. The six groups identified are: 0 billion–1 billion VND, 1 billion–10 billion VND, 11 billion–50 billion VND, 51 billion–100 billion VND, 101 billion–500 billion VND, and 501 billion–1,000 billion VND.

Some Results (see Table 5.3)

Of the number of companies interviewed, the three largest groups (each equally having a 17.3% share) state that they are currently having business dealings with overseas companies either in manufacturing, textiles, or construction.

Next in the descending order of ranking, 11.1% indicate that their current international dealings involve electronics, and 9.9% are in other non-specified business. Only 6.2% of the companies are in consumer goods, and 4.9% in chemical goods.

No company is involved in the until now popular area of hotel business, but business in electrics accounts for 3.7%.

Dealings in communications, tourism and forestry total each 2.5% of the number of companies interviewed.

The above findings appear to indicate that the growing areas of commercial transactions in Vietnam are in the manufacturing, textile, and construction industries. When we combine the two industries of electronics and electrics together however, they also account for a sizable share of 14.8%.

Hotels and tourism which were all the rage in investment activity until recently seem to be a no-go industry as far as the interviewed companies are concerned.

3.4 Business Experience with Australia

Objective and Definition

In order to assess to what extent Vietnamese companies know about Australia and Australian companies, one question in our questionnaire asked whether the Vietnamese companies or their executives in our sample have had any experience in business with Australia.

The responses are classified into three types: yes, no, and a little. These response are again cross-tabulated against six revenue-based groups of companies. The six groups of companies identified are: 0 billion–1 billion VND, 1 billion–10 billion VND, 11 billion–50 billion VND, 51 billion–100 billion VND, 101 billion–500 billion VND, and 501 billion–1,000 billion VND.

Some Results (see Table 5.4)

No response to this question in our survey was received from 9.9% of all companies interviewed.

Table 5.3 Vietnamese Business Distribution Annual Company Income by Business Activity (1995)
Annual Company Income (Row) by Main Activity (Column)

	1	2	4	5	6	7	8	9	10	11	12	13	14	15	16	RT
0	0	1	0	0	2	0	1	0	0	1	1	0	0	2	0	8
na																
% R	0	12.5	0	0	25.0	0	12.5	0	0	12.5	12.5	0	0	25.0	0	9.9
%C	0	20.0	0	0	100.0	0	7.1	0	0	50.0	33.3	0	0	25.0	0	
%T	0	1.2	0	0	2.5	0	1.2	0	0	1.2	1.2	0	0	2.5	0	
1	0	0	0	0	0	1	0	0	0	0	0	0	1	1	0	3
0–1b																
%R	0	0	0	0	0	33.3	0	0	0	0	0	0	33.3	33.3	0	3.7
%C	0	0	0	0	0	7.1	0	0	0	0	0	0	25.0	12.5	0	
%T	0	0	0	0	0	1.2	0	0	0	0	0	0	1.2	1.2	0	
2	2	1	1	0	0	7	4	0	0	0	0	3	2	2	0	22
1–10b																
%R	9.1	4.5	4.5	0	0	31.8	18.2	0	0	0	0	13.6	9.1	9.1	0	27.2
%C	22.2	20.0	50.0	0	0	50.0	28.6	0	0	0	0	21.4	50.0	25.0	0	
%T	2.5	1.2	1.2	0	0	8.6	4.9	0	0	0	0	3.7	2.5	2.5	0	
3	6	3	1	1	0	4	5	1	1	1	1	8	1	1	1	35
11–50b																
%R	17.1	8.6	2.9	2.9	0	11.4	14.3	2.9	2.9	2.9	2.9	2.9	22.9	2.9	2.9	43.2
%C	66.7	60.0	50.0	100	0	28.6	35.7	100	100	50.0	33.3	57.1	25.0	12.5	100	
%T	7.4	3.7	1.2	1.2	0	4.9	6.2	1.2	1.2	1.2	1.2	9.9	1.2	1.2	1.2	

Table 5.3 Continued

	1	2	4	5	6	7	8	9	10	11	12	13	14	15	16	RT
4 51–100b	0	0	0	0	0	1	3	0	0	0	1	3	0	0	0	8
%R	0	0	0	0	0	12.5	37.5	0	0	0	12.5	37.5	0	0	0	9.9
%C	0	0	0	0	0	7.1	21.4	0	0	0	33.3	21.4	0	0	0	
%T	0	0	0	0	0	1.2	3.7	0	0	0	1.2	3.7	0	0	0	
5 101–500b	1	0	0	0	0	1	1	0	0	0	0	0	0	2	0	5
%R	20.0	0	0	0	0	20.0	20.0	0	0	0	0	0	0	40.0	0	6.2
%C	7.1	0	0	0	0	7.1	7.1	0	0	0	0	0	0	25.0	0	
%T	1.2	0	0	0	0	1.2	1.2	0	0	0	0	0	0	2.5	0	
CT	9	5	2	1	2	14	14	1	1	2	3	14	4	8	1	81
%	11.1	6.2	2.5	1.2	2.5	17.3	17.3	1.2	1.2	2.5	3.7	17.3	4.9	9.9	1.2	100

Notes: %R: % Row, %C: % Column, %T: % Total. RT: Row total, CT: Column total. Columns refer to 16 types of main activity. See also footnotes to Table 5.1.

Table 5.4 Vietnamese Business Distribution Annual Company Income by Business Experience (1995)
Annual Company Income (Row) by Business Experience (Column)

	1	2	3	Row Total
0	0	8	0	8
na				
%R	0	100.0	0	9.9
%C	0	11.4	0	
%T	0	9.9	0	
1	0	3	0	3
0–1b				
%R	0	100.0	0	3.7
%C	0	4.3	0	
%T	0	3.7	0	
2	1	20	1	22
1–10b				
%R	4.5	90.9	4.5	27.2
%C	50.0	28.6	11.1	
%T	1.2	24.7	1.2	
3	1	28	6	35
11–50b				
%R	2.9	80.0	17.1	43.2
%C	50.0	40.0	66.7	
%T	1.2	34.6	7.4	
4	0	7	1	8
51–100b				
%R	0	87.5	12.5	9.9
%C	0	10.0	11.1	
%T	0	8.6	1.2	
5	0	4	1	5
101–500b				
%R	0	80.0	20.0	6.2
%C	0	5.7	11.1	
%T	0	4.9	1.2	
Column Total	2	70	9	81
%	2.5	86.4	11.1	100.0

Notes: Columns refer to 1 (yes), 2 (no), and 3 (a little). See also footnotes to Tables 5.1 and 5.3.

All of the fairly small companies in our sample (100%) having an annual revenue of up to 1 billion VND (3.7% of all companies) indicate that they have had no experience in this case.

For companies with an annual revenue of between 1 billion and 10 billion VND (27.2% of all companies interviewed), the responses are almost all (90.9%) no. Only 4.5% of these companies say they have had some business experience with Australia, and also 4.5% say they have had only a little bit of experience with Australia.

The largest group of companies that have had no business experience with Australia is companies with an annual revenue of between 11 billion and 50 billion VND (43.2% of all companies interviewed). In this group, only 1.2% have had experience, and 11.1% have had only a little bit of experience with Australian companies. A total of 86.4% of the companies in this revenue-based group have had no business experience with Australia.

For the 51 billion–100 billion VND companies (9.9% of all companies interviewed) 87.5% say no to our question, and 12.5% indicate they have had some business experience with Australia.

The picture is similar for the companies in the 101 billion–500 billion VND range of activity (6.2% of all companies). Here 80.0% say no and 20.0% say a little business experience with Australia.

For a combination of all six revenue-based groups of companies, 86.4% say they have had no experience with Australia or Australian companies. 11.1% say they have had some experience. Only 2.5% say they have already had business experience with Australia.

This kind of information coupled with that found earlier about Vietnamese companies' desire to do business with Australia indicates that the opportunity is there for Australia to expand further its business presence in Vietnam if it wishes. Although the climate for business is present and inviting for Australia, competition with other countries does exist however, according to our findings previously.

3.5 Knowledge of Investment Laws

Objective and Definition

Investment and business are often subject to the prevailing laws, regulations, controls, and economic policy of both the host and recipient countries. Any serious and practical plans or strategy for investment and business expansion must therefore take into account these important restrictions or guidelines.

This knowledge is all the more important when the business climate has changed so quickly as is the case with Vietnam and with Australia in the past few years.

Implied in this case is the fact that within this climate of rapid change in the business environment, existing means of communication between companies and between the government representatives and the companies may not be that effective at all levels. If this flow of information is not adequate or effective, then remedial approaches have to be implemented in order to improve business and trade activity.

Therefore, one question in our survey has been designed to gather the information about two issues. First, it is to gauge the awareness of Vietnamese companies of the various laws, regulations, controls, policies etc. that are operative in Australia regarding foreign investment and business expansion as sourced from Australia. Second, it is to accommodate this awareness or unawareness by implementing appropriate policy or action.

The responses from the companies in our survey again are classified into three types: yes, no, and a little.

These responses are cross-tabulated against six income or revenue-based groups of companies. The six groups of companies identified are: 0 billion–1 billion VND, 1 billion–10 billion VND, 11 billion–50 billion VND, 51 billion–100 billion VND, 101 billion–500 billion VND, and 501 billion–1,000 billion VND.

Some Results (See Table 5.5)

A total of 9.9% of all companies interviewed were unable to answer this question in our survey. Also, all companies with an annual revenue of between 501 billion and 1000 billion VND could not provide any information asked.

The fairly small companies in our sample having an annual revenue of up to 1 billion VND (3.7% of all companies) indicate that they have no knowledge (2.7%) or only a little knowledge (1.2%) of any of Australia's laws, regulations, controls, policy etc. on foreign investment or business.

For companies with an annual revenue of between 1 billion and 10 billion VND (27.2% of all companies interviewed), almost all (86.4%) say they are not aware of these laws etc. and only 13.6% indicate that they have some knowledge about them.

The largest group of companies that responded to this question in our survey (43.2% of all companies interviewed) involved the companies

Table 5.5 Vietnamese Business Distribution Annual Company Income by Knowledge of Law (1995)
Annual Company Income (Row) by Knowledge of Investment Laws (Column)

	1	2	3	Row Total
0	0	7	1	8
na				
%R	0	87.5	12.5	9.9
%C	0	10.1	9.1	
%T	0	8.6	1.2	
1	0	2	1	3
0–1b				
%R	0	66.7	33.3	3.7
%C	0	2.9	9.1	
%T	0	2.5	1.2	
2	0	19	3	22
1–10b				
%R	0	86.4	13.6	27.2
%C	0	27.5	27.3	
%T	0	23.5	3.7	
3	1	29	5	35
11–50b				
%R	2.9	82.9	14.3	43.2
%C	100.0	42.0	45.5	
%T	1.2	35.8	6.2	
4	0	8	0	8
51–100b				
%R	0	100.0	0	9.9
%C	0	11.6	0	
%T	0	9.9	0	
5	0	4	1	5
101–500b				
%R	0	80.0	20.0	6.2
%C		5.8	9.1	
%T		4.9	1.2	
Column Total	1	69	11	81
%	1.2	85.2	13.6	100.0

Notes: Columns refer to 1 (yes), 2 (no), and 3 (a little). See also footnotes to Tables 5.1 and 5.3.

with an annual revenue of between 11 billion and 50 billion VND. In this group, only 2.9% are aware of the laws etc., 82.9% are not aware of them, and 14.3% only know a little about them.

For the 51 billion–100 billion VND companies (9.9% of all companies interviewed), 100% say they are not aware of the investment laws etc..

The picture is similar for the companies in the 101 billion-500 billion VND range of activity (6.2% of all companies), with 80.0% of them saying not aware and 20.0% saying they know only a little bit about Australia's investment laws etc..

For a combination of all six revenue-based groups of companies, only 1.2% say that they are aware of the prevailing laws, regulations, controls, policy etc., 85.2% say they are not. Only 13.6% indicate they have some knowledge about these laws.

From these findings, it is obvious that there is a need for Vietnamese companies to know about the laws, regulations etc. in Australia that can affect foreign investment and business expansion in Vietnam.

Government agencies and private organizations can do much better to inform the Vietnamese business community about this kind of information.

Scope for rectifying this requirement is enormous. It can be done via information or trade training, academic or technical workshops, specialist seminars – general or industry – or commodity-specific conventions, and short courses by private information providers, or via trade promotion and other active efforts by Australia's trade representatives in Vietnam. However, existing vehicles of communication in this case appear to be inadequate.

4 FUTURE TRENDS OF BUSINESS AND INVESTMENT

4.1 Areas of Future Preferred Foreign Investment and Business

Objective and Definition

The above two cross-tabulation studies deal with the current state of foreign investment and business between Vietnamese companies and their overseas counterparts. It is however useful also to have some information on what Vietnamese companies would like to see taking place in Vietnam in the near future. This kind of information can be used to build up scenarios and make forecasts for foreign investment and business development in Vietnam in cooperation with overseas companies.

The questions in our survey ask for information about preferred future business expansion covering the different sectors of the economy in detail.

There are 16 types of business the Vietnamese companies we interviewed would like to know about for future cooperation and business expansion. They are identical to the list of businesses in the preceding section and include: electronics, consumer goods, hotels, communications, transport, tourism, manufacturing, textiles, agriculture, mining, forestry, electrics, construction, chemical goods, other goods, and unspecified industry.

These types of business are cross-tabulated against the six groups of companies. The groups are defined in terms of the size of their annual revenue. The six groups identified are: 0 billion–1 billion VND, 1 billion–10 billion VND, 11 billion–50 billion VND, 51 billion–100 billion VND, 101 billion–500 billion VND, and 501 billion–1,000 billion VND.

Some Results (see Table 5.6)

The largest group of companies (17.3%) indicate that they would prefer to have more foreign investment and overseas business in the area of textiles, followed by 12.3% in manufacturing, 11.1% in electronics, and 9.9% in construction.

Of the 81 companies interviewed, 8.6% say they are interested in any business, and 6.2% are interested in more foreign investment and further business in chemical goods.

The three industries of consumer goods, communications, and electrics all equally have a preference rate of 4.5% for further business and overseas investment.

No company wants further business and investment in the hotel or agricultural industry.

14.8% of the companies interviewed have no information about more foreign investment or further business expansion with overseas counterparts.

The four industries of textiles, manufacturing, construction and electronics account for most of the preferred future foreign investment and overseas business. The same industries also constitute the current principal activity of the companies interviewed.

Scope for further investment and business by overseas companies should therefore be concentrated in these sectors of the economy.

Table 5.6 Vietnamese Business Distribution Annual Company Income by Investment Area (1995)
Annual Company Income (Row) by Preferred Investment Area (Column)

	1	2	4	5	6	7	8	10	11	12	13	14	15	16	RT
0	0	0	0	0	1	0	0	0	1	1	0	0	2	3	8
na															
%R	0	0	0	0	12.5	0	0	0	12.5	12.5	0	0	25	37.0	9.9
%C	0	0	0	0	100	0	0	0	100	25	0	0	28.6	25.0	
%T	0	0	0	0	1.2	0	0	0	1.2	1.2	0	0	2.5	3.7	
1	0	0	0	0	0	1	0	0	0	0	0	1	1	0	3
0–1b															
%R	0	0	0	0	0	33.3	0	0	0	0	0	33.3	33.3	0	3.7
%C	0	0	0	0	0	10.0	0	0	0	0	0	20.0	14.3	0	
%T	0	0	0	0	0	1.2	0	0	0	0	0	1.2	1.2	0	
2	1	1	1	0	0	5	5	0	0	0	1	2	2	4	22
1–10b															
%R	4.5	4.5	4.5	0	0	22.7	22.7	0	0	0	4.5	9.1	9.1	18.2	27.2
%C	11.1	25.0	25.0	0	0	50.0	35.7	0	0	0	12.5	40.0	28.6	33.3	
%T	1.2	1.2	1.2	0	0	6.2	6.2	0	0	0	1.2	2.5	2.5	4.9	
3	7	3	3	1	0	3	5	1	0	1	5	1	1	4	35
11–50b															
%R	20.0	8.6	8.6	2.9	0	8.6	14.3	2.9	0	2.9	14.3	2.9	2.9	11.4	43.2
%C	77.8	75.0	75.0	100	0	30.0	35.7	100	0	25.0	62.5	20.0	14.3	33.3	
%T	8.6	3.7	3.7	1.2	0	3.7	6.2	1.2	0	1.2	6.2	1.2	1.2	4.9	

Table 5.6 Continued

	1	2	4	5	6	7	8	10	11	12	13	14	15	16	RT
4	0	0	0	0	0	1	3	0	0	1	2	0	1	0	8
51–100b															
%R	0	0	0	0	0	12.5	37.5	0	0	12.5	25.0	0	12.5	0	9.9
%C	0	0	0	0	0	10.0	21.4	0	0	25.0	25.0	0	14.3	0	
%T	0	0	0	0	0	1.2	3.7	0	0	1.2	2.5	0	1.2	0	
5	1	0	0	0	0	0	1	0	0	1	0	1	0	1	5
101–500b															
%R	20.0	0	0	0	0	0	20.0	0	0	20.0	0	20.0	0	20.0	6.2
%C	11.1	0	0	0	0	0	7.1	0	0	25.0	0	20.0	0	8.3	
%T	1.2	0	0	0	0	0	1.2	0	0	1.2	0	1.2	0	1.2	
CT	9	4	4	1	1	10	14	1	1	4	8	5	7	12	81
%	11.1	4.9	4.9	1.2	1.2	12.3	17.3	1.2	1.2	4.9	9.9	6.2	8.6	14.8	100

Notes: Columns refer to 16 preferred areas for future investment. See also footnotes to Tables 5.1 and 5.3.

4.2 Forms of Preferred Business with Overseas Companies

Objective and Definition

The form or type of business cooperation is important in the different stages of economic development in a country. This is due either to the government policy of the developing country or to purely business acumen which can be detrmined case by case, goods by goods, sector by sector, or country by country.

Six forms of business cooperation were identified in our questionnaire. They are:

0 Any
1 100% foreign owned
2 Joint venture
3 Subsidiary
4 Representative office
5 Other

These types of business have been cross-tabulated against the level of company revenue. There are six levels of company revenue in our questionnaire. The six groups identified are: 0 billion–1 billion VND, 1 billion–10 billion VND, 11 billion–50 billion VND, 51 billion–100 billion VND, 101 billion–500 billion VND, and 501 billion–1,000 billion VND.

Some Results (see Table 5.7)

Of the 81 companies we interviewed, 47 or 58.0% indicate that they prefer business cooperation with overseas companies and in the form of joint ventures. 31 companies or 38.3% say that they prefer any kind of business cooperation. Only one company (1.2%) prefers the cooperation in the form of a representative office. Two companies (2.5%) have no preference.

For small companies with an annual revenue of up to 1 billion VND which account for 3% of all companies, joint ventures are the only preferred form of cooperation.

For larger companies with an annual revenue of up to 10 billion VND, the preference is between joint ventures (16.0%) and any business cooperation (11.1%).

For larger companies with an annual revenue of between 11 billion and 50 billion VND, the preference is 27.2% for joint ventures and 16.0% for any kind of business.

Table 5.7 Vietnamese Business Distribution Annual Company Income by Cooperation Type (1995)
Company Annual Income (Row) by Preferred Type of Cooperation (Column)

	0	2	4	5	Row Total
0	2	4	1	1	8
na					
%R	25.0	50.0	12.5	12.5	9.9
%C	100.0	8.5	100.0	3.2	
%T	2.5	4.9	1.2	1.2	
1	0	3	0	0	3
0–1b					
%R	0	100.0	0	0	3.7
%C	0	6.4	0	0	
%T	0	3.7	0	0	
2	0	13	0	9	22
1–10b					
%R	0	59.1	0	40.9	27.2
%C	0	27.7	0	29.0	
%T	0	16.0	0	11.1	
3	0	22	0	13	35
11–50b					
%R	0	62.9	0	37.1	43.2
%C	0	46.8	0	41.9	
%T	0	27.2	0	16.0	
4	0	3	0	5	8
51–100b					
%R	0	37.5	0	62.5	9.9
%C	0	6.4	0	16.1	
%T	0	3.7	0	6.2	
5	0	2	0	3	5
101–500b					
%R	0	40.0	0	60.0	6.2
%C	0	4.3	0	9.7	
%T	0	2.5	0	3.7	
Column Total	2	47	1	31	81
%	2.5	8.0	1.2	38.3	100.0

Notes: Columns refer to 'Don't Know' (0) and 5 types of cooperation: 1 (100%), 2 (joint venture), 3 (subsidiary), 4 (representative office), 5 (other). See also footnotes to Tables 5.1 and 5.3.

This kind of preference ranking (that is joint ventures) for business cooperation is not observed for bigger companies with an annual revenue of between 51 billion and 100 billion VND or between 101 billion and 500 billion VND. In fact, for the first group of companies, only 3.7% prefer joint ventures against 6.2% for any kind of business cooperation. For the second group, 2.5% prefer joint ventures whereas a slightly larger number of companies (that is, 3.7%) prefer any kind of business cooperation.

The above findings indicate that generally joint ventures are the preferred form of business cooperation (58.0%) by Vietnamese companies with their overseas counterparts. In fact, a large proportion of the companies interviewed (38.3%) prefer any kind of business be it joint ventures or otherwise.

Almost all Vietnamese companies we interviewed prefer business cooperation with their overseas counterparts.

4.3 Labour Supply and Business Cooperation

Objective and Definition

In the process of business expansion or utilization of foreign investment, the problem of supply of personnel (either for administration, finance, service, or production) having adequate skills or experience is not unimportant. The justification for this kind of information in our case can be found from the traditional neo-classical theory of economics.

One of the questions to the companies in our survey is whether they perceive any serious problems in finding suitably qualified staff in all areas of activity to assist in the process of business expansion or in managing foreign investment portfolios.

The answers are to be classified into three types:

1. Yes
2. No
3. No but with difficulty.

Again, the three types of response are cross-tabulated against six income groups of companies. The six groups of companies identified are: 0 billion–1 billion VND, 1 billion–10 billion VND, 11 billion–50 billion VND, 51 billion–100 billion VND, 101 billion–500 billion VND, and 501 billion–1,000 billion VND.

Some Results (see Table 5.8)

For fairly small companies with an annual revenue of up to 1 billion VND and for very large companies with an annual revenue of more than 501 billion VND per year, no response regarding the problem of skilled or trained labour supply was available for recording.

For companies with an annual revenue of between 1 billion and 10 billion VND (27.2% of all companies interviewed) however, the responses are almost all (90.9%) yes. Only 9% of these companies say they see no problem with the supply of skilled or trained labour mentioned here.

The largest group of companies that see a serious problem with skilled or trained labour supply is those companies with an annual revenue of between 11 billion and 50 billion VND (43.2% of all companies interviewed). In this group, only 5.7% see no problem with skilled or trained labour supply.

For the 51 billion–100 billion VND companies (9.9% of all companies interviewed) 87.5% say yes to our question, and 12.5% say no. For the 101 billion–500 billion VND group of companies (6.2% of all companies interviewed), all say they perceive a serious problem of skilled or trained labour supply. For a combination of all six groups of companies, 88.9% see it is difficult to find suitably qualified personnel to handle further business expansion or increased foreign investment. 7.4% reply no, and 3.7% reply no but with difficulty.

The implication is fairly obvious in this case. More education, training, or retraining of the existing labour force in Vietnam is urgently required to handle business expansion and to accommodate further foreign investment. This requirement would involve both the government and the private sectors with the express purpose of accelerating human and physical technology transfer from overseas to Vietnam.

The scope for investment in general or in-house technical education provision by Australia or any other country capable of doing so is enormous in this case.

4.4 Infrastructure and Business Cooperation

Objective and Definition

As was discussed above, the process of business expansion or utilization of foreign investment requires not only that the supply of skilled or trained personnel (either for administration, finance, service, or production) has to be amply satisfied, but also that the amount of

Table 5.8 Vietnamese Business Distribution Annual Company Income by Labour Problem (1995)
Annual Company Income (Row) by Labour Skills Problem (Column)

	1	2	3	Row Total
0	4	3	1	8
na				
%R	50.0	37.5	12.5	9.9
%C	5.6	50.0	33.3	
%T	4.9	3.7	1.2	
1	3	0	0	3
0–1b				
%R	100.0	0	0	3.7
%C	4.2	0	0	
%T	3.7	0	0	
2	20	1	1	22
1–10b				
%R	90.9	4.5	4.5	27.2
%C	27.8	16.7	33.3	
%T	24.7	1.2	1.2	
3	33	2	0	35
11–50b				
%R	94.3	5.7	0	43.2
%C	45.8	33.3	0	
%T	40.7	2.5	0	
4	7	0	1	8
51–100b				
%R	87.5	0	12.5	9.9
%C	9.7	0	33.3	
%T	8.6	0	1.2	
5	5	0	0	5
101–500b				
%R	100.0	0	0	6.2
%C	6.9	0	0	
%T	6.2	0	0	
Column Total	72	6	3	81
%	88.9	7.4	3.7	100.0

Notes: Columns refer to 1 (yes), 2 (no), and 3 (with difficulty). See also footnotes to Tables 5.1 and 5.3.

infrastructure necessary to carry out the expansion or utilization must be available.

One of the questions to the companies in our survey is whether they can foresee any serious problems in existing infrastructure or in the provision of extra infrastructure necessary to carry out the process of business expansion or in managing increased foreign investment portfolios.

The responses are again to be classified into three types:

1. Yes
2. No
3. No but with difficulty.

These responses are cross-tabulated against six income groups of companies. The six groups of companies identified are: 0 billion–1 billion VND, 1 billion–10 billion VND, 11 billion–50 billion VND, 51 billion–100 billion VND, 101 billion–500 billion VND, and 501 billion–1,000 billion VND.

Some Results (see Table 5.9)

On the question of infrastructure availability, 9.9% of all companies we interviewed did not provide an answer. The companies with an annual revenue of more than 501 billion VND also did not provide an answer.

For fairly small companies (according to our definition) with an annual revenue of up to 1 billion VND (3.7% of all companies), the response is 100% yes in relation to the difficulty of providing necessary infrastructure for business expansion and further foreign investment.

For companies with an annual revenue of between 1 billion and 10 billion VND (27.2% of all companies interviewed), the responses are also almost all (95.5%) yes. Only 4.5% of these companies say they see no problem with the infrastructure availability issue.

The largest group of companies that see a serious problem with available infrastructure is those companies with an annual revenue of between 11 billion and 50 billion VND (43.2% of all companies interviewed). In this group, only 5.7% see no infrastructure problem.

For the 51 billion–100 billion VND companies (9.9% of all companies interviewed) 100% say yes to our question. A 100% yes response is also obtained for companies in the 101 billion–500 billion VND range of activity (6.2% of all companies).

Table 5.9 Vietnamese Business Distribution Annual Company Income by Infrastructure (1995)
Annual Company Income (Row) by Infrastructure Problem (Column)

	1	2	Row Total
0	7	1	8
na			
%R	87.5	12.5	9.9
%C	9.1	25.0	
%T	8.6	1.2	
1	3	0	3
0–1b			
%R	100.0	0	3.7
%C	3.9	0	
%T	3.7	0	
2	21	1	22
1–10b			
%R	95.5	4.5	27.2
%C	27.3	25.0	
%T	25.9	1.2	
3	33	2	35
11–50b			
%R	94.3	5.7	43.2
%C	42.9	50.0	
%T	40.7	2.5	
4	8	0	8
51–100b			
%R	100.0	0	9.9
%C	10.4	0	
%T	9.9	0	
5	5	0	5
101–500b			
%R	100.0	0	6.2
%C	6.5	0	
%T	6.2	0	
Column Total	77	4	81
%	95.1	4.9	100.0

Notes: Columns refer to 1 (yes), 2 (no), and 3 (with difficulty). See also footnotes to Tables 5.1 and 5.3.

For a combination of all six revenue-based groups of companies, 95.1% see it is difficult not only to use existing infrastructure to carry out business expansion or to manage more foreign investment but also to provide extra necessary infrastructure. Only 4.9% reply no to our question on infrastructure availability.

There is scope here for investment in infrastructure in Vietnam. Some international organizations are in the process or are already involved in this kind of investment. There is still scope for transnational companies to consider investment of this kind in Vietnam.

4.5 Special Issues with Some Major Industries

Objective and Definition

The findings above indicate that (a) the four major industries the companies interviewed in our survey sample are currently engaged in are manufacturing textiles, construction and electronics; and (b) the four preferred industries for further business expansion and increased investment development by our companies are these same sectors. Using the first grouping (a), the rankings are 17.3% of all companies interviewed each for manufacturing, textiles, and construction, and 11.1% for electronics. Using the second grouping (b), the rankings are: 17.3% for textiles, 12.3% for manufacturing, 11.1% for electronics, and 9.9% for construction.

There thus appears to be a preferred planned reduction in the future activity by the companies in our survey in manufacturing and construction.

For the preferred industries for planned future business expansion and investment development, we asked (a) whether the companies concerned would like to receive assistance from the government (through the Ministry of Trade) and (b) which kind of assistance they would like to receive.

The answer to (a) is yes, no and maybe. The answer to (b) is;

0 Dont know
1 General information only on business and foreign investment
2 Export promotion activity
3 Information on a specific area of business or industry
4 Information on finding business partners
5 Other

For the definition of the major industries above, electronics includes both electronics and electrics.

These responses are cross-tabulated against six income or revenue-based groups of companies. The six groups of companies identified are: 0 billion–1 billion VND, 1 billion–10 billion VND, 11 billion–50 billion VND, 51 billion–100 billion VND, 101 billion–500 billion VND, and 501 billion–1,000 billion VND.

Some Results (see Tables 5.10 and 5.11)

Major Industries at the Current Level of Activity (Table 5.10)
There are a total of 45 companies currently engaging in business in the four major industries of textiles, manufacturing, construction, and electronics. These account for 55.6% of all companies interviewed in our survey.

Of these 45 companies, 39 (or 86.7%) indicate that they would like to receive some assistance from the Ministry of Trade, and 13.3% say no.

One company from this group of major industries (2.2%) provided no information about its annual income, but said yes to the question of assistance or not. The only one company in the annual income level of between 0 and 1 billion VND (2.2%) also said yes.

For larger (that is between 1 billion and 10 billion VND income per year) companies (26.7% of all companies in the group), 83.3% of these companies said yes, and 16.7% said no.

The largest number of companies is those companies earning between 11 billion and 50 billion VND per year (46.7% of all companies in the group). 85.7% of these companies said yes, and 14.3% said no to the question of assistance.

For the companies earning between 51 billion and 100 billion VND per year (15.6% in the group), again 85.7% said yes and 14.3% said no.

Finally for the companies earning more than 100 billion but less than 500 billion VND per year (6.7% in the group), all said that they would need assistance from the government.

For all companies of all annual revenue levels, 86.7% indicated that they require information from the Ministry of Trade for their business expansion and foreign investment development, 13.3% said that they do not need this information.

Table 5.10 Vietnamese Business Distribution Annual Company Income by Investment Information Assistance (1995)
Annual Company Income (Row) by Need for Investment Information Assistance (Column)

	1	2	3	Row Total
0	6	2	0	8
na				
%R	75.0	25.0	0	9.9
%C	9.2	13.3	0	
%T	7.4	2.5	0	
1	3	0	0	3
0–1b				
%R	100.0	0	0	3.7
%C	4.6	0	0	
%T	3.7	0	0	
2	16	5	1	22
1–10b				
%R	72.7	22.7	4.5	27.2
%C	24.6	33.3	100.0	
%T	19.8	6.2	1.2	
3	29	6	0	35
11–50b				
%R	82.9	17.1	0	43.2
%C	44.6	40.0	0	
%T	35.8	7.4	0	
4	7	1	0	8
51–100b				
%R	87.5	12.5	0	9.9
%C	10.8	6.7	0	
%T	8.6	1.2	0	
5	4	1	0	5
101–500b				
%R	80.0	20.0	0	6.2
%C	6.2	6.7	0	
%T	4.9	1.2	0	
Column Total	65	15	1	81
%	80.2	18.5	1.2	100.0

Notes: Columns refer to 1 (yes), 2 (no), 3 (a little). See also footnotes to Tables 5.1 and 5.3.

Table 5.11 Vietnamese Business Distribution Annual Company Income by Assistance Type (1995)
Annual Company Income (Row) by Assistance Type (Column)

	0	1	2	3	4	5	Row Total
0	2	2	0	0	3	1	8
na							
%R	25.0	25.0	0	0	37.5	12.5	9.9
%C	11.8	8.7	0	0	10.3	10.0	
%T	2.5	2.5	0	0	3.7	1.2	
1	0	2	0	0	1	0	3
0–1b							
%R	0	66.7	0	0	33.3	0	3.7
%C	0	8.7	0	0	3.4	0	
%T	0	2.5	0	0	1.2	0	
2	6	7	0	0	6	3	22
1–10b							
%R	27.3	31.8	0	0	27.3	0	27.2
%C	35.3	30.4	0	0	20.7	0	
%T	7.4	8.6	0	0	7.4	0	
3	7	6	1	0	17	4	35
11–50b							
%R	20.0	17.1	2.9	0	48.6	11.4	43.2
%C	41.2	26.1	100.0	0	58.6	40.0	
%T	8.6	7.4	1.2	0	21.0	4.9	
4	1	3	0	1	1	2	8
51–100b							
%R	12.5	37.5	0	12.5	12.5	25.0	9.9
%C	5.9	13.0	0	100.0	3.4	20.0	
%T	1.2	3.7	0	1.2	1.2	2.5	
5	1	3	0	0	1	0	5
101–500b							
%R	20.0	60.0	0	0	20.0	0	6.2
%C	5.9	13.0	0	0	3.4	0	
%T	1.2	3.7	0	0	1.2	0	
Column Total	17	23	1	1	29	10	81
%	21.0	28.4	1.2	1.2	35.8	12.3	100.0

Notes: Columns refer to 0 (any), 1 (general information), 2 (exports), 3 (specific area), 4 (partners), 5 (other). See also footnotes to Tables 5.1 and 5.3.

Major Industries for Planned Future Increased Business and Investment (Table 5.11)

For the companies with either no information about their annual revenue or with a turnover of up to 1 billion VND per year, the answer is that assistance from the government is needed and it is in the form of general information only. These companies represent 2.2% each of the major companies.

For the companies with an annual turnover of between 1 billion and 10 billion VND (26.7% in the group), 16.7% provided no information about their need, and 33.3% indicated that they would need general information only for business expansion and foreign investment. Also 33.3% said that they were interested in information leading to finding business partners. 16.7% indicated that they would need other information.

The companies that make between 11 billion and 50 billion VND per year account for 46.7% of all major companies defined earlier. 14.3% of these companies indicated that they would need general information from the government, 4.8% would require export promotion activity, and 52.4% seek information leading to finding business partners. 14.3% said they would need other information. 14.3% of the companies here provided no information about their need.

For the companies in the 51 billion–100 billion VND per year range (15.6% in the group), 14.3% provided no information about their need, 28.6% said they require general business and investment information, 14.3% want information on a specific area of business, also 14.3% want information leading to finding business partners. Finally, 28.6% require other information.

For the companies in the 101 billion–500 billion VND per year range (6.7% in the group), 66.7% want general information from the government, and 33.3% require information leading to finding business partners.

In general, when we combine all companies of all annual income levels, 13.3% provided no information about their kind of need, 28.9% want general business and investment information, 2.2% want to receive export promotion and also 2.2% require information in specific areas of business and investment. Finally, 37.8% require information for finding business partners, and 15.6% need other information.

5 SUMMARY OF MAIN FINDINGS

From the the preceding analysis, we now can summarize the main and pertinent findings from our survey. The findings are of general interest to governments, institutions, business, syndicates, and individual investors. They can also be used as relevant and timely information to develop industry- or commodity-specific practical policy and to formulate operational and effective implementations of this policy on business and trade development by all sectors of the economy.

1. The survey is the first rigorous effort to understand foreign investment and business development in Vietnam.
2. The survey of business in Vietnam is a pioneering and systematic work to provide much needed information about Vietnamese businesses and their business and trade expectations.
3. The companies interviewed in the survey cover the major businesses in Vietnam, and include most sectors of the economy.
4. The list of countries doing business with Vietnam currently stands at 18, covering countries in Asia, North America, and Europe. The countries in these geographical regions are likely to form the core of the trading countries in the near future.
5. Australia at present plays only a small part in business with Vietnam.
6. Active current business in Vietnam as identified in the survey is mainly in the manufacturing, textiles, construction, and electronics/electrics sectors.
7. Hotels and tourism in Vietnam have declined in interest and importance.
8. Preferred business and investment in the future in Vietnam are in the manufacturing, textiles, construction, and electronics/electrics sectors.
9. Almost all Vietnamese companies interviewed would like business cooperation with overseas companies.
10. Joint ventures are the preferred form of business cooperation between Vietnamese companies and their overseas counterparts.
11. All companies interviewed see serious problems with the supply of adequately skilled and trained personnel to support business expansion and increased foreign investment in Vietnam.
12. All companies interviewed see serious problems with having or providing adequate infrastructure to support business expansion and increased foreign investment in Vietnam.
13. Almost all companies interviewed indicate they have had no business experience with Australia.
14. Almost all companies interviewed say they are not aware of investment laws, regulations, controls, guidelines etc. in Australia.
15. The scope for investment by Australian companies in Vietnam is

enormous, as most Vietnamese companies want to do business with Australia, and as her share of business in Vietnam is low compared to other countries' involvement.

16. Australian companies wanting to do business in Vietnam should be made aware that business and trade competition from overseas countries in Vietnam is strong. A laid-back or complacent attitude may not be desirable in this case.
17. The scope for business development and expansion by Australian companies in Vietnam is substantial either in the form of business cooperation, general and technical education and training provision, or increased trade promotion activity.
18. Among the companies interested in planning business expansion and foreign investment cooperation, a large proportion (37.8%) want help in finding overseas business partners, and 28.9% require general information on business and foreign investment.
19. The existing methods of business exploration and trade promotion in Vietnam by Australia are inadequate, as the responses from the Vietnamese business community indicate.
20. There is an urgent need for more utilization of existing resources both at the company and government levels as well as for ways to improve trade and investment information flows (Table 5.12).
21. A good cooperation between Austrade and Australian companies to develop business and to expand investment in Vietnam would be more effective than the one-party approach (Table 5.13).
22. A cohesive approach combining both the private and government sectors in Australia would be a good way to promote trade, investment, and business in Vietnam for Australia.

6 CONCLUSIONS

In this chapter, we have reported the first business survey in Vietnam carried out in conjunction with the ICTC staff, the Ministry of Trade, in Hanoi, during January–April 1995, as part of our ARC-RIFER research project's activity. The survey is important in our view because it provides cross section data to supplement time series data which are currently scarcely available. For the first time the survey provides first-hand information about business and foreign investment activity and its preferred forms of business and investment activity in the future in Vietnam.

Table 5.12 Vietnamese Businesses Distribution Annual Company Income by Investment Information (1995)
Annual Company Income (Row) by Information about Investment Area (Column)

	1	2	3	Row Total
0	7	1	0	8
na				
%R	87.5	12.5	0	9.9
%C	9.6	14.3	0	
%T	8.6	1.2	0	
1	3	0	0	3
0–1b				
%R	100.0	0	0	3.7
%C	4.1	0	0	
%T	3.7	0	0	
2	20	2	0	22
1–10b				
%R	90.9	9.1	0	27.2
%C	27.4	28.6	0	
%T	24.7	2.5		
3	30	4	1	35
11–50b				
%R	85.7	11.4	2.9	43.2
%C	41.1	57.1	100.0	
%T	37.0	4.9	1.2	
4	8	0	0	8
51–100b				
%R	100.0	0	0	9.9
%C	11.0	0	0	
%T	9.9	0	0	
5	5	0	0	5
101–500b				
%R	100.0	0	0	6.2
%C	6.8	0	0	
%T	6.2	0	0	
Column Total	73	7	1	81
%	90.1	8.6	1.2	100.0

Notes: Columns refer to the four levels of information on investment available: 1 (no), 2 (little), 3 (adequate), 4 (100%). See also footnotes to Tables 5.1 and 5.3.

Table 5.13 Vietnamese Business Distribution Annual Company Income by Information Source (1995)
Annual Company Income (Row) by Sources of Information (Column)

	0	1	3	4	5	Row Total
0	7	0	0	0	1	8
na						
%R	87.5	0	0	0	12.5	9.9
%C	9.5	0	0	0	50.0	
%T	8.6	0	0	0	1.2	
1	3	0	0	0	0	3
0–1b						
%R	100.0	0	0	0	0	3.7
%C	4.1	0	0	0	0	
%T	3.7	0	0	0	0	
2	20	0	1	1	0	22
1–10b						
%R	90.9	0	4.5	4.5	0	27.2
%C	27.0	0	50.0	50.0	0	
%T	24.7	0	1.2	1.2	0	
3	31	1	1	1	1	35
11–50b						
%R	88.6	2.9	2.9	2.9	2.9	43.2
%C	41.9	100.0	50.0	50.0	50.0	
%T	38.3	1.2	1.2	1.2	1.2	
4	8	0	0	0	0	8
51–100b						
%R	100.0	0	0	0	0	9.9
%C	10.8	0	0	0	0	
%T	9.9	0	0	0	0	
5	5	0	0	0	0	5
101–500b						
%R	100.0	0	0	0	0	6.2
%C	6.8	0	0	0	0	
%T	6.2	0	0	0	0	
Column Total	74	1	2	2	2	81
%	91.4	1.2	2.5	2.5	2.5	100.0

Notes: Columns refer to six sources of information: 0 (none), 1 (Austrade), 2 (media), 3 (partners), 4 (Ministry of Trade), 5 (other). See also footnotes to Tables 5.1 and 5.3.

Strategies for business expansion, investment direction and allocation, and trade promotion can be based on some of the information revealed in this survey.

While the sample may be relatively small in our returned questionnaires, it is the best that our research staff were able to achieve under the present circumstances of no response and apathy from the companies we contacted during the period under study. When we compare our sample with that from other studies that use the survey technique (for example, Nguyen Van Anh, 1995), the size of our sample is decidedly superior.

In spite of this, it may be best however to regard our survey as a pilot study of current patterns and future trends of business and foreign investment in Vietnam. More substantial business surveys can be carried out in the future if resources permit. In fact, it is our intention to carry out a business survey among the Australian companies currently doing business in Vietnam in the near future. This would provide another perspective (that is, from trading partners or seekers) about business cooperation, investment opportunities, and trade potentials in Vietnam.

For what is available, the kind of information we have collected in our present study about what the Vietnamese business community is doing and wants to be done in the future would be of interest not only to us, the researchers, but also to the Australian business community or other business community overseas. It is of interest to Australian government trade agencies or commissions for whom the objective is to promote business and trade between Australia and Vietnam.

The information we have collected here could form a database of business activity in Vietnam from which current and future businesses, corporations, institutions, government agencies, and individual investors from Australia and other trading countries with Vietnam could draw upon to formulate their business, investment, and trade policy.

APPENDIX 5.1
FIRST BUSINESS SURVEY OF VIETNAMESE COMPANIES
HANOI, VIETNAM
JANUARY–FEBRUARY 1995

QUESTIONNAIRE AND CODES USED

Q01 The number of employees on the payroll in your company:

(0) : Don't know
(1) : 0–30 persons
(2) : 31–50 persons
(3) : 51–100 persons
(4) : 101–200 persons
(5) : 201–500 persons
(6) : 501–1,000 persons

Q02 Your company's estimated annual income:

(0) : No answer
(1) : 0–1 billion VND
(2) : 1–10 billion VND
(3) : 11–50 billion VND
(4) : 51–100 billion VND
(5) : 101–500 billion VND
(6) : 501–1,000 billion VND

Q1 The main trading/manufacturing/service etc. activity of your company:

(1) : Electronics
(2) : Consumer
(3) : Hotels
(4) : Communications
(5) : Transport
(6) : Tourism
(7) : Manufacturing
(8) : Textiles
(9) : Agriculture
(10) : Mining
(11) : Forestry
(12) : Electrics
(13) : Construction
(14) : Chemical
(15) : Other
(16) : No answer

Q2 Countries which you currently have business dealings with:

(1) : Australia
(2) : Canada
(3) : China
(4) : England
(5) : France
(6) : Germany
(7) : HongKong
(8) : Italy
(9) : Japan
(10) : Singapore
(11) : SNG
(12) : South Korea
(13) : Switzerland
(14) : Taiwan/Cuba
(15) : Thailand
(16) : USA
(17) : EU
(18) : Other
(19) : No answer

Q3 Which preferred area for future investment, trade and business do you want to know about?

(1) : Electronics
(2) : Consumer
(3) : Hotels
(4) : Communications
(5) : Transport
(6) : Tourism
(7) : Manufacturing
(8) : Textiles
(9) : Agriculture
(10) : Mining
(11) : Forestry
(12) : Electrics
(13) : Construction
(14) : Chemical
(15) : Other
(16) : Any

Q4.1 Have you got information about this area now?

(1) : No
(2) : Little
(3) : Adequate
(4) : 100%

Q4.2 If you have got information, through which organization or group have you got it?

(0) : None
(1) : Austrade
(2) : Media
(3) : Partners
(4) : Ministry of Trade
(5) : Other

Q5 What kind of business cooperation do you prefer to have with foreign investors?

(0) : None
(1) : 100% foreign owned
(2) : Joint venture
(3) : Subsidiary
(4) : Representative office
(5) : Other

Q6 Can you foresee any skilled or trained labour supply problem in your area for foreign investment?

(1) : Yes (2) : No (3) : With difficulty

Q7 Can you foresee any infrastructure problem in your foreign investment area?

(1) : Yes (2) : No (3) : With difficulty

Q8 Have you had any business experience with Australia in the past?

(1) : Yes (2) : No (3) : A little

Q9 Are you familiar with investment policy and aware of various foreign investment, trade and business laws in Australia?

(1) : Yes (2) : No (3) : A little

Q10.1 Do you need any help from the Ministry of Trade to get the information on foreign investment, trade and business for your company?.

(1) : Yes (2) : No (3) : Maybe

Q10.2 What specific kind of information on investment, trade and business do you want to have?

(0) : Any
(1) : General information
(2) : Export promotion
(3) : Specific area
(4) : Seeking partners
(5) : Other

References

Helleiner, G. K., *Direct Foreign Investment and Manufacturing for Export in Developing Countries: A Review of the Issues*, Aldershot, UK, 1990.

Hill, H., 'Foreign Investment and East Asian Economic Development', *Asian Pacific Economic Literature*, Vol. 4, 1990, pp. 21–58.

Lee, C. H., 'Direct Foreign Investment, Structural Adjustment, and International Division of Labour: A Dynamic Macroeconomic Theory of Direct Foreign Investment', *Hitotsubashi Journal of Economics*, Vol. 31, 1990, pp. 61–72.

Lee, K., *New East Asian Economic Development: Interacting Capitalism and Socialism*, Armonk, New York, and London: Sharpe, 1993.

Lucas, R. E. B., 'On the Determinants of Direct Foreign Investment: Evidence from East and Southeast Asia', *World Development*, Vol. 21, 1993, pp. 391–406.

Maitland, E., 'Australian Companies in Vietnam', *Vietnam Economic and Political Update*, Australian National University, Canberra, Australia, 1995.

Nguyen Thi Van Anh, 'Foreign Investment in Vietnam', MA Thesis, Faculty of Economics, Thammasat University, Bangkok, Thailand, 1995.

Ramstetter, E. D., *Direct Foreign Investment in Asia's Developing Economies and Structural Change in the Asia Pacific Region*, Boulder and Oxford, 1991.

Tran Van Hoa, 'Studies of Foreign Investment in Vietnam: Methodologies', *Foreign Trade Review*, forthcoming.

Tsai, P. L., 'Foreign Investment, Technology Transfer and Foreign Capital Impact Function', *International Economic Journal*, Vol. 3, 1989, pp. 43–56.

6 Vietnam Tourism, 1995 to 2010: Development Strategy and Plan

Le Nhat Thuc and Tran Van Hoa

1. INTRODUCTION

In recent years, the number of foreign tourists to Vietnam has been wildly fluctuating from year to year. However, the general underlying trend that we have observed is that, like most other economic activity in Vietnam, it has been increasing at an exponential rate.

More specifically, the statistical data shows that the number of foreign tourists to Vietnam was only 7,000 in 1986, 40,000 in 1987, and 60,000 in 1988, but it rose to 187,000 in 1989. In 1990, the number fell down to 99,721, and since then it has grown rapidly to 231,973 in 1992, 375,700 in 1993, and 738,661 in 1994 (Vietnam Statistical Yearbook, 1994).

It has been generally accepted by the travel industry outside Vietnam that the potentials and prospects of Vietnam's tourism are enormous for both local and foreign operators. This can be translated more concretely into the existence of an industry that is highly profitable to manage and, as a result, is highly attractive for the flow of foreign direct investment into it. In spite of this assessment, the tourism industry in Vietnam is still in its infancy in almost all aspects by international standards. There are a number of reasons for this state of affairs.

First, the open door policy of the government of Vietnam started with the promulgation of the economic reform or Doi Moi at the end of 1987, and the results of its implementation really took off only in 1991 or so.

Second, while Vietnam's tourists consist of both (1) local residents travelling the width and the 2,000 kilometre breadth of Vietnam for business or leisure and (2) foreign tourists looking for unexplored cultures and untrodden landscapes and exotic adventures (431,308 out of 738,661 or 58.3% in 1994) or for business opportunities (31.9% also in 1994), a large proportion (27.4%) of all foreign tourists coming to Vietnam are Vietnamese expatriates from the US, France, Australia, and other countries which have accepted Vietnamese nationals as residents in the past 20 years. This type of foreign tourist is being encouraged by the government of Vietnam to make the visits, through the relaxation of a number of previously restrictive procedures.

Third, while the crowd-pulling features of Vietnam's landscape, culture, history, ethnicity and commerce that are known to be attractive to tourists are many and various, Vietnam has not been able, due to a number of reasons, to exploit or develop these features sufficiently to take advantage of them for the purposes of commerce expansion. Some of these reasons and their possible remedies are to be discussed below.

Fourth, the state of undevelopment or under-development of the tourist industry in Vietnam reflects a lack of required capital and necessary management personnel as well as of domestic and foreign investment in it.

From an economic modernization process perspective then, and from the point of view of economic growth, international trade, investment, and business, there is an urgent need for a development of tourism in Vietnam. As two corollaries of this, there is also a need for a formal policy for tourism development and a need to attract domestic and foreign capital funds to support this development.

The need for tourism development in Vietnam comes from its economically and socially beneficial multiplier effects on many aspects of the economy.

The impact of tourism on the economy of a country has been assessed theoretically within the framework of the OECD's SNA or empirically within the modelling approach in many studies in recent years. From the past experience in other Asian developing economies (such as Thailand) for example, income from tourism can also be a, if not the, major component of GDP in a country. It should also be said that the need for tourism development has, to be consistent with good and balanced economic management, to be measured against the aspects of development sustainability and environment conservation as well as other economic and social considerations.

This chapter argues as its main theme that tourism is a beneficial aspect of a modern economy, and focuses on the strategy and plan by the government of Vietnam to develop tourism in Vietnam for the period 1995 to 2010. The prospects arising from this strategy and plan, and the subsequent foreign investment requirement to achieve the government's target are also discussed qualitatively and quantitatively.

2 VIETNAM'S TOURISM IN THE REGIONAL AND WORLD CONTEXT

General Features

Geographically and strategically, Vietnam is a major country in the South-East Asia region. It is located in the South China Sea and lies between Laos to the West and the Philippines to the East. It also provides a good sea route linking Asia to Australia, and other transportation needs from the Middle East to East Asia through two oceans (the Pacific and the Indian).

Vietnam's territory has two parts: land with more than 3,444 km of the coastline and large adjoining seas. On land, it stretches from the latitude 23°22' and shares a border with China in the North, Laos and Cambodia in the West, the East Sea and Thailand in the South-East and South-West. The land boundary of Vietnam is 3,818 km.

The land mass of Vietnam is 331,041 km^2, of which 325,360 km^2 is on land. Three-fourths of the land area covers hills and mountains and this is mainly in the central highlands and in the north and the north-west of the country. The rest is the low and flat alluvial plains, with two large deltas: the Red River delta in the North and the Mekong delta in the South.

As of early in 1996, Vietnam has 3,059 km of railroads, 85,000 km of highways, and 17,702 km of waterways. The main ports of Vietnam are Danang, Hai Phong, and Ho Chi Minh City. About 100, mainly small, airports are scattered around the country.

The population of Vietnam reached more than 73 million in 1994, and is ranked second (after Indonesia) in the ASEAN region. This population has a composition of a multi-ethnic community whose history of independence and foreign rule and internal conflict goes back more than two thousand years.

Internationally and geographically, Vietnam is also in a prime position of being a gateway for transnational transport and communication. It provides potential to develop rail, sea, road, and air links between Vietnam and other countries in Greater Indochina and in the Asia Pacific region, the subcontinent, and the rest of the world. One of these examples is the planned construction of a trans-Asian railway line from Beijing in China through Vietnam and on to the subcontinent, the Middle East, and Europe.

Tourism Potential

The potential of Vietnam's tourist industry, in terms of development of both existing and planned tourist centres, is abundant and diversified. It is the features of existing tourist centres that have in part attracted a growing number of both domestic and international tourists in recent years as mentioned above.

It has also been assessed that if existing tourist centres in Vietnam are properly planned and suitably developed to attract tourists and to draw both local and foreign investment to them, then Vietnam's tourist industry will be expanded to a critical mass and can therefore compete with other tourist destinations in the other countries in the region and in the world.

Some of these existing tourist centres which have been identified by the Vietnam Tourism Commission for planning and development are: Hanoi, the districts of Ha Tay, Ninh Binh, Vinh Phu, Hoa Binh, Ha Long – Cat Ba – Do Son (Quang Ninh, Hai Phong), Dai Lanh – Van Phong, Nha Trang (Khanh Hoa), Phu Quoc Island (Kien Giang), Hue – Da Nang, Ho Chi Minh City, and the Mekong delta.

The potential for development of tourist resorts in Vietnam is great since the attractions of these resorts are themselves diversified and rich in natural endowments. These natural endowments include beaches, caves, hot springs, islands, flora, rare and precious fauna, and unique natural wonders such as the Bay of Ha Long and the Sapa mountain resort in the North.

The attractions of Vietnam tourism are also numerous in terms of culture, and the people: history, historical relics, art, architecture, traditional customs and practices, and distinctive cultural traditions of the ethnic people. These attractions could be used to facilitate the development of both seaside and highland tourist resorts, catering for long-term and short-term tourists and for other various different purposes of visit. Some of these purposes are short-term visits, recreation, relaxation, sports, scientific researches, conferences, and fairs.

The distribution of tourism resources is at present concentrated near the big cities in Vietnam. And this kind of development of near urban tourist resorts might neglect the regional nuances or characteristics outside these big cities. It is however these different nuances that are typically non-transferable that provide diversity in the character of regional tourist resorts. On the other hand, the allocation of tourism resources near big cities has its rationale. Since these big city resorts form a significant gateway to international tourist routes they could create favourable conditions for travelling, visiting, food, and accommodation for the tourists.

In the future, the Indochinese tourist route (Vietnam–Laos–Cambodia) is seen as being capable of providing an important feature in the international visitors' itinerary in South-East Asia. It will form one of the most attractive intra-regional tourist routes in the region (for example, the circular Indochina route: Hanoi – Hue – Danang – Nha Trang – Ho Chi Minh City – Phnom Peng – Angkor Vat – Angkor Thom – Bangkok – Vientiane – Hanoi). With further extension and connection, this route can be linked to the international tourist route by land to Malaysia, Singapore and Myanmar.

Vietnam has a huge supply of human resources which are endowed with intelligence, good work ethics, technical skills, a customer friendly approach, and currently low wages. In addition, these working people are learning very fast many aspects and skills of international tourist management that international tourists are accustomed to expecting in other developing countries in the ASEAN and the Asia Pacific.

3 CURRENT TRENDS IN TOURISM IN SOUTH-EAST ASIA

In recent years, as a result of the government of Vietnam's Doi Moi or renovation policy with a special emphasis on foreign economic policy, Vietnam's tourism has made great progress and the effect of this progress is pervasive on many aspects of the social and economic life in the country.

As has been mentioned earlier, in the past few years, Vietnam has received a large number of foreign tourists and this number has been on the steady rise. However, the number of present international tourists to Vietnam is small in comparison with that to other countries in the region. The reasons for this relatively low volume of tourism are many, but they can be summarized as follows:

1. Vietnam's tourism infrastructure is currently backward.
2. Technical support for tourism is bare and in poor quality.
3. Staff in the tourist industry possess only limited professional skills and foreign languages.
4. The state management of the tourist industry is loose and strictly uniform so the result does not correspond to the country's diverse tourist development potentials.

This state of affairs is in stark contrast to the world development in tourism and the subsequent substantial revenue collection for the countries that foreign tourists have found attractive enough to visit.

For example, during the 30 years from 1960 to 1991, the revenue from tourism across the world increased 15 times from USD 6.8 billion in 1960 to USD 102 billion in 1980, and USD 260 billion in 1991. An estimated revenue of USD 324 billion was made for 1993. With such an increased turnover on a global basis, many countries (such as Thailand where tourism revenue had exceeded its main and traditional export: rice) have regarded the tourist industry as a crucial sector in their socio-economic development and growth strategies.

Within the past two decades, the East Asia and Pacific region has played a more and more important role in international tourist activities. The increase in the tempo (in the number of international tourists and the increased turnover of tourist journeys) in this region is indeed leading the world in tourism development.

More specifically, in 1992, the number of international tourists to South-East Asia achieved an annual increase of 9.49%, reaching 21.859 million people and making up 4.6% of the world's total number of international tourists. It has been predicted that South-East Asia will receive up to 39 million tourists by 2000 and 72 million by 2010.

In 1993, South-East Asia's tourist revenue increased by 15.61% to USD 17.40 billion. The most international tourist receiving countries in the South-East Asian region in 1993 were Singapore with a revenue of USD 6,230 million, Malaysia with USD 6,570 million, Thailand with USD 5,620 million, and Indonesia with USD 3,500 million. It should be noted that, in Singapore, the number of tourists might have included business people on business trips to the city state. In spite of this qualification, Singapore is a leading country in South-East Asia in terms of foreign currency earnings from tourism. In 1992, it received 5.9 million tourists and earned USD 6.1 billion. After Singapore comes Thailand with 5.1 million tourists, earning USD 4.5 billion (Source: National Tourist Organization).

Malaysia is the country that received most international tourists in South-East Asia with 6.57 million in 1993, and nearly 22% of the country's manpower resources working in the tourist industry. The position of tourism in Malaysia's national economy has changed from the sixth place in 1989 to the third place in 1990.

4 OBJECTIVES FOR TOURISM DEVELOPMENT IN VIETNAM

The objectives for tourism development in Vietnam are many and varied but they can be summarized as follows:

1. To acquire tourist development experience in the region despite a recognition that tourist competitiveness there is fierce.
2. To narrow the gap between tourist growth and development and the present capacity of hotel accommodations and infrastructure development.
3. To reconcile an open door policy attracting international visitors with national security and social order. This last objective has posed a number of big obstacles to Vietnam's tourism development.

To affirm, however, the important position of Vietnam's tourism industry in the restrictive period and in the context of tourism development in the region and the world, the governmnent of Vietnam has issued many decrees and has developed policies creating favourable conditions for tourism development.

On 22 June 1993 for example, the government issued Resolution No 45/CP on 'renovative management and tourist development'. On 24 May 1995, the government promulgated Decision No 307 TT9, approving a 'tourist development master plan towards 2010'.

4.1 Vietnam's Tourism: Target, Strategies and Plan to 2010

The following are the objectives in detail of the target, strategy, and plan to develop Vietnam's tourism to 2010.

1. Goal of the economy: To optimize the tourist industry's contribution to national income and to create employment.
2. Goal of the environment: To combine tourist development with preservation of ecological and social environments.
3. Social aim: To acquire tourist development experience of high quality from other countries and at the same time to assure positive effects on the society of tourism by diversification of tourist products, and improvement of standard quality of products.
4. Together with international tourism development, to push forwards domestic tourism development with a focus on the people's needs for travelling, visiting and excursion, to help to improve the local people's spiritual and material life, especially in remote areas of the country, in ethnic minorities' regions and to protect public benefit.

4.2 Quantitative Targets

The quantitative targets for tourist development in Vietnam to 2010 are given in Table 6.1.

It should be noted that, in Table 6.1, the fastest growth rate is in the revenue component. Between 2000 and 2010, the revenue growth rate increases by eight times. During this period, the number of tourists increases by only slightly over 100%.

4.3 Organization of Tourist Territories

The allocation of tourist territories or areas for development is one of the most difficult problems in the tourism development strategy in Vietnam.

In principle, the allocation is simple. The tourist territory organization and the tourist space distribution in Vietnam are based on:

1. The available resources
2. Existing infrastructure
3. The supply of technical materials, labour, and office management
4. Connections with the growing demand for resources and with other industries in the area
5. Futher expansion to the countries in the region, especially the countries in South-East Asia

In spite of the problems in the allocation of the tourist areas for development, a plan for development priorities has been identified by the government of Vietnam.

More specifically, by the year 2000, Vietnam needs to centralize its planning and to exploit four tourist regions:

* The tourist sites in the North,
* The North-Central,
* The South-Central,
* The South.

The planning consists of specific tourism development projects. This includes many long-term projects as the country prepares to cater for increasing tourist demand in the twenty-first century.

Table 6.1 Targets for Tourism Development in Vietnam to 2010

Year	Number of international tourists (million turnover)	Revenue of international tourists (excluding transport) (USD billion)	Number of domestic tourists (million turnover)
1995	1.4	0.4	4.5
2000	3.8	1.06	11.0
2010	8.7	8.00	25.0

1995: Revenue of tourism accounted for 2.8% (5.8%) of the whole country's GDP
2000: Revenue of tourism to account for 5.0% (9.0%) of the whole country's GDP
2010: Revenue of tourism to account for 10.0% (20.0%) of the whole country's GDP

The details of these areas for tourism development are given below.

1. Pac Po (Northern tourism sites)

The Pac Po tourist development plan includes 23 provinces, stretching from Ha Giang to Ha Tinh, with Hanoi being the centre of the tourist area, and the Ha Noi – Hai Phong – Quang Ninh tourism triangle having the growth impetus.

At the moment, the local tourism industry is still ranked as in a modest low position among other regional industries. In the coming years, however, tourism will become an important industry in this area. This is due to the growth of national tourism and the remarkable increase in the number of international visitors to the area.

More importantly, tourism service infrastructure and special material or physical facilities are being improved, and greater tourism resources (both natural and human resources) are contributing to a generation of favourable conditions to attract foreign and domestic visitors.

The development plan for the Pac Po tourism sites includes the following focus points:

Key Focus

* Making tourism one of the most important industries in the region.

* Linking tightly controlled resource exploitation programmes to the

specialized products of the area thus making local features attractive to the visitors' consumption habits and preferences.

* Embellishing, upgrading and conserving tourism resources as well as the environment, tourism service infrastructure, and a gradual completion of special material or physical facilities.

* Paying attention to improving the types of tourism and making them available to the tourists. These types include regular holidays, seabathing, weekend holidays, city outskirt visits, seminars and tours, conferences, fairs, health resorts, sports and other exercising activities (mountain climbing, canoeing, sailing etc.).

* Focusing on the planning and development of

(a) Key tourism resorts in the triangle: Hanoi – Hai Phong – Quang Ninh so as to create an impetus to the whole tourism industry

(b) International–national tourism resorts especially in the key prime area Hanoi and its neighbouring areas such as the Ha Long Bay, Cat Ba beaches, and the Do Son seaside resort.

* Investing in the construction of highland tourism resorts in Ba Be (Cao Bang), and Dien Bien Phu (Lai Chau).

2. North Central Tourism Resorts

This tourist resort region includes five provinces: Quang Binh, Quang Tri, Thua Thien-Hue, Quang Nam – Da Nang, and Quang Ngai.

Despite the present potential for considerable tourist development in this area, the tourism industry is still barely in existence when we compare it to other regional economic industries. A major reason for this lack of development is the region's slow economic development, out-of-date infrastructure and severe shortfall in tourism service material facilities.

In the years to come, the tourism industry in the area could be boosted into a large scale development and supported by a faster forward plan for improvement.

The development plan for the North Central resorts includes the following focus points:

Key Focus

* In the north of the area (Quang Binh, Quang Tri, Thua Thien-Hue): Excursion touring activities as well as tours connected to Laos and Thailand must be focused on for improvement or development.

* In the south of the area where many natural sites and touring hotspots can be found, such activities as seabathing, health care, excursions, scientific study tours, and sports could be improved.

* Diving and marine-based tourism: cultural and sea tours together with sports activities are the strong points for exploitation, depending on the local geographical characteristics. These activities are sand-dunes motor racing, rafting, boating, mountaineering, hunting, fishing, yachting, sailing, etc.

* Programmes should be developed to focus on tourism environment and conservation, to stop random tree-cutting and water contamination (especially from the city-overflowing rivers such as the Huong River [Hue], the Han River [Da Nang]), and to stop fresh water contamination in the urban environment, and in seaside and coastal areas.

* Conservation of historical places of interest.

* Investing in and upgrading of infrastructures, especially airports, transportation systems, and water and electricity supply.

3. South Central and Southern Tourist Resorts

These two tourist resort regions include 25 provinces from Kon Tum to Minh Hai and are divided into two small tourist districts:

* South Central (nine provinces) and Southern (16 provinces) with Ho Chi Minh City being the centre of the region

* Ho Chi Minh City, Nha Trang and Da Lat, forming the tourism growth triangle

The local tourism industry in the area has been rapidly improved and its growth has also been accelerated in all aspects. In the near future, tourism in the region will be developed and it is expected to become one of the key industries. However, Ho Chi Minh City's tourism will hold an especially crucial position.

The South Central and Southern areas, in comparison to the North and North Central regions, have better infrastructure and supporting tourism facilities. And these characteristics of the region give favourable conditions to tourism development to cope with the increasing number of both domestic and foreign visitors to the areas.

The development plan for the South Central and South resorts areas includes the following focus points:

Key Focus

* Tightly linking natural tourism resources to human exploitation.

This means that places of historical, art, and architectural interest are preserved and restored so as to make them attractive high-quality local tourism products to attract visitors.

* Developing different types of tourism, according to the special regional characteristics. These include excursions, winter holidays, seabathing, summer vacations, sports, mountaineering, short and long leave, seminars or study tours, conferences, etc..

* Conserving the tourism environment and gradually improving material facilities, and re-planning national and international tourism environment and surroundings.

These actions are especially important in the coastal ranges stretching from Nha Trang, Van Phong Bay, Dai Lanh (Khanh Hoa province), Lam Dong (Da Lat), to Ba Ria – Vung Tau, and several of Ho Chi Minh City's neighbouring areas such as Tay Ninh, Dong Nai, Con Dao, and Phu Quoc island.

5 IMPROVING AND RENOVATING TOURISM MANAGEMENT

It can be argued that it will be impossible to implement the development plans and to put the strategies as described above in place in Vietnam if no suitable method to improve and renovate tourism management in the country is contemplated or formulated and used or implemented.

The discussion below gives a survey of a number of possible ways to implement the identified plans and strategies, through a combination of tourism management and tourism administration. There are two targets in this case:

* Legal procedures: Improving and renovating management systems from the central committee to the local committees.

* Tourism marketing: Rearranging the tourism marketing system based upon tourism environmental specialization and planning.

5.1 Management Measures and Implementation Mechanism

As a first step to renovate and improve a system of tourism management, a separation of the government management from the business enterprises' trading practices is necessary.

The General Department of Tourism will be part of the government functioning as a governing board of management to control nationwide tourism and to help the government to prepare:

- discussion papers
- legal documents
- policy measures
- government resolutions
- government policies on tourism

and to formulate:

- laws of passage (corridors) for tourism enterprises working under the control of the government.

In some regions, where the bureaux of tourism and trade (departments, offices) manage, control, and operate tourism activities in their locality, the General Department of Tourism has to:

- administer directly international tourist activities, and nationwide planning
- develop regional constructional activities
- monitor the main focus as well as to guide specialized developing and training
- promote the tourist industry operation between the tourism enterprises and businesses, as determined in the government's Resolution No 09/CP.

The setting up of professional organizations such as travelling associations, a travel agents federation and a hotels association will be beneficial to the tourist industry once the favourable conditions are available.

5.2 Technological Solutions and Settlements

When a dispute arises in travel or tourist matters, the mechanism for dispute solution and settlement should be available. This involves:

* Enforcing the tourism industry standards with three targets:
  1. International and technological standards
  2. Traditional characteristics
  3. Objective, simple, and easy-to-understand implementation so as to be easily checked and observed
* Making inter-branch documents integrated and coherent.

6. STRATEGIES FOR TOURISM DEVELOPMENT

In this section, the strategies to develop tourism in Vietnam are discussed. In total, six aspects of tourism development can be identified.

6.1 Product Differentiation

Vietnam's essential strategies for tourism development include first and foremost, differentiation of Vietnam's tourist attractions or products.

These strategies have two purposes. First the strategies could exploit the country's unique tourism features such as traditional (especially with culturally traditional characteristics), historical, and art products. Second, this kind of focus would enable Vietnam to compete with neighbouring countries in tourism and to expand its markets to foreign visitors from Asia, North America, and Europe.

This is reinforced by recent estimates that predict that Vietnam will, in the coming years, receive its visitors chiefly from the Asia Pacific, West Europe, and North America. Tourism development strategies should be focused on this source of foreign tourists and also on the development of suitable products, marketing programmes and tours to attract them to Vietnam. Some of the development activities that can be seriously considered are: creating seminar-tourism products for health care tours, sea-convalescing therapy, cave exploring, golf, sports, fishing, boating.

For those who are fond of handicraft arts, the activities may include traditional craft, ethnic village tours, bonsai cultivation, festivals, national cultural festivities, conferences, business meetings etc.

6.2 Developing Strategies

Some of the development strategies for Vietnam's tourism which have been considered by the government are:

* Diversification of tourism products
* Making sure that these products meet the required product standards and meet the needs or demand of the international tourist market.
* Aggressive marketing of Vietnam's tourism products in the main sources of international tourists.

6.3 Tourism Heritage's Conservation Strategies (including natural and human heritages)

Some of the conservation strategies of Vietnam's tourism which have been considered are:

* Planning to zone and to locate fully protected or preserved regions (such as national parks, natural reserves areas, and listed scenic spots),
* Planning reserve land and upgrading scenic areas,
* Planning future long- and medium-term urbanized reserve areas,
* Listing cultural, historical heritage and natural sites,
* Promulgating and listing regulations and scenic landscapes protection laws.

6.4 Forecasts and Investment and Tourism Strategies

Once Vietnam's tourism strategies have been adopted, resources are necessary to implement some of these strategies. Domestic and foreign investment will have an important impact on this implementation.

Some of the programmes to generate investment are:

1. Encouraging, by advertising in the media and by promotional campaigns, foreign and domestic investors to support Vietnam's tourism development plans and to invest in the projects they consider appropriate and profitable.

To protect investors in Vietnam in this case, there must be legislation or other legal documents in such matters as laws of tourism together with general laws of investment.

2. Investment in hotels: It is advisable to focus on the construction and erection of the two following kinds of hotels

* Transitional and temporary hotels (1–3 star standard)
* High standard hotels (4–5 star standard)

Transitional and temporary hotels provide tourism services along the tourism routes. It has been estimated that by the year 2000, there will be a demand for 16,200 rooms from this kind of hotel in Vietnam.

Luxury 4–5 star hotels should be around the well-known and big tourist centres.

Our focus is on the investment in building up-market high-scale hotels in Hanoi and Ho Chi Minh City with a capacity of over 200 rooms each. It has been estimated that by the year 2000, there will be a need for more than 6,700 rooms in this class of hotel.

This demand for up-market hotel rooms is distributed over three economic sectors of the Vietnamese economy: 2,000 rooms in Sector 1 200 rooms in Sector 2, and 4,500 rooms in Sector 3. For this kind of demand, there is a need for investment of up to USD 830 million (with USD 120 million per year on average). By the year 2010, there will be a need for more than 15,850 hotel rooms (4,960 rooms in Sector 1 550 rooms in Sector 2, and 10,340 rooms in Sector 3). To meet this demand for hotel rooms in Vietnam, an amount of USD 1,708 million is required for investment.

Up to now, Vietnam's tourism has received nearly 100 foreign investment projects with a total investment capital of approximately USD 1.4 billion. Given its ability to develop and construct hotels of international standard to meet the demand for hotel rooms from now to the year 2010 as mentioned above, Vietnam will need USD 6.44 billion in investment capital. This amount is required to build up to 98,250 international standard hotel rooms within 16 years.

One of the most important activities on the part of Vietnam's tourism department in order to attract foreign capital is the promotion of joint ventures with foreign investors to build 4–5 star business hotels and, to a lesser extent, health care hotels in the urban sectors or in other important tourism sectors. The mobilizing of domestic investment and capital to support development in the tourism industry is also another important aspect of Vietnam's macroeconomy and, especially, tourism department.

3. Investment in the tourism sectors and in the amusement and entertainment areas: Generally, investment in these activities must be focused to diversify and upgrade high-quality products of Vietnam's tourism industry. Once this area of priority has been implemented, Vietnam's tourism industry would be better equipped to increase its capability to attract touring guests.

Some of the investment urgently required at present is investment for upgrading Nha Trang (Khanh Hoa) by re-establishing Ninh Thuan as a tourist resort, and for upgrading Da Lat's sawtoothed railway routes.

Planning is currently under way to develop the tourist route Ho Chi Minh City – Da Lat-Nha Trang, and to build the Tay Nguyen cultural village in the Da Lat District.

6.5 Weekend Resort Development at Vung Tau-Long Hai-Con Dao

An important weekend retreat earmarked for development is the Long Hai-Phuoc Hai area. This is a coastal resort. There is also a plan for a private development to convert Con Dao into a holiday resort. Another plan exists to develop Con Dao-Vung Tau into a tourist area.

6.6 Ho Chi Minh City and its Surrounding Areas

Plans should be developed to take full advantage of the potential of Ho Chi Minh City in order to explore and create tourist routes along the Bach Dang river.

The areas in the delta of the Cuu Long river and along the Phnom Peng river would also be suitable for developing into tourism resorts with connections further to Laos and Thailand.

In addition, there is a project to develop a cultural village in Ho Chi Minh City.

6.7 Ha Tien – Phu Quoc (Kien Giang)

Substantial gains will be obtained by Vietnam's tourism industry when the island of Phu Quoc is fully developed as an off-shore holiday resort. However, the development of Phu Quoc must be conceived as a comprehesive and integrated investment project with a long-term planning.

In this context, Vietnam could learn some experience on island resort development from Thailand which already has successful off-shore resorts on Ko Samet and Ko Samui. These two resorts have been exceptionally popular with foreign tourists to Thailand, and as a result, have provided a large proportion of foreign currency to the country.

Emphasis by Vietnam's tourism industry has often been placed on the prices of tourism products in the country. In a nutshell, in comparison with the local standard of living and the costs of tours in neighbouring countries such as Thailand, Malaysia, and Indonesia, Vietnam cannot afford to price itself out of the tourist market.

While tourism goods have to be unique and of high quality to be able to sell to foreign tourists, the prices of these goods and other related services in the tourism industry in Vietnam also have to be attractive (competitive) to these tourists. Vietnam's tourism department must devise ways to monitor this situation.

Product differentiation and price competitiveness are therefore two important elements in the strategies for a successful development of the tourism industry in Vietnam in the years to come.

7 CONCLUSIONS

The government of Vietnam has clearly realized the importance of the tourism industry in Vietnam's economy and its present need for development as a priority of the country. Over the past few years, we have seen passed or promulgated a large number of regulations, provisions and measures to develop tourism throughout the country.

The experience from tourism in other countries in the region and the attractions of Vietnam as an outstanding destination for foreign tourists and the international business community will both indicate one course of action. And that is that there is a great opportunity for Vietnam to develop its tourism industry. This kind of development is in concert with the modernization process and, especially, with the open door policy of the government of Vietnam.

The benefits of tourism development in Vietnam, if the development is well planned and well implemented and is consistent with environmental and social concerns, are substantial not only for the tourism industry in Vietnam but also for other economic sectors of the country. This is because of the multiplier effects of a major economic activity such as tourism development on the whole economy. In other words, the benefits from the tourism industry are also there for other sectors of the economy.

These benefits are both in the short-term as well as in the long-term, since tourism development involves investment in infrastructure and in human resources, both of which are characterized by long-term investments.

A well planned tourism development strategy must include a detailed study of the tourism industry, its potentials and prospects and international competition.

To implement this strategy effectively, suitable policy has to be formulated. This policy must be concerned with human resources development, domestic and foreign capital formation, simple and effective laws on investment and investment protection and guarantee, the mechanism of international finance, and an efficient management system to implement this policy.

Thus a good policy encompasses four important players: the government and its advisers, the local people, the international visitors, and the transnational finance experts.

Since only a good policy for tourism development in Vietnam would bring about overall benefits both for the industry itself and also for the other sectors of the macroeconomy as a whole, the outcomes of the various strategies for tourism development described above are conditional upon the policy adopted, given a stable political environment.

APPENDIX 6.1
FOREIGN INVESTMENT IN TOURISM IN VIETNAM FROM 1988 TO 1994

Total Number of Projects

Total number of licensed projects	129
Joint venture projects	117
100% foreign capital projects	5
Cooperation projects	7
Licence-revoked projects	10

Total Investment Capital in 119 Licensed Projects

– 2 billion USD of which

– Legal capital	1.5 billion USD
– Contribution from the Vietnamese side	31%
– Contribution from the foreign side	69%
– Projects currently in operation	30%

Among these 119 licensed projects are projects involving:

12 5-star hotels providing 2,800 rooms
26 4-star hotels providing 5,400 rooms
46 3-star hotels providing 5,200 rooms

Biggest Investors in Vietnam:

- Hong Kong
- Taiwan
- Australia
- Japan

- India
- Canada
- Italy
- Czechoslovakia
- Singapore
- Philippines

7 Foreign Investment and Growth in Some Developing Economies in Asia Pacific: Leading Patterns for Vietnam?

Tran Van Hoa

INTRODUCTION

This chapter investigates the causal patterns of foreign investment, growth, external debts, and inflation in some major developing economies in the Asia Pacific in recent times, and the possible implications of these patterns for the formulation and implementation of development and growth policy in the transition countries in Indochina (Vietnam, Laos, and Cambodia) and Myanmar.

The chapter therefore assumes that the 'flying geese pattern', representing the sequential stages of growth for an economic region while being endowed with diverse natural resources supply conditions, may exist. It goes on to study which part of this pattern may be relevant to policy formulation for newly developing economies.

The basis of the analysis is a focus on the results of an application of the general cointegration or long-term causal tests (Engle and Granger, 1987: Johansen, 1991) applied to relevant economic causality models (Granger, 1969: Tran Van Hoa, 1992a and 1992c) and fitted to data on foreign direct investment, external debts, GDP, inflation and other relevant macroeconomic aggregates from three countries in the ASEAN (Indonesia, Malaysia, and Thailand) and one NIC from East Asia (Korea). The objective is an investigation into the asymptotically persistent or long-term relationships between these major macroeconomic aggregates. The existence of these relationships is relevant to a useful formulation of development and growth policy of newly developing economies.

Using the data from the World Bank database for the period 1970 to 1992, the findings indicate that, for these important developing economies (Indonesia, Korea, Malaysia, and Thailand) in the Asia Pacific region, foreign direct investment, external debts, GDP and inflation as defined in our econometric models are generally statistically nonstationary and fluctuating with discernible patterns.

More importantly, foreign direct investment is cointegrated (that is, related in the long term) with economic growth in Malaysia and Thailand, and, unfortunately, also with inflation rates in these countries. As a result, a national economic policy which concentrates only on capital inflows may produce an imbalance of benefits to an economy. A policy that combines both growth and the rising costs of living (resulting in the so called misery index) may be more appropriate.

External debts are relevant causal factors to FDI in Korea, to growth in Malaysia, and to inflation in Indonesia. Also in Indonesia, terms of trade affect inflation, and human resources and the government budget strongly influence foreign direct investment.

The utility of our findings has wide implications for other LDCs in the ASEAN and the Asia Pacific, especially Vietnam (which on 28 July 1995 joined the ASEAN as its seventh member) where the lessons and past experience from other Asian NICs and developing economies on the direction of causation for foreign investment and its effects on other economic and social activity of a country are important for policy formulation, implementation, monitoring, success, or failures.

In this context, our findings indicate that the country with a clear pattern of development and growth consistent with established economic theory and published official statistical data is Thailand. The economic policy and development paths of Thailand thus would provide a good example for Vietnam, Laos, Cambodia, and Myanmar to follow in their development.

This is buttressed further by the fact that all these countries are in a contiguous state with a long standing cultural and historical link and with a possibility for setting up a regional economic integration bloc.

Since investment and economic growth in a country (developed or developing) are intimately linked to such aspects as environment, sustainability, and global pollution issues, our findings on growth and investment would have a significant impact on discussions about these important and current issues. An analysis of this impact is however within the scope of another study.

OBJECTIVES

It is well known in the theories of economics, international economic relations, and international finance that foreign investment and external debts play an important role in microeconomic and macroeconomic activity and policy (Dornbusch and Fisher, 1990). The role is also pervasive in all sectors of an economy. These postulates are valid, it is assumed, in many developed countries in which the savings are low and especially in developing countries where capital for instituting economic developments is in short supply (World Bank, 1991). As a result, a study of the linkage between these issues is amply justified.

In the case of developed countries, the transmission mechanism of the effect of foreign investment and, to some extent, external debts can be investigated formally by means of the Mundell-Fleming model (Pippenger, 1984), whilst in the case of developing countries, it can be studied by means of such Keynesian models as the conventional Harrod-Domar specification or the multi-gap multi-equation growth framework popularized by McKinnon and Chenery and others (Gillis *et al.*, 1992).

More important for our paper is perhaps the observation that the level of foreign investment in developing countries has rapidly grown in the past few decades, and this has generated serious problems for external debts, their risk exposure, and their repayments or relief (Bulow and Rogoff, 1990: Kenen, 1990: Sachs, 1990). In spite of these problems, foreign investment or, its important component in the sense of international finance or transnational corporation operations, direct investment, is usually seen as a necessary ingredient of economic growth in the short run as well as in the long run, and is capable of reducing unemployment and affecting the exchange rates, the balance of payments, and inflation (Pippenger, 1984) or other major economic and social indicators (Gillis *et al.*, 1992).

The purpose of this chapter is fourfold.

First, as a significant contribution to macroeconomic analysis in general and to development economics in particular, we propose to rigorously investigate the asymptotically persistent or long-term relationships between foreign direct investment and external debts with respect to economic growth in some major and growing economies in the Asia Pacific region. The analysis goes therefore beyond the standard theory of unidirectional causation of FDI determination as proposed initially by Helleiner in his PhD thesis (see for example the cited publication in 1990) and developed further by Dunning (1993) and others in this context.

The countries included in this study at this stage are three countries of the ASEAN , namely, Indonesia, Malaysia, and Thailand, and one country from North Asia, namely, Korea.

The second purpose is methodological in nature in that the chapter departs from the applied modelling approaches of conventional regression, simultaneous equation, or seemingly unrelated regression (Tran Van Hoa, 1992a, 1992b and 1992c), and makes use of the theory of cointegration (Engle and Granger, 1987) to provide substantive high level evidence on the possible existence of these long-term relationships.

Third, as a contribution to a balanced economic policy or to an effective economic cost-benefit analysis of foreign direct investment and external debts in Indonesia, Malaysia, Thailand, and Korea, the possible negative effects of these macroeconomic growth indicator aggregates on the country's inflation rates are also investigated. Here, the balance is between economic growth and the possible worsening of the standard of living of a country. This balance has not been adequately studied in the current literature for both developed and developing economies.

Finally, the findings of the chapter will be used as a background information database to support micro and macroeconomic policy formulation analysis to determine whether the observed and econometrically significant pattern of development and growth and inflation from these major economies would be relevant to the national development and growth policy of other newly developing and/or transitional economies in general and of the South Asia peninsula, including thus Vietnam (the seventh member of the ASEAN), Laos, Cambodia, and Myanmar in particular.

TESTS OF LONG-TERM RELATIONSHIPS IN CAUSALITY MODELS

It has been generally accepted that the validity or effectiveness of economics, economic theory, and economic policy is simply based upon a set of strong causal statements or relationships between micro and macroeconomic activities in both closed and open economies. The causal relationships can stand alone (the case of single equation models) or they can be derived from a system of many inter-related relationships (the case of simultaneous equation models).

However, it is a fact that the fundamental relationships used by economists or model builders and policy forecasters are in many instances mere postulates without empirical support from collected real life statistical data. It is also well known in the current economic literature that a theory which is not supported by data (from national accounts, financial statements, surveys, etc.) has no relevance to meaningful policy. In spite of these facts, the question of verifying causation for economic variables has often been overlooked in serious economic analysis with national and international impact.

The testing for causation between economic variables can be carried out by informal methods or rigorous analysis. While causation at the elementary level can be done by means of tabular representations or graphs of the relevant variables accompanied by a simple description of them, this tabular or graphical approach lacks the rigour of scientific precision for both the linear and nonlinear or higher order relationships.

A more appropriate testing procedure with more scientific foundations would be correlation analysis, regression models, Granger causation procedures, or Engle-Granger cointegration protocols. The correlation analysis also has the drawback of ignoring higher order relationships among the variables. And the regression analysis while being well known among applied economists can produce spurious or unreliable results in the sense of Granger and Newbold.

The early concept of causality in the sense of Wiener was formalized and proposed for testing by Granger (1969) to investigate possible causation between economic variables. In its essence, the concept is based on the cross spectrum decomposition of the variables and, using current and lagged correlations among these variables, deals specifically with short-run fluctuations. Empirical applications of this Granger causality test have been extensive in the past two decades or so and involve many important areas of economics. These include studies of causation between money and income (Sims, 1972), and wage and price inflation (Fels and Tran Van Hoa, 1981), to name a few.

The theory of cointegration (Engle and Granger, 1987) also deals with causation between economic variables, but is focused particularly on a determination of the long-term relationships. The basic idea of the theory is that 'causal or correlated' economic series may wander in the short run, but they will not drift apart in the long run or in the equilibrium. Thus, in the short run, the equilibrium error may not be zero, but in the long run, systematic differences between the causal or cointegrated variables should disappear.

The empirical tests of the Granger-Wiener causality theory assume that the variables in the models should be statistically stationary or fluctuating randomly and perennially around the zero level (that is, $I(0)$).

The empirical tests of the Engle-Granger cointegration assume on the other hand that the variables should be stationary in their first differences (that is, $I(1)$). A variable is $I(1)$ if its first difference is $I(0)$. An important application of this result is in the use of the rate of change of a variable (see below). Since a rate of change is equivalent, if the change is small, to a log-difference, a variable in log is $I(1)$ if its rate of change is $I(0)$. The use of the rate of change also avoids the problem of taking logs of the economic variables having negative values (such as government budget or current account deficits).

It should be noted that these requirements of $I(1)$ for cointegration tests are generally not strictly defined (see Engle and Granger, 1987, pp. 252–254). It is also well known that the reliability of the results of causality or cointegration tests depends not only on the correct information set used for the model under study but also crucially on the usually unknown delayed impact or lag structure of these variables.

In the application of the cointegration theory, the appropriate tests include cointegration regression analysis, Dickey-Fuller and augmented Dickey-Fuller regression procedures, and restricted and unrestricted vector autoregressive methods (Engle and Granger, 1987). More recent developments of the cointegration theory include the maximum likelihood approach of Johansen (1991) within the unified framework of vector autoregressive and error correction models. Within the maximum likelihood approach, two sets of economic variables can be cointegrated in a number of ways. There is however only one maximum eigenvalue for a dataset. It is always advisable to focus on this eigenvalue and its eigenvector.

Below, we depart significantly from these studies and make use of a simple procedure (Pindyck and Rubinfeld, 1991: Tran Van Hoa, 1993) to test for unit roots or random walks among our variables of interest. This procedure is a prerequisite for further tests of cointegration (or causality). We then apply the convenient cointegration regression method (Engle and Granger, 1987) to investigate the possible existence of the long-run relationships (a) between foreign direct investment, external debts and output growth, and (b) from another important perspective in the composition of the well known misery index, also between foreign direct investment, external debts and inflation.

Thus, in our study, the test of unit roots or random walks for a variable Y consists simply of estimating the unrestricted regression equation (also known as the reduced form error correction model)

$$Y_t - Y_{t-1} = a1 + a2T_t + (a3-1)Y_{t-\infty 1} + a4DY_{t-1} + u_t \qquad (1)$$

and the restricted regression equation (with $a2 = 0$ and $a3 = 1$)

$$Y_t - Y_{t-1} = a1 + a4DY_{t-1} + u_t \tag{2}$$

In (1) and (2), T is a linear time trend, $DY_{t-1} = Y_{t-1} - Y_{t-2}$ or any other similarly defined error correction factors to take into account higher order impact or correlation of Y. The a's are the parameters to be estimated, and the u's the error terms.

In the case that this preliminary test yields the results of unit roots or random walks for the variable Y, a second-stage reduced form error correction model can be similarly constructed in which second differences replace first differences, lags of first differences replace past levels, etc. (see Engle and Granger, 1987). The remainder of the tests follow the same procedure as described in (1) and (2) above.

In the second stage of the cointegration tests, we use the resulting OLS (ordinary least squares) estimated residual sums of squares from (1) and (2) or their second-stage procedures, and compute an F statistic and compare it to the critical values of the distribution tabulated by Dickey and Fuller (1981) or any other subsequently tabulated critical values. The hypothesis of random walk for Y is rejected if the estimated F value is greater than the critical F value tabulated for an appropriate significance level and for an appropriate sample size.

In the case of bivariate (Y and X for example) models in which both Y and X are statistically $I(1)$, an effective test of cointegration (which avoids in practical applications and to some extent the arbitrary selection of the unknown true lags of the variables) between Y and X is as follows:

First, we simply estimate by OLS the cointegrating regression equation (Engle and Granger, 1987)

$$Y_t = b1 + b2X_t + e_t \tag{3}$$

where e is a new disturbance. Second, we test to determine whether the residuals (i.e., the estimated e) from this equation are statistically stationary.

In view of the definition of our economic variables in the form of the rates of change as described in Tran Van Hoa (1992a, 1992c) and used in the causal models in our study below however, if our variable is $I(0)$ then it implies that its first difference based on the level data in logs is approximately $I(0)$. In other words, if our rate of change variable is $I(0)$, the variable in log in the level must be $I(1)$ (see Engle and

Granger, 1987, p. 271). This argument to justify the transformation of the variables into logs is on a sounder economic theoretic basis than other *ad hoc* procedures and is used below in our empirical study.

The implication of the cointegration results is as follows:

If Y and X which are say $I(1)$ are not cointegrated, then any linear combination of Y and X will not be stationary. In this case, the residual e will be nonstationary. However, for the series e to be a random walk (nonstationary), $E(et - et - 1) = 0$, and accordingly, the Durbin-Watson (DW) statistic which is defined as $DW = 2(1 - r)$ must be zero (r is the correlation parameter between et and $et - 1$).

The test of cointegration between Y and X which are $I(1)$ is therefore the test whether $DW = 0$ (Engle and Granger, 1987). Similar tests can be used for $I(2)$ variables.

The testing procedures as described above will be applied below to determine the possiblity of long-term relationships between the various economic variables in our models for Indonesia, Korea, Malaysia, and Thailand.

DATASET AND DATA TRANSFORMATION

The required data are dictated as usual by the universe of information specified for the economic model we formulate for our study. This universe of information consists of the form of the functional relationships and the explicit variables present in the relationships. Two structures of an econometric model should be identified however: single equation models and multi-equation models.

In our case, a study of growth can be done via the expenditure sector of the Standardized National Account (SNA) of the OECD in which GDP in its simplest form is made a function of private consumption, total (i.e., domestic and foreign) investment, government expenditure, exports and imports. In a standard three-equation Keynesian econometric model with (a) private consumption following the standard specification by Keynes, Friedman, Duesenberry, and Modigliani, and (b) investment obeying the neo-classical or Tobin Q-theory framework, GDP is simply a function of lagged consumption, lagged GDP, current and lagged interest rates, government expenditure, exports and imports or the balance of payments.

In a system context, these economic activities or macroeconomic variables are also the instrumental variables for the growth equation in the reduced form. In this system, it can also be verified that investment (or more properly the domestic and foreign components of investment) has the same reduced form and the same instrumental variables.

Alternatively, GDP at factor cost can be made a function of labour, capital, and entrepreneurial or management skills. In its differential form however, the rate of change in GDP (or output growth) is a function of (a) a rate of change in the labour force, (b) investment growth (which is a rate of change in national capital stocks), and (c) technical progress or efficiency in both capital and human resources. Investment can therefore be derived as an inverse function of GDP, labour, and efficiency.

In our study below, we depart from this system approach and instead propose to test for the presence of the fundamental pairwise relationships between the four major economic variables of interest to us: output growth, foreign investment, external debts, and inflation rate. Other relevant macroeconomic, institutional, or demographic variables can be incorporated into these relationships to characterize the special features of each economy for the period under study.

We therefore formulate for each of the four countries in our study (i.e., Indonesia, Korea, Malaysia, and Thailand) four principal bivariate causality models of the forms (1) – (2) using $I(1)$ variables – or their $I(2)$ counterparts as the case may be – for four pairs of macroeconomic variables: (a) foreign direct investment (denoted by *FDI*) and output growth (*GDP*), (b) *FDI* and inflation rate (*INFLATION*), (c) external debts (*DEBT*) and *GDP*, and (d) *DEBT* and *INFLATION*.

In addition, a multivariate causality model using some relevant economic variables is formulated to study empirically possible causes of foreign investment in the four countries under observation. In this model, the relevant variables are the domestic and local market demand condition represented by *GDP*, local labour force (*LABOUR*), the terms of trade (*TT*), inflation rate (*INFLATION*), government budget surplus or deficit (*G*), and money supply (*M*1).

The justification for the use of these variables is based on standard macroeconomic postulates for a multi-equation econometric model for an open economy. Some exposition of this kind of multi-equation econometric model has been reported recently (see for example Harvie and Tran Van Hoa, 1995a, 1995b, and Tran Van Hoa, 1995).

The raw data used to calculate *FDI*, *DEBT*, *GDP*, *INFLATION*, *LABOUR*, *TT*, *G*, and *M*1, for Indonesia, Korea, Malaysia, and Thailand are obtained from the 1994 World Bank database made available via the DX retrieving facilities. The data are annual data and are available for the period 1970 to 1992.

For *FDI*, *DEBT*, *GDP*, *G* and *M1*, the data are in real terms with the base period being 1987. The real variables are obtained by dividing the nominal variables by the *GDP* deflator. For *LABOUR*, the data are in millions of workers. For the index variables *INFLATION* and *TT*, the base year is 1987. Each variable has an effective sampling size of 21 years.

To approximate inflation, we use the *GDP* deflator.

The dataset described above contains only raw variables. These variables have to be transformed to conform to our general modelling methodology.

In other words, making use of the general economic modelling approach of total differentials we proposed earlier (Tran Van Hoa, 1992a and 1992c), the variables in each of these four bivariate causality models and a multivariate model for each of the four countries under study are expressed in terms of their percentage rates of annual change.

The functional justification for using the rates of change in our models is simply mathematical in the sense of total differentiation of a function. In terms of economic theory, the models may be interpreted as macroeconometric models of the general Johansen-class that are fundamental specifications in applied or computable general equilibrium macroeconomic analysis. The parameters of these models can be verified to be the elasticities that affect the variables of interest in a linear manner.

SUBSTANTIVE UNIT ROOT AND COINTEGRATION RESULTS

The results of the tests of unit roots or random walks as based upon Eqts (1) and (2) for the eight economic variables *FDI*, *DEBT*, *GDP*, *INFLATION*, *LABOUR*, *TT*, *G*, and *M*1 are given in Tables 7.1 and 7.2. These variables in our models are defined as the annual rates of change for the four countries under study (Indonesia, Malaysia, Thailand, and Korea) . Also, as required case by case (see Engle and Granger, 1987), both the first and second differences as the dependent variables have been experimented with.

The main results of our experiments are given in Table 7.1 for first differences of the eight variables and in Table 7.2 for second differences of the eight variables.

A summary of the findings are interesting in that they appear to confirm generally what Nelson and Plosser (1982) have observed for similar economic aggregates in other countries, our major economic

Table 7.1 Behaviour of Macroeconomic Aggregates in Three Main ASEAN Countries and Korea
Tests of Unit Roots – First Differences 1970 to 1992

Economic Activity	*Indonesia*		*Malaysia*		*Thailand*		*Korea*	
	DW	*F*	*DW*	*F*	*DW*	*F*	*DW*	*F*
Inflation	2.17	8.41	1.84	10.53	2.40	7.45	1.35	4.38
Output (GDP) Growth	1.78	9.31	2.02	3.15	1.62	5.50	1.90	3.89
Government Budget	1.88	5.19	2.06	7.50	1.84	7.54	2.24	11.45
FDI	2.13	6.23	1.54	3.53	2.06	6.43	2.02	3.10
Labour Force	1.99	7.25	2.05	1.76	2.16	3.20	2.06	1.68
External Debts	2.05	6.53	2.16	8.54	2.07	7.19	1.90	2.70
Terms of Trade	1.09	11.10	1.83	14.30	2.22	12.12	2.18	8.66
Money (*M1*)	2.09	16.96	1.45	11.42	1.88	6.35	2.26	13.56

Notes: The results are based on Eqts (1) and (2). All variables are expressed in terms of the annual rates of change which are equivalent to log differences. *DW* = Durbin Watson statistic from Eqt (1), *F* = estimated *F* value from Eqts (1) and (2). The critical *F* value is 3.77, 3.17, and 2.84 at the 1%, 5% and 10% siginificance levels respectively.

Source: All the data used are from the 1994 World Bank database.

Table 7.2 Behaviour of Macroeconomic Aggregates in Three Main ASEAN Countries and Korea
Tests of Unit Roots – Second Differences 1970 to 1992

Economic Activity	Indonesia		Malaysia		Thailand		Korea	
	DW	*F*	*DW*	*F*	*DW*	*F*	*DW*	*F*
Inflation	1.90	31.06	1.32	41.56	1.83	15.11	1.50	13.45
Output (GDP) Growth	1.28	43.75	1.89	11.24	1.51	13.56	1.80	17.83
Government Budget	1.97	33.38	1.86	31.23	1.84	69.05	1.19	34.70
FDI	2.07	28.41	1.56	19.81	1.99	52.00	1.94	11.29
Labour Force	1.84	58.09	2.23	7.13	2.34	4.62	2.39	4.78
External Debts	1.63	16.52	1.86	24.44	1.95	13.02	2.35	20.93
Terms of Trade	1.19	57.96	1.38	63.95	2.02	50.83	2.03	6.02
Money (*M1*)	1.67	53.30	1.14	19.24	1.68	26.79	1.92	49.13

Notes: see Table 7.1.

variables (*FDI*, *DEBT*, *GDP*, *INFLATION*, *LABOUR*, *TT*, *G*, and *M*1) as defined for the models are in fact random walks or *I*(1).

Indonesia

From the results given in Table 7.1, we note that, for Indonesia, all estimated *F* statistics based on the first difference or error correction reduced form representations are greater than the tabulated critical *F* values at the 5% significance level. We can thus reject the hypothesis of random walks for all eight variables as defined in the models we use in this case.

In other words, all variables *FDI*, *DEBT*, *GDP*, *INFLATION*, *LABOUR*, *TT*, *G*, and *M*1 as expressed as the annual rates of change in our study are therefore *I*(1).

Using these *I*(1) variables in the Sargan-Bhargava *DW* cointegration tests (see above), it is found that foreign direct investment (*FDI*) has a positive long-term relationship with labour force and a negative long-term relationship with government budget.

The implications appear to be that *FDI* is principally related to human capital investment in Indonesia. Further, the public sector's expenditure and revenue seems to have the effect of discouraging *FDI* here.

Foreign direct investment is surprisingly found not to be a significant factor for either growth or inflation in the equilibrium.

Judged from the same cointegration however, exernal debts (*DEBT*) do not appear to have any influence on growth or inflation. But, in conjunction with the terms of trade (*TT*), inflation is negatively affected by *DEBT* and positively by the terms of trade (*TT*).

Malaysia

Also from Table 7.1, we note that, for Malaysia, the six variables *INFLATION*, *G*, *FDI*, *DEBT*, *TT*, and *M*1 have their *F* values greater than the tabulated critical *F* value at the 5% significance level. Therefore, their first differences do not have a nonstationary behaviour. Thus, the annual rates of change of these variables are *I*(1).

However, for *GDP* and *LABOUR*, some statistical evidence of random walks exists in the equations using the first differences as the dependant variables (Table 7.1). This necessitates the specification of second differences as the dependant variables, and the results of the unit root tests in this case are given in Table 7.2. Using the second differences for these variables as the dependant variables in Eqts (1) and (2) and their appropriate *RHS* variables, their resultant *F* values now are greater than the critical *F* value (see Table 7.2).

GDP and *LABOUR* are in the case of Malaysia *I*(0) in their second differences. In other words, the first differences of the annual rates of change in *GDP* and *LABOUR* in Malaysia are *I*(1).

Using these *I*(1) variables in the Sargan-Bhargava *DW* cointegration tests (see above), it is found that foreign direct investment does not have a long-term relationship with either labour force or with government budget as is the case of Indonesia, but rather significantly only with output growth. The local demand condition is in fact an inducement or attraction to *FDI* to Malaysia.

FDI is on the other hand found to have a positive equilibrium effect on inflation. And inflation has just a small and negligible contribution from external debts.

Equally important here is the finding that, in Malaysia, growth is positively and significantly affected by FDI in the long run. Unfortunately, higher external debts are also seen as an impediment to growth.

Thailand

For Thailand, all eight variables *FDI*, *DEBT*, *GDP*, *INFLATION*, *LABOUR*, *TT*, *G*, and *M*1 have their *F* values greater than the critical *F* value at the 5% significance level (see Table 7.1).

All of these variables are *I*(0) in their first differences, or equivalently, *I*(1) in their rates of change.

An application of these variables in a cointegration analysis has produced interesting results that are not available to other ASEAN countries under study. First, the joint force of both local demand conditions and inflationary pressure in Thailand between 1970 and 1992 has had a significant and positive impact on the inflow of FDI. High prices and strong demand (as a result of higher income) for the general level of goods and services can be identified as the main causes of FDI inflow.

However, higher FDI also causes higher growth. More importantly, higher FDI in combination with higher money supply causes strong growth. The findings appears to indicate that Thailand is the only country in the ASEAN that has an effective monetary policy for economic growth.

External debts appear to have some positive impact on inflation and some negative influence on growth. However, these effects are not statistically significant or strong at the conventional critical level.

Korea

From Table 7.1, we note that only five variables in our study are $I(0)$ in their error correction reduced form. They are *GDP*, *INFLATION*, *TT*, *G*, and *M*1. These variables are therefore $I(1)$ in their annual rates of change.

For the remaining three variables *FDI*, *DEBT*, and *LABOUR*, the second difference representations have to be carried out. The results of this are reported in Table 7.2, and the evidence is that these representations are stationary or $I(0)$. From these results, we conclude that the differences of *FDI*, *DEBT*, and *LABOUR* are $I(1)$.

As has been discussed earlier, external debts have no significant effect on both inflation and growth in Thailand. In our long-term analysis using data on Korea, external debts and also foreign direct investment are found to have similar effects.

The only significant effect in the case of Korea is that of external debts on FDI. Here FDI is closely related to external debts in the long run. This result is not obtained for the three countries in the ASEAN, namely Indonesia, Malaysia, and Thailand.

POLICY IMPLICATIONS

The economic implications of our tests of unit roots and cointegration based on the data on foreign direct investment, external debts, *GDP* and inflation for three major and growing economies in the ASEAN (Indonesia, Malaysia, and Thailand) and one NIC in East Asia (Korea) for the period under study (i.e., from 1970 to 1992) are interesting and need recapitulating.

First, our observed data on foreign direct investment, external debts, inflation and, more importantly, output growth in all four Asian countries studied are random walks as observed by Nelson and Plosser. This provides further statistical evidence to support previous macroeconomic studies for similar aggregates in other developed and developing countries.

Second, for Indonesia and Korea, there exist no significant long-term relationships between foreign direct investment and the standard of living and also between external debts and economic growth. However, there is strong evidence to support the presence of such relationships for Thailand and Malaysia.

For Malaysia and Thailand then, a balanced macroeconomic management would require a carefully planned fiscal and monetary policy

Table 7.3 Long-term Relationships between Major Macroeconomic Aggregates in Three Main ASEAN Countries and Korea
Sargan-Bhargava DW Cointegration Regression Tests 1970 to 1992

Tested Relationship	*Indonesia*	*Malaysia*	*Thailand*	*Korea*
Foreign Direct Investment on				
Output Growth	no	yes (+)	yes (+)	no
Inflation	no	no	yes (+)	no
Labour	yes (+)	no	no	no
External Debts	no	no	no	yes (+)
Government Budget	yes (−)	no	no	no
Output Growth on				
Foreign Direct Investment	no	yes (+)	yes (+)	no
External Debts	no	yes (−)	no	no
Money M1	no	no	yes (+)	no
Government Budget	no	no	no	no
Inflation on				
Foreign Direct Investment	no	yes (+)	yes (+)	no
External Debts	yes (−)	no	no	no
Money (*M1*)	no	yes (−)	no	no
Terms of Trade	yes (+)	no	no	no
Government Budget	no	no	no	no

Notes: no = no significant long-term relationship exists, yes = significant long-term relationship exists with significant (+) positive causation or significant (−) negative causation. Both bivariate and multivariate cointegration models using only $I(1)$ variables are experimented with. All 'yes' results reported are based on the estimated *DW* statistics in the Sargan-Bhargava cointegration regressions being greater than the tabulated critical *DW* value of 0.386 for two variables and 0.367 for three variables at the 5% significance level.

that takes into account both economic growth and development and a possible decline in the standard of living as manifested in the form of higher inflation in these countries.

Third, it is in the case of Malaysia and Thailand that some determinants of foreign direct investment can be quantitatively identified. In both countries, output growth or the growing local demand pressure attracts FDI. In the case of Thailand alone, inflationary pressure or higher domestic prices (coupled perhaps with a stable exchange rate regime in the past two decades or so) also attract foreign direct investment.

Finally, while the cause of FDI into Korea cannot be identified from our study, it is the existence of human capital development that attracts

FDI into Indonesia. Also in Indonesia, the revenue and disbursement of the government sector are seen as presenting an impediment to FDI.

LEADING PATTERNS FOR INDOCHINA AND MYANMAR

In this chapter, we have proposed four simple bivariate causality models incorporating the concept of growth (i.e., the rate of change) for eight major economic variables to investigate the presence of a long-term relationship between foreign direct investment, external debts, output growth and inflation in three major and growing economies in the ASEAN, namely, Indonesia, Malaysia, and Thailand, and an advanced developing (NIC) economy in the Asia Pacific, namely Korea.

While our study uses only a bivariate form and a simple but effective methodology, it nevertheless addresses (and provides evidence for) the important questions of (a) the causes of foreign direct investment in developing economies in the Asia Pacific, and (b) the economic benefits (output growth) and costs (higher inflation) of foreign investment and external debts. These issues we believe are important and useful for policy analysis in both the developing countries and may be of significant interest to the industrially advanced and open economies.

Our study argues that the concept of growth is, as a general methodology, natural in both economic theory and in economic modelling studies. Our empirical evidence indicates that the concept is natural to applications of many recent important statistical methods that depend on the property of stationarity in economic series.

While we have found statistical evidence to support the thesis that, in Malaysia and Thailand, foreign direct investment is a co-movement of economic growth, it is also seen to be associated with inflation. Since economic growth reflects the standard of living or measures the welfare of a country, it is the main preoccupation of economics. We have therefore provided statistical evidence to support the view that, in these two ASEAN countries in the Asia Pacific region and for the period under study, foreign direct investment does make a contribution to economic growth and development.

This positive contribution is attenuated nevertheless by the findings that foreign direct investment is also a co-movement of the cost of economic growth and development, namely rising prices of goods and services in the country.

Whilst our findings are limited by the small size of the data and their usual reliability feature as well as the bivariate features of the models used, to some significant extent they provide a useful perspective on the economic benefits and costs of an important component of international capital mobility and of external debts in the developing countries in the Asia Pacific.

A more complete study of the benefits and costs of these components in Indonesia, Malaysia, and Thailand in particular or in any developed and developing economies that are engaged in international trade and capital movements can be achieved for more realistic purposes by means of economy-wide econometric models incorporating many sectors and many economic activities. This is however beyond the scope of the present chapter.

As far as some useful features of our findings are concerned, we believe it is more appropriate for other newly developing economies in the Asia Pacific region or in the Indochina peninsula such as Vietnam, Laos, Cambodia, and possibly Myanmar to learn some lessons in macroeconomic fiscal and monetary policy as well as economic growth and development policy from Thailand.

It is Thailand that has had a remarkable achievement in economic development and economic growth in recent years. This achievement can further be substantiated by modern economic and data analysis and in accordance with standard economic theoretic postulates.

In this context, it is Thailand with its social, cultural, geographic, economic, and traditional characteristics very much akin to those in Vietnam, Laos, Cambodia, and Myanmar that can best provide a good example for economic modernization in Indochina and Myanmar, concurrent especially with the objectives of the government of Vietnam in recent times.

Perhaps, the 'flying geese' pattern does exist in this case. A national economic policy that makes use of other similarly endowed and historically similar economies in the neighbourhood might be able to accelerate economic progress and modernization one or two steps faster into prosperity in the near future and might at the end of the day not hurt national pride but instead be a socially and nationally optimal policy after all.

References

Bulow, J. and Rogoff, K., 'Cleaning up Third World Debt without Getting Taken to the Cleaners', *Journal of Economic Perspectives*, Vol. 4, 1990, 31–42.

Dickey, D. A. and Fuller, W. A., 'Likelihood Ratio Statistics for Autoregressive Time Series with a Unit Root', *Econometrica*, Vol. 49, 1981, 1057–1072.

Dornbusch, D. and Fischer, S., *Macroeconomics*, 5th Edition, Sydney: McGraw Hill, 1990.

Dunning, J. H., *Multinational Enterprises and the Global Economy*, Wokingham: Addison-Wesley, 1993.

Fels, A. A. and Tran Van Hoa, 'Causal Relationships in Australian Wage Inflation and Minimum Award Rates', *Economic Record*, Vol. 57, 1981, 23–34.

Engle, R. F. and Granger, C. W. J., 'Co-integration and Error Correction: Representation, Estimation and Testing', *Econometrica*, Vol. 55, 1987, 251–276.

Gillis, M., Perkins, D. H., Roemer, M. and Snodgrass, D. R., *Economics of Development*, 3rd edition, New York: Norton, 1992.

Granger, C. W. J., 'Investigating Causal Relations by Econometric Models and Cross Spectral Methods', *Econometrica*, Vol. 37, 1969, 424–438.

Harvie, C. and Tran Van Hoa (1995a), 'Terms of Trade and Macroeconomic Adjustments in a Resource Exporting Economy: The Case of Australia', *Resources Policy*.

Harvie C. and Tran Van Hoa (1995b), 'Long Term Relationships between Oil Production, Oil Prices, and the Current Account, Real Exchange Rate, Capital Stock, Nonoil Output, Manufacturing Output and Growth: The UK Experience', *Journal of Energy and Development*.

Helleiner, G. K., *Direct Foreign Investment and Manufacturing for Export in Developing Countries: A Review of the Issues*, Aldershot, 1990.

Johansen, S., 'An I(2) Cointegration Analysis of the Purchasing Power Parity between Australia and the United States', Australasian Economic Modelling Conference, 27–30 August 1991, Port Douglas, Australia, 1991.

Kenen, P. B., 'Organizing Debt Relief: The Need for a New Institution', *Journal of Economic Perspectives*, Vol. 4, 1990, 7–18.

Nelson, C. R. and Plosser, C. I., 'Trends and Random Walks in Macroeconomic Times Series: Some Evidence and Implications', *Journal of Monetary Economics*, Vol. 10, 1982, 139–162.

Pindyck, R. S. and Rubinfeld, D. L., *Econometric Models and Economic Forecasts*, 3rd Edition, Sydney: McGraw Hill, 1991.

Pippenger, J. E., *Fundamentals of International Trade*, New York: Prentice Hall, 1984.

Sachs, J. D., 'A Strategy for Efficient Debt Reduction', *Journal of Economic Perspectives*, Vol. 4, 1990, 19–29.

Sims, C. A, 'Money, Income and Causality', *American Economic Review*, Vol. 62, 1972, 540–552.

Tran Van Hoa, 'Modelling Output Growth: A New Approach', *Economics Letters*, Vol. 38, 1992a, 279–84.

Tran Van Hoa, 'A Multi-equation Model of Energy Consumption in Thailand', *International Journal of Energy Research*, Vol. 16, 1992b, 381–385.

Tran Van Hoa, 'A New and General Approach to Modelling Short Term Interest Rates: with Application to Australian Data 1962–1990', *Journal of Economics and Finance*, Vol. 16, 1992c, 327–335.

Tran Van Hoa, 'Foreign Investment, External Debts, Growth and Inflation in

Thailand: Does a Long Term Relationship Exist?', *Thammasat Economic Journal*, Vol. 11, 1993, 29–38.

Tran Van Hoa, 'Foreign Investment in Vietnam: Methodologies', *Foreign Trade Review*, 1995.

World Bank, 'The Challenge of Development', *World Development Report*, Oxford: Oxford University Press, 1991.

8 Foundation for Better Forward Planning Policy in Developing Economies: Improved Forecasts of Macroeconomic Aggregates

Tran Van Hoa

This chapter deals with recent advances in information technology (IT) and their applications to modelling and forecasting in the social sciences in both developed and developing economies. First, it briefly describes a new general forecasting approach with superior accuracy – the two-stage hierarchical information (2SHI) average mean squared errors-based estimating and forecasting theories for the linear models (Tran Van Hoa, 1985, 1986a, 1993a, Tran Van Hoa and Chaturvedi, 1988, 1990, 1993) – for use in economics, business, trade, and, finance. Second, it reports an application of this approach to forecasting, by use of a multi-activity macroeconomic model of investment and ouput growth using the World Bank data over two decades 1970 to 1992 in three major developing economies in the ASEAN: Indonesia, Malaysia, and Thailand, and one NIC country in the Asia Pacific: Korea.

A comparison of our empirical findings with the results based on the more traditional methods in current use such as the OLS or ML and positive Stein is also made. In all cases under study, a gain of up to 51% in increased accuracy or information extraction is achieved in our 2SHI *ex post* forecasts for investment and output growth for these countries.

Our findings have important implications for applications of recent IT advances to the social sciences, and also an appropriate selection of current methodologies to make better forecasts in practical applications in economics, business, finance, investment, trade, and statistics. More specifically, the use of our new forecasting approach will significantly help economic analysts and business planners to formulate better strategic forward policy with more successful commercial outcomes in both developed and especially developing economies where, because of their fast growth and subsequent wide fluctuations in economic activities, a high level and more accurate modelling and forecasting approach is necessarily required.

1 INTRODUCTION

In the past few decades, high technology has penetrated all areas of scientific and social research as well as mass communications and brought with it some would say beneficial effects. In economic and business studies, this can be seen more clearly in the case of a number of advances in information technology being applied to many aspects of economic and business analysis and its ensuing academic or commercial policy. These applications are important in the sense that they can (a) enhance the accuracy and robustness (that is, the continuing accuracy in spite of possible changes to the event under observation), of economic and business decisions, and (b) increase the speed of processing or of the availability of the desirable and timely solutions to major economic and business issues. The former is done through the use of high level and sophisticated applied modelling experiments, and the latter through the use of high power computing facilities.

While the use of forward planning strategies by the government, the corporations, and even individual business people has firmly established their importance in governmental and commercial enterprises, and has in addition gained increased popularity in a global context, these strategies depend to a large extent on the integrity of the underlying analysis and, more importantly for government economic policy and electoral credibility and commercial financial success, on the accuracy of the forecasts upon which the strategies crucially depend.

The integrity issues can be handled by up-to-date and sound theoretical considerations. The accuracy issue has to be handled by means of current and high level modelling and forecasting methodologies. The accuracy issue is, in addition, more important in practice in the economies which, due to their necessary catch-up modernization or transition process and successful economic developments, have achieved in recent years fast rising and widely fluctuating economic, business, trade, and finance activities. These very wide fluctuations which have taken place in some major developing economies in the ASEAN and the Asia Pacific entail a high spectrum frequency and sudden structural breaks in their movements in the terminology of econometrics and statistics and, as a result, make them more difficult or elusive to model adequately and forecast accurately.

The purpose of the chapter is threefold. First, as a contribution to macroeconomic analysis in general and to business, trade, investment, and finance studies, and development economics in particular, we propose to investigate rigorously the causal structure and provide empirical forecasts of two important macroeconomic aggregates, namely, investment (see Pippenger, 1984 for a discussion on the implications of investment for international finance and economic development) and economic growth (or the standard of living) in some major and growing economies (the economic tigers) in the ASEAN and the Asia Pacific region.

For rather pragmatic reasons, the countries included in this study at this stage are Indonesia, Malaysia, Thailand (three ASEAN economies), and Korea (a NIC country in the Asia Pacific region). The causal structure for our study is based upon the conventional dynamic multi-equation Keynesian theory of macroeconomics and the standardized national accounting (SNA) framework of the United Nations.

The second purpose is methodological in nature in that the paper departs from the conventional modelling approaches of linear multiple regressions, simultaneous equations, or seemingly unrelated regressions, and makes use of a fairly simple and flexible modelling approach by means of differential analysis in economics (Tran Van Hoa, 1992a, 1992d) to provide the fundamental equations in the reduced or policy form for estimation and forecasting purposes.

Finally, the chapter offers a contribution to recent advances in the statistical theory of forecasting using information technology with real applications to a better formulation of policy in economics, business, trade, investment, and finance in the cases of Indonesia, Malaysia, Thailand, and Korea (and possible applications to other developing or developed countries in the region or beyond). Additionally the discussion covers forecasts of investment and output growth as indicated above under different plausible scenarios. The forecasts are based on the empirical Bayes or hierarchical information (Tran Van Hoa, 1985, 1986a, 1993a, 1995: Tran Van Hoa and Chaturvedi, 1988, 1990, 1993) as well as other well known forecasting theories currently available.

In order to evaluate the magnitude of the success (or failure) of this new modelling and forecasting approach to economics, business, investment, trade, and finance, the *ex post* (see Pindyck and Rubinfeld, 1991) performance of these forecasts in the almost universal context of average mean squared errors (MSE) or Wald risk criteria is then calculated and compared against some more traditional forecasts based on the ordinary least squares (OLS), the maximum likelihood (ML), or the explicit (Baranchik, 1973) positive part Stein-like (Anderson, 1984) methodologies.

The implications of our results are as follows: If a substantial gain in *ex post* forecasting error reduction is achieved by the 2SHI methods in relation to other conventional procedures currently in use, then our findings will point to a new direction of rigorous forecasting analysis for analysts in economics, business, trade, investment, and finance in their everyday strategic planning applications in the countries under study and also in other developing economies in the region and beyond.

2 STRUCTURAL MODELS TO EXPLAIN INVESTMENT AND GROWTH

Consider a simple static nonstochastic three interdependent activity macroeconomic model of an open economy in its arbitrary functional form in a neoclassical framework within the Johansen class

$$C = C(Y) \tag{1'}$$

$$I = I(Y, R) \tag{2'}$$

$$Y = Y(C, I, G, X, IM) \tag{3'}$$

where C = private final consumption expenditure, Y = gross domestic product, I = private gross fixed capital expenditure, G = public expenditure, X = exports of goods and services, IM = imports of goods and services, and R = short-term money market interest rate or its equivalent variable.

In its well known linearized dynamic multi-equation Keynesian stochastic form, this model is usually written as:

$$C_t = \alpha 11 + \alpha 12Y_t + \alpha 13C_{t-1} + u1_t \tag{1}$$

$$I_t = \alpha 21 + \alpha 22Y_t + \alpha 23Y_{t-1}\ \alpha 23R_t + \alpha 23R_{t-1} + u2_t \tag{2}$$

$$Y_t = C_t + I_t + G_t + X_t - IM_t \tag{3}$$

The *α's* denote the structural parameters, and the *u's* the error terms. All variables are expressed in terms of current prices.

The model (1) – (3) is a dynamic macroeconomic model (Pindyck and Rubinfeld, 1991) for an open economy and takes into account (a) a partial adjustment process in consumption behaviour encompassing the hypotheses of relative and permanent income, liquid assets, wealth, and life cycles in the sense of Duesenberry, and two Nobel laureates Friedman and Modigliani, and (b) a flexible accelerator investment behaviour, augmented by user's costs.

In the model, consumption, investment, and GDP are endogenous.

It can be verified that, using the order condition for identifiability or mathematical consistency in econometrics, the investment equation (2) in the model is identified. As a result, it can be written in its complete differential form (see Allen, 1960) in the reduced form (see Tran Van Hoa, 1992a and 1992d, Harvie and Tran Van Hoa, 1993, 1995a, 1995b) as

$$I\%_t = a11 + a12C\%_{t-1} + a13Y_{t-1} + a14R\%_t + a15R_{t-1} + a16G\%_t + a17X\%_t - a18IM\%_t + e1_t \quad (4)$$

where $I\%$, $C\%$, $Y\%$, $R\%$, $G\%$, $X\%$, and $IM\%$ indicate the rate of change of I, C, Y, R, G, X and IM respectively, and a's indicate the reduced form parameters.

Similarly, the GDP identity (3) can be verified to be identified and it can be written in its differential reduced form as

$$Y\%_t = a21 + a22C\%_{t-1} + a23Y_{t-1} + a24R\%_t + a25R_{t-1} + a26G\%_t + a27X\%_t - a28IM\%_t + e2_t \quad (5)$$

with a's being the reduced form parameters.

Equations (4) and (5) are equations characterizing respectively the investment and output growth relationships from the three-equation macroeconomic model (1) – (3). By conventional definition, the parameters from these equations are in fact either static or dynamic elasticities associated with either current or lagged variables.

The derivation of (4) and (5) by means of total differentiation is simple and, more importantly, consistent with the procedure usually adopted for neoclassical macroeconomic models of the applied or computable general equilibrium kind. In these neoclassical models, the endogenous and exogeneous variables in the economy are linked by a (usually first order) approximate transmission mechanism in terms of the elasticities. There are however at least five important differences between our investment and growth equations given in (4) and (5) above and the investment and growth specification from applied or computable general equilibrium Johansen-class models.

First, in our case, the important linking elasticities have to be estimated for the models as a whole using economic time series data. Our equations thus are completely data-based, although clearly we do not preclude the use of prior or extraneous information in the equations in other theoretical or judgemental contexts.

Second, in view of the above arguments, our models are capable of accommodating sub- and add-factors as well as structural change and other institutional considerations (for a discussion supporting the use of these factors in macroeconomic models, see Johansen, 1982). Third, our equations must be mathematically consistent as required by the identifiability conditions for complete systems of structural simultaneous equations in econometrics.

Fourth, by its construct, our modelling approach encompasses a wide class of linear and nonlinear multi-equation econometric models in which the exact functional form of each of the individual structural equations is usually unknown or needs not be specified.

Finally, for an important group of $I(1)$ economic variables, our equations by their construct include as the special cases the co-integration or long-term equations of the Engle-Granger (1987) class (see Tran Van Hoa, 1993b, 1993c, and Harvie and Tran Van Hoa, 1993, 1995a, 1995b, for further detail).

To evaluate the performance of (a) the I and Y equations in this macroeconomic model and (b) our forecasting methodology using real-life data from major economies in the Asia Pacific, we have fitted the two equations to data for the period 1970 to 1992 for four selected countries: Indonesia, Korea, Malaysia, and Thailand. This will optimally produce the necessary elasticity estimates. These estimates are then used in a comparative study which is based on stochastic simulation to measure the relative MSE performance or operational success of our equations and also of our new forecasting approach and other current modelling methodologies.

The implications of our results on further forecasting and planning studies in business, economics, finance, investment and trade in these economies as well as other developing and transition economies in the ASEAN, the Asia Pacific, Africa, and South America are wide-ranging.

3 ALTERNATIVE FORECASTING METHODOLOGIES

Now, both the investment and output growth equations in differential and reduced form (4) and (5) can be written more generally with a sampling size T and k independent variables as

$$y = Z\beta + u \qquad (6)$$

where y is a $T \times 1$ vector of the observations on the dependent variable, Z is a $T \times k$ matrix of the observations on the explanatory variables with full column rank, β is a $k \times 1$ vector of the structural parameters, and u the $T \times 1$ vector of the disturbance with a multivariate normal distribution with 0 mean vector and $\sigma^2 I$ dispersion matrix.

In our models, the following Stein-like estimation conditions for dominance (see Baranchik, 1973: Anderson, 1984) are true: $k > 2$, and $T > k + 2$.

Model (6) can be used for forecasting purposes in a number of ways, and the quality of the performance of the forecasts depends on which way is adopted. Among the well known *bona fide* forecasting approaches are the standard OLS and ML and other alternative methodologies which have been developed in the literature of econometrics and statistics over the past 40 years or so. These new methodologies include the Stein, Stein-like, improved Stein-like, and empirical Bayes theories.

The traditional method used routinely by almost all quantitative economists is the OLS or the ML which produces an estimator

$$b = (X'X)^{-1} X'y \qquad (7)$$

with variance-covariance

$$V(b) = \sigma^2 (X'X)^{-1} \qquad (8)$$

The OLS estimator b is a BLU (best, linear, and unbiased) estimator satisfying the Cramer lower bounds when all basic assumptions about the model are satisfied. When a model is known or proved to have BLU properties, conditional and unconditional as well as stochastic and non-stochastic forecasts can then be made from this estimated model to assist economic policy and financial corporate forward planning if required.

For many years, this method had been regarded as being able to produce the best estimates and the best forecasts for the linear model of the type (6).

In the 1950s however, Charles Stein from Columbia University (now at Stanford University) proved in a series of papers that the OLS estimator b is suboptimal or inadmissible in relation to the almost universally used criterion of a quadratic loss function (see Baranchik, 1973; Anderson, 1984). That is, given a quadratic loss function say $L(\beta a, \beta)$ which is a reasonable criterion in forecasting evaluation (see Baranchik, 1973; Pindyck and Rubinfeld, 1991)

$$L(\beta a, \beta) = (1/\sigma^2)(\beta a - \beta)' Q(\beta a - \beta) \tag{9}$$

where βa is an arbitrary estimator and Q a positive definite symmetric matrix, there exists an estimator with a smaller risk [or average MSE with $MSE((\beta a) = E(\beta a - \beta)' Q(\beta a - \beta)]$ than the OLS or ML. In other words, there exists an estimator with better (or more accurate) forecasting MSE properties.

The so-called Stein estimator βs was then proposed, having this property

$$\begin{aligned} \beta s &= [1 - c(y - Xb)'(y - Xb)/b'X'Xb]\ b \\ &= [1 - c(1 - R^2)/R^2]\ b \end{aligned} \tag{10}$$

where c is a scalar satisfying the bounds $0 < c < 2(k - 2)/T - k + 2)$, and $R^2 = (b'X'Xb/y'y)$ is the sample (observed) multiple correlation coefficient. The following inadmissibility result also known as the famous Stein effect or inequality for the linear regression model has been proved

$$\text{MSE}(b) \geq \text{MSE}(\beta s) \tag{11}$$

with equality somewhere in the parameter space. The dominance is greatest when the characterizing scalar $c = (k - 2)/(T - k + 2)$.

Extensions of the Stein estimator include the positive part Stein estimator which is defined as (Anderson, 1984).

$$\begin{aligned} \beta s^+ &= [1 - c(y - Xb)'(y - Xb)/b'X'Xb]^+\ b \\ &= [1 - min\{1, c(1 - R^2)/R^2\}]\ b \end{aligned} \tag{12}$$

The positive part Stein estimator constrains the flattening or Stein factor $\{c(1 - R^2)/R^2\}$ to lie between 0 and 1. This restriction is appropriate for many problems in economics. It is well known that this estimator dominates the usual Stein estimator in MSE (Anderson, 1984). That is,

$$MSE(b) \geq MSE(\beta s) \geq MSE(\beta s^+) \tag{13}$$

with equality somewhere in the parameter space.

The positive part Stein estimator here has a special appeal to economics, because it implies that, in important empirical studies in economics, many economic postulates (such as the positive marginal propensity to consume) cannot change its sign from say positive to negative when the Stein procedure is used in the case of low coefficient of determination. For many years, the positive part Stein estimator was regarded as the best estimator in MSE among all estimators that can be obtained in the context of multiple linear regression models.

It should be noted that this positive part Stein estimator also dominates another important class of estimators in econometrics, the so-called pre-test estimators (Judge and Yancey, 1986).

In 1985, Tran Van Hoa demonstrated that the Stein estimator is itself suboptimal or inadmissible under quadratic loss (Tran Van Hoa, 1985, 1986a: Tran Van Hoa and Chaturvedi, 1988, 1990, 1993). In other words, there exists a class of fully operational or explicit (the so-called two stage hierarchical information [2SHI]) estimators that dominate in MSE the Stein estimator. The class of 2SHI estimators is defined as (Tran Van Hoa, 1985)

$$\begin{aligned}\beta h &= [1 - c(y - Xb)'(y - Xb)/b'X'Xb - c(y - Xb)'(y - Xb)/ \\ &\quad \{b'X'Xb + c(y - Xb)'(y-Xb)\}]\ b \\ &= [1 - c(1 - R^2)/R^2 - c(1 - R^2)/\{R^2(1 + c(1 - R^2)/R^2)\}]\ b \end{aligned} \tag{14}$$

The following important result in MSE dominance has been proved (Tran Van Hoa and Chaturvedi, 1988, 1990) for the 2SHI estimators

$$MSE(b) \geq MSE(\beta s) \geq MSE(\beta h) \tag{15}$$

with equality somewhere in the parameter space.

It is important to note that the positive part 2SHI estimator which is defined similarly to the Stein estimator restricted to the positive parameter space can be written as

$$\begin{aligned}\beta h^+ &= [1 - c(y - Xb)'(y - Xb)/b'X'Xb - c(y - Xb)'(y - Xb)/ \\ &\quad \{b'X'Xb + c(y - Xb)'(y - Xb)\}]^+\ b \\ &= [1 - min\{1, c(1 - R^2)/R^2\} \\ &\quad - min\{1, c(1 - R^2)/\{R^2(1 + c(1 - R^2)/R^2)\}\}]\ b \end{aligned} \tag{16}$$

It has been demonstrated that this positive 2SHI estimator dominates in MSE the positive part Stein estimator (Tran Van Hoa, 1986a). That is the following sequence of MSE dominance or inequality is valid

$$MSE(b) \geq MSE(\beta s) \geq MSE(\beta h) \tag{17}$$

$$MSE(\beta s) \geq MSE(\beta s^{+}) \geq MSE(\beta h^{+}) \tag{18}$$

The foundation for the various improved Stein-like or 2SHI estimators discussed above has been interpreted in a number of ways. The most interesting interpretation is that these estimators are a special case of the empirical Bayes estimators.

More specifically, the flattening or Stein-like factor $\{c(1 - R^2)/R^2\}$ in Eqt (10) described earlier contains in fact prior information on the parameters of the linear regression model but this information is not used by the OLS or ML. This information comes objectively however from the sample dataset and not from a subjective knowledege as is often the case in proper Bayesian analysis with informative prior. In other words, the OLS or ML is unable to extract all information available from the sample dataset. The fact that the Stein estimator which is an explicit or fully operational estimator in the sense of Baranchik (1973) can do this is one of the most remarkable achievements in the theory of estimation and forecasting in recent times (Anderson, 1984).

In this context, the foundation of the 2SHI estimators which are explicit and fully operational is also Bayesian, and the prior information used in the estimation of the regression model comes entirely from the sample dataset and not from subjective extraneous information. The amount of hierarchical information retrieved from the sample dataset increases with the higher order stage of iterations of the Stein-like estimation procedure. In an empirical context, the 2SHI estimators are obtained simply by applying the OLS to the model (6) after that model has been adjusted for the Stein effect. The adjusted model contains prior information in the sense of Stein.

More specifically, if the Stein estimator $(1 - \{c(1 - R^2)/R^2\})\, b$ is a better estimator in MSE of the regression coefficient vector β in (6), then *a fortiori* $X\beta s$ must be a better forecast of y than Xb. Equivalently, Xb must be a better forecast of $y + X\{c(1 - R^2)/R^2\}b$ and not of y. The question that the 2SHI theory of estimation and forecasting seeks to answer is whether some further gain in information extraction can be obtained by applying the Stein procedure to this adjusted model.

In this context, the 2SHI estimator is simply obtained as a Stein estimator being derived from an application of the OLS or ML to the adjusted linear regression model

$$y + X\{c(1 - R^2)/R^2\}\, b = X\,\beta + e \tag{19}$$

where e is a new disturbance with classical statistical properties. The MSE dominance of the 2SHI over the Stein has been discussed earlier.

Other well known estimators such as the Ullah-Ullah (1978) double-k class (Tran Van Hoa, 1987a) or the Strawderman generalized ridge can be generated as special cases of the 2SHI (Tran Van Hoa, 1987b), and are dominated by it in MSE.

Later work (see Tran Van Hoa, 1993a, and Tran Van Hoa and Chaturvedi, 1990) proves that the 2SHI is a mixture or encompassing estimator, and it includes the OLS and the Stein as subsets. Other extensions of the 2SHI estimator or its subsets to the dynamic, heteroskedastic or autocorrelated models have also been reported (see for example Tran Van Hoa, 1995; Tran Van Hoa, Chaturvedi, and Lal, 1992; Chaturvedi, Tran Van Hoa, and Shukla, 1993; and Tran Van Hoa and Chaturvedi, 1993).

Important applications of the 2SHI estimator to energy consumption and forecasts to the year 2000 in Thailand (Tran Van Hoa, 1992b) have also been reported. In these studies, the gain in MSE reduction from an application of the 2SHI to the linear model is substantial in an empirical context.

What are the implications of the results of this section? The above discussion indicates that for modelling and forecasting studies that are based on the linear economic, financial or whatever model, the use of the OLS or ML will not produce the best results. Rational decision-makers in economic or financial management studies will (or should) not attempt to use a suboptimal method for their investigations and report the findings of it to government planning agencies, shareholders or for corporate policy analysis.

It is more interesting in an empirical context, while the improvement in forecasting accuracy can be calculated analytically for arbitrary values of the parameters and the sampling size of the models used for forecasting, what is the gain in actual applications? In other words, how much different will the forecasts from the alternative methods be is an empirical question to be answered case by case in practical applications.

Below, we report our study on the superiority of the 2SHI in estimation and forecasting by investigating the performance of alternative estimation and forecasting methodologies for two classic examples used in economics (growth or Eqt (5)) and finance (investment or Eqt (4)) as derived earlier for illustration purposes.

While some application of these forecasting methodologies to predictions of economic activity in some developed countries such as Australia (see Tran Van Hoa, 1992d, and 1995) has been made, the extent of the significance of the MSE dominance, or equivalently, the informational gain or relative forecasting success between the alternative estimators above has not been investigated in an empirical context using economic data from the major economies in the ASEAN and the Asia Pacific regions. Some of these economies are Indonesia, Korea, Malaysia, and Thailand. This issue is taken up in the study below.

Another interesting feature of our study is that, since all data from the ASEAN and Asia Pacific countries have as usual a small sample size, our study is therefore designed to look at the finite sample performance of alternative forecasting methods. Finally, since the poor quality of economic data from the ASEAN, Asia Pacific and other LDC economies is well known, *one by-product of our study is that we in fact investigate the performance of the alternative forecasting methodologies in the case of serious measurement errors on the variables of the macromodel of an economy however it is defined.*

The substantive findings reported below are based on the three-equation macreconomic model described earlier in (1)–(3), and the appropriate estimating equations to produce elasticity parameters or the forecasting equations to produce policy impact are given in (4) for investment and (5) for output growth.

4 WELL KNOWN CRITERIA FOR EVALUATION OF FORECASTS

In our study, we have fitted both the investment equation (4) and the growth equation (5) to annual data from Indonesia, Korea, Malaysia, and Thailand. The sample period is 1970 to 1992, giving, when the dynamic (lag) structure is taken into account, an effective sample size of 21 observations for each variable. In our comparative study, only the OLS or ML, the positive-part Stein, and the positive-part 2SHI estimators are used.

The data are in nominal terms and obtained from the 1994 World Bank Asia Pacific database, using Australia's DX extracting procedure.

The research strategy of our study includes a number of features:

First, to investigate the effects of the sampling size on the performance of the various estimators (this study is also known as structural change or stability analysis), we split the total sample size of 21 observations for the equations into three overlapping subsamples of 13, 19, and 21 observations respectively. The division is used to approximate chiefly the second oil crisis of 1981 and the crash of the world-wide stock markets in 1987 which have changed the course of investment and growth behaviour in both developed and developing economies.

Second, to investigate the possible informational gain under different situations from the data, the *ex post* forecasts (Pindyck and Rubinfeld, 1991) of investment and output growth from our macroeconomic model are derived rather pragmatically for three, three, and five years ahead. These are called Subsamples 1, 2, and 3 respectively. In other words, for our investment and growth equations, the *ex post* forecasts are made three years ahead from 1982 to 1984 (Subsample 1), three years ahead from 1988 to 1990 (Subsample 2), and five years ahead from 1988 to 1992 (Subsample 3). The consistency of the *ex post* forecasts in Subsamples 2 and 3 (which are based on the same historical simulation period), if it exists, describes to some extent the possible presence of rationality (i.e., the forecasts match the data generating process) in the forecasting equations.

Third, for each of these subsamples, the MSE of the forecasts from Equations (4) and (5) is computed from a stochastic simulation and is based on 100 (smaller or larger simulations yielded similar results) statistical trials. In stochastic simulation, both the estimated parameters and the disturbances are allowed to vary from trial to trial (see Pindyck and Rubinfeld, 1991, for further detail). The distributions used to generate these parameter and disturbance trial-to-trial variations are based upon their OLS-based sample distributions.

Finally, in the case of the disturbance or error term distribution, the simulation for each subsample takes respectively the value of s^2, $10s^2$, and $100s^2$, where s^2 is the sample disturbance variance. This strategy is adopted to investigate the impact of the size of the disturbance variances (or the measurement errors or mis-specification of the investment and output growth functions) on the relative performance of the various forecasting methodologies in our macroeconomic equations.

Thus, in our empirical study, the *ex post* forecasting MSE is obtained, by stochastic simulation, for a total of 36 investment equations and 36 growth equations, different from each other in terms of T (the sample size), σ^2 (the disturbance variance), and the country of origin.

The relative performance of the OLS, positive-part Stein $\beta + s$, and positive-part 2SHI $\beta + h$ estimators for each of these equations and for each of the four countries (Indonesia, Korea, Malaysia, and Thailand) in the Asia Pacific between 1970 and 1992 is given in Tables 8.1–8. Relative performance between say the OLS and the positive-part Stein is defined formally as

$$R(b/\beta + s) = 100[MSE(b) \,/\, MSE(\beta + s) - 1] \tag{20}$$

and dominance or informational gain in *ex post* forecasting MSE of $\beta + s$ over b exists whenever *ex post* forecasting $R(b/\beta + s) \geq 0$, with equality somewhere in the parameter space.

It can be further verified that, for the forecasting equation of the functional form defined in (6), when historical and future values of Z are known, dominant *ex post* forecasting MSE implied dominant *ex ante* forecasting MSE. This extension is useful for policy analysis into the future.

For *ex post* forecasting, the relative performance of the OLS, $\beta + s$, and $\beta + h$ estimators for each of these models is also expressed in terms of its standard criteria such as mean per cent errors, RMS per cent errors, and per cent improvement in *ex post* forecasting MSE (see Pindyck and Rubinfeld, 1991). This relative performance is given in Tables 8.1–8.

The relative performance in *ex post* forecasting MSE between say the OLS-based forecasts and the positive-part Stein-based forecasts, as reported in Tables 8.1–8, is in fact defined as

$$R(b/\beta + s) = 100[(MSE(yb - y) \,/\, MSE(ys - y)) - 1] \tag{21}$$

with MSE($yb - y$) being the MSE of the forecasting errors based on the OLS estimates, and MSE($ys - y$) the MSE of the forecasting errors based on the positive-part Stein. The calculation of MSE($yh - y$) is similar.

5 SUBSTANTIVE EVIDENCE ON BETTER FORECASTS

From the results given in Tables 8.1–8, we observe that all relative MSE values $R(ml/s)$, $R(ml/h)$, and $R(s/h)$ for the 72 investment and growth equations for Indonesia, Korea, Malaysia, and Thailand, are greater than zero for the specified model (1)–(3) and for the period under study, namely, from 1970 to 1992. As a result, the positive-part

Table 8.1 Forecasting Investment and Output Growth in some Asia Pacific Economies: Results of Stochastic Simulation

Indonesia: 1970 to 1992 Investment									
Average R^2									
	0.981	0.949	0.917	0.939	0.782	0.708	0.941	0.797	0.699
OLS-based disturbance variance $(\sigma 1^2\ \sigma 2^2\ \sigma 3^2)$									
	0.148633E-01	0.148633	1.48633						
Estimation period									
	1972 to 1981			1972 to 1987			1972 to 1987		
Forecasting period									
	1982 to 1984			1988 to 1990			1988 to 1992		
	$\sigma 1^2$	$\sigma 2^2$	$\sigma 3^2$	$\sigma 1^2$	$\sigma 2^2$	$\sigma 3^2$	$\sigma 1^2$	$\sigma 2^2$	$\sigma 3^2$
Ex Post Forecasting Relative Mean Error (%)									
OLS	2.16	−85.57	−2160.62	7.40	7.59	3.17	8.12	3.06	−34.00
STEIN	1.63	−93.61	−1838.99	6.83	5.27	0.93	7.57	1.10	−25.99
2SHI	1.16	−96.93	−1622.60	6.28	3.38	−0.86	7.03	−0.43	−20.64
Ex Post Forecasting Relative RMS Error (%)									
R(ml/s)	22.47	355.23	1766.28	1.34	3.14	7.86	1.80	4.90	20.16
R(ml/h)	21.71	324.31	1583.30	1.27	2.70	6.32	1.72	4.00	15.18
R(s/h)	21.07	299.55	1463.12	1.20	2.38	5.34	1.64	3.37	12.73
Ex Post Forecasting Relative MSE – Informational Gain (%)									
R(ml/s)	5.97	19.36	26.13	11.83	35.08	54.52	10.49	49.53	72.99
R(ml/h)	11.64	38.71	49.53	24.63	71.46	116.94	21.70	108.81	145.96
R(s/h)	5.35	16.21	18.56	11.45	26.92	40.40	10.14	39.64	42.19

Notes: b = OLS, βs = positive-part Stein (STEIN), βh = positive-part 2SHI. R(ml/s) = R(b/βs) = 100[MSE(b)/MSE(βs)-1], where MSE(b) = E(b-β)'(b-β) with β calculated from the OLS estimates of each equation using 500 repetitions (with the error terms only random from trial to trial), and used as the true parameter vector. Similarly for βh and βs, i.e., R(ml/h)=R(b/βh) and R(s/h)=R(βs/βh). Relative efficiency in *ex post* forecasting MSE of say βh over βs exists whenever R(s/h) = R(βs/βh) ≥ 0. σ^2 = OLS-based disturbance variance. In our stochastic simulation study, all results are based on 100 statistical trials and c is arbitrarily set = (k−2) /(T−k+2). All data are extracted from the 1994 World Bank DX database.

Table 8.2 Forecasting Investment and Output Growth in some Asia Pacific Economies: Results of Stochastic Simulation

Indonesia: 1970 to 1992 Output growth									
Average R^2									
	0.945	0.934	0.911	0.830	0.720	0.700	0.844	0.717	0.705
OLS-based disturbance variance $(\sigma 1^2\ \sigma 2^2\ \sigma 3^2)$									
	0.383907E-03	0.383907E-02	0.383907E-01						
Estimation period									
	1972 to 1981			1972 to 1987			1972 to 1987		
Forecasting period									
	1982 to 1984			1988 to 1990			1988 to 1992		
	$\sigma 1^2$	$\sigma 2^2$	$\sigma 3^2$	$\sigma 1^2$	$\sigma 2^2$	$\sigma 3^2$	$\sigma 1^2$	$\sigma 2^2$	$\sigma 3^2$
Ex Post Forecasting Relative Mean Error (%)									
OLS	12.72	7.40	79.22	16.74	17.71	22.57	16.95	12.23	−8.15
STEIN	10.42	4.66	66.24	12.12	9.81	10.01	12.77	4.00	−10.14
2SHI	8.44	2.45	56.86	8.34	3.96	1.23	9.33	−1.86	−11.73
Ex Post Forecasting Relative RMS Error (%)									
R(ml/s)	3.08	6.92	28.84	1.17	2.29	6.23	1.19	1.98	5.87
R(ml/h)	2.78	6.12	25.66	0.93	1.84	4.70	0.98	1.42	4.54
R(s/h)	2.56	5.56	23.63	0.80	1.63	3.90	0.86	1.24	3.79
Ex Post Forecasting Relative MSE – Informational Gain (%)									
R(ml/s)	27.28	27.95	28.69	57.03	53.13	72.57	48.75	94.46	67.20
R(ml/h)	53.30	54.91	53.77	111.02	95.76	148.92	93.15	157.76	141.76
R(s/h)	20.44	21.07	19.49	34.38	27.84	44.25	29.85	32.55	44.59

Stein-based forecasts of investment and output growth uniformly dominate the OLS-based forecasts. In addition, the positive-part Stein-based forecasts of investment and output growth here are uniformly dominated by the positive-part 2SHI forecasts.

The implications from these findings are important and wide-ranging to government planners, business forecasters, corporate strategists, and statistical scientists.

The evidence here indicates that the traditional methods (such as the OLS, the ML, and other improved Stein-like, generalized ridge, double k-class, and pre-test) that are often routinely used in modelling and forecasting in business, economics, finance, investment, and statistics

Table 8.3 Forecasting Investment and Output Growth in some Asia Pacific Economies: Results of Stochastic Simulation

Korea: 1970 to 1992 Investment									
Average R^2									
	0.996	0.975	0.968	0.979	0.907	0.839	0.981	0.907	0.837
OLS-based disturbance variance $\{\sigma 1^2\ \sigma 2^2\ \sigma 3^2\}$									
	0.269270E-02 0.269270E-01 0.269270								
Estimation period									
	1972 to 1981			1972 to 1987			1972 to 1987		
Forecasting period									
	1982 to 1984			1988 to 1990			1988 to 1992		
	$\sigma 1^2$	$\sigma 2^2$	$\sigma 3^2$	$\sigma 1^2$	$\sigma 2^2$	$\sigma 3^2$	$\sigma 1^2$	$\sigma 2^2$	$\sigma 3^2$
Ex Post Forecasting Relative Mean Error (%)									
OLS	6.28	2.68	84.61	4.39	6.08	7.62	6.33	1.16	−19.87
STEIN	6.20	2.30	88.36	4.28	5.51	6.54	6.20	0.97	−17.31
2SHI	6.13	1.97	89.63	4.17	4.99	5.58	6.08	0.78	−15.21
Ex Post Forecasting Relative RMS Error (%)									
R(ml/s)	2.40	5.22	40.99	1.39	3.37	10.01	2.53	6.21	20.36
R(ml/h)	2.38	5.07	39.00	1.37	3.20	9.07	2.50	5.84	18.56
R(s/h)	2.37	4.95	37.66	1.34	3.04	8.30	2.48	5.52	17.14
Ex Post Forecasting Relative MSE – Informational Gain (%)									
R(ml/s)	1.23	5.47	9.55	3.38	11.06	21.92	2.75	12.40	18.16
R(ml/h)	2.45	10.46	17.21	6.85	22.53	45.34	5.55	25.30	36.71
R(s/h)	1.21	4.74	6.99	3.36	10.33	19.21	2.73	11.48	15.70

are cumbersome, inflexible, and suboptimal using the usual or universal criterion of *ex post* forecasts and average mean squared forecasting errors. This result holds even if these methods are found to be superior to the technical (or time series) analysis which is based not on sound theoretical foundations of the subject matter but solely on past observations of the data.

A better forward planning strategy is more likely to be achieved therefore if more recent advances in modelling and forecasting theories (such as the differential and 2SHI approaches) are adapted for use in these areas. This comment is robust even for the different data characterized by different behaviours in different countries at different stages of their economic developments.

Table 8.4 Forecasting Investment and Output Growth in some Asia Pacific Economies: Results of Stochastic Simulation

Korea: 1970 to 1992 Output Growth									
Average R^2									
	0.990	0.966	0.967	0.959	0.872	0.833	0.964	0.874	0.834
OLS-based disturbance variance $\{\sigma1^2\ \sigma2^2\ \sigma3^2\}$									
	0.619527E-03	0.619527E-02	0.619527E-01						
Estimation period									
	1972 to 1981			1972 to 1987			1972 to 1987		
Forecasting period									
	1982 to 1984			1988 to 1990			1988 to 1992		
	$\sigma1^2$	$\sigma2^2$	$\sigma3^2$	$\sigma1^2$	$\sigma2^2$	$\sigma3^2$	$\sigma1^2$	$\sigma2^2$	$\sigma3^2$
Ex Post Forecasting Relative Mean Error (%)									
OLS	15.60	5.96	249.43	8.48	11.58	14.36	10.01	5.30	−14.45
STEIN	15.18	4.50	256.24	8.02	9.70	11.34	9.58	3.70	−13.56
2SHI	14.78	3.40	257.17	7.58	8.06	8.84	9.17	2.37	−12.82
Ex Post Forecasting Relative RMS Error (%)									
R(ml/s)	2.47	5.42	40.37	1.32	3.09	8.86	1.44	2.70	9.08
R(ml/h)	2.44	5.24	38.50	1.27	2.84	7.96	1.39	2.46	8.36
R(s/h)	2.41	5.11	37.17	1.22	2.64	7.26	1.35	2.29	7.78
Ex Post Forecasting Relative MSE – Informational Gain (%)									
R(ml/s)	2.67	6.71	9.75	8.23	17.63	23.94	6.33	20.18	17.88
R(ml/h)	5.33	12.13	17.76	16.94	35.86	48.95	12.87	38.80	35.95
R(s/h)	2.59	5.08	7.30	8.05	15.49	20.18	6.16	15.49	15.33

Some interesting sectoral and country features are described and commented on below.

Indonesia

Using just ten annual data points for making three year ahead *ex post* forecasts, we observe that these short-term forecasts for Subsample 1 (from 1982 to 1984) of investment and output growth in Indonesia improve by 26.13% and 28.69% respectively between the OLS and the Stein. However, between the OLS and the 2SHI, the improvement is 49.53% and 54.91%. The gain between the Stein and the 2SHI is 18.56% and 21.07%.

Table 8.5 Forecasting Investment and Output Growth in some Asia Pacific Economies: Results of Stochastic Simulation

Malaysia: 1970 to 1992 Investment

Average R^2

	0.991	0.966	0.958	0.970	0.883	0.856	0.975	0.873	0.829

OLS-based disturbance variance $\{\sigma 1^2\ \sigma 2^2\ \sigma 3^2\}$

0.369337E-02 0.369337E-01 0.369337

Estimation period

1972 to 1981 1972 to 1987 1972 to 1987

Forecasting period

	1982 to 1984			1988 to 1990			1988 to 1992		
	$\sigma 1^2$	$\sigma 2^2$	$\sigma 3^2$	$\sigma 1^2$	$\sigma 2^2$	$\sigma 3^2$	$\sigma 1^2$	$\delta 2^2$	$\delta 3^2$
Ex Post Forecasting Relative Mean Error (%)									
ML	35.37	7.45	145.86	3.72	3.63	2.05	4.67	−0.44	−12.94
STEIN	34.72	6.73	145.58	3.63	3.32	2.22	4.57	−0.25	−11.20
2SHI	34.10	6.43	143.94	3.53	3.05	2.28	4.48	−0.12	−09.77
Ex Post Forecasting Relative RMS Error (%)									
R(ml/s)	45.49	51.32	171.26	1.61	3.93	13.26	2.43	6.79	19.85
R(ml/h)	45.03	49.66	166.63	1.59	3.72	12.34	2.39	6.14	17.71
R(s/h)	44.60	48.22	163.12	1.56	3.56	11.56	2.35	5.65	16.20
Ex Post Forecasting Relative MSE – Informational Gain (%)									
R(ml/s)	2.77	6.94	5.81	3.21	11.03	15.35	3.36	17.72	22.42
R(ml/h)	5.47	13.40	10.64	6.47	21.43	31.37	6.77	35.15	43.34
R(s/h)	2.62	6.04	4.56	3.15	9.37	13.89	3.30	14.81	17.09

Using 50% more data (from 1970 to 1987) for making three year ahead *ex post* forecasts, these short-term forecasts for Subsample 2 (from 1988 to 1990) of investment and output growth in Indonesia improve by 54.52% and 72.57% respectively between the OLS and the Stein. However, between the OLS and the 2SHI, the improvement is 116.94% and 148.92%. The gain between the Stein and the 2SHI is 40.40% and 44.25%.

Long-term (five year ahead) *ex post* forecasts for Subsample 3 (from 1988 to 1992) of investment and output growth in Indonesia that are based on 15 annual data points (from 1970 to 1987) improve by 72.99% and 94.46% respectively between the OLS and the Stein. However, between the OLS and the 2SHI, the improvement is 145.96% and

Table 8.6 Forecasting Investment and Output Growth in some Asia Pacific Economies: Results of Stochastic Simulation

Malaysia: 1970 to 1992 Output Growth									
Average R^2									
	0.976	0.963	0.956	0.931	0.852	0.853	0.938	0.841	0.836
OLS-based disturbance variance $\{\sigma 1^2\ \sigma 2^2\ \sigma 3^2\}$									
	0.513214E-03	0.513214E-02	0.513214E-01						
Estimation period									
	1972 to 1981			1972 to 1987			1972 to 1987		
Forecasting period									
	1982 to 1984			1988 to 1990			1988 to 1992		
	$\sigma 1^2$	$\sigma 2^2$	$\sigma 3^2$	$\sigma 1^2$	$\sigma 2^2$	$\sigma 3^2$	$\sigma 1^2$	$\sigma 2^2$	$\sigma 3^2$
Ex Post Forecasting Relative Mean Error (%)									
OLS	14.98	11.66	53.75	18.31	18.52	1.20	20.93	−4.22	−81.46
STEIN	13.82	9.65	50.43	16.98	16.06	2.55	19.57	−4.84	−70.43
2SHI	12.81	8.06	47.64	15.74	13.99	3.12	18.29	−5.43	−61.92
Ex Post Forecasting Relative RMS Error (%)									
R(ml/s)	2.11	4.90	17.61	2.48	6.19	26.14	2.19	5.81	20.76
R(ml/h)	2.02	4.64	17.12	2.38	5.77	24.32	2.09	5.28	18.80
R(s/h)	1.96	4.47	16.73	2.30	5.43	22.76	2.01	4.87	17.42
Ex Post Forecasting Relative MSE Informational Gain (%)									
R(ml/s)	9.06	11.58	5.91	8.02	14.99	15.55	9.15	20.97	21.91
R(ml/h)	16.49	20.49	10.94	16.16	29.50	31.93	18.40	41.86	41.94
R(s/h)	6.81	7.98	4.74	7.53	12.62	14.17	8.48	17.27	16.43

157.76%. The gain between the Stein and the 2SHI is 42.19% and 44.59%.

A general remark from the results of this dataset for Indonesia is that the longer historical data are used for making *ex post* forecasting, the better are the *ex post* forecasts of investment and growth. As expected, when longer *ex post* forecasts are made, some efficiency is lost for all forecasting methods. However, the informational gain hierarchy $MSE(b) \geq MSE(\beta s) \geq MSE(\beta h)$ as described above still persists.

Table 8.7 Forecasting Investment and Output Growth in some Asia Pacific Economies: Results of Stochastic Simulation

Thailand: 1970 to 1992 Investment									
Average R^2									
	0.980	0.946	0.934	0.904	0.754	0.684	0.905	0.738	0.679
OLS-based disturbance variance $\{\sigma 1^2\ \sigma 2^2\ \sigma 3^2\}$									
	0.993986E-02 0.993986E-01 0.993986								
Estimation period									
	1972 to 1981			1972 to 1987			1972 to 1987		
Forecasting period									
	1982 to 1984			1988 to 1990			1988 to 1992		
	$\sigma 1^2$	$\sigma 2^2$	$\sigma 3^2$	$\sigma 1^2$	$\sigma 2^2$	$\sigma 3^2$	$\sigma 1^2$	$\sigma 2^2$	$\sigma 3^2$
Ex Post Forecasting Relative Mean Error (%)									
OLS	13.12	11.80	308.21	6.51	14.47	11.38	5.74	58.25	223.33
STEIN	12.49	11.65	306.14	5.66	10.42	−43.64	4.97	55.53	186.69
2SHI	11.89	11.31	301.36	4.87	7.47	−68.99	4.22	51.06	154.51
Ex Post Forecasting Relative RMS Error (%)									
R(ml/s)	3.87	27.39	186.97	5.05	11.31	130.79	20.61	89.21	239.46
R(ml/h)	3.74	25.66	170.71	4.73	9.59	102.99	19.16	68.95	174.36
R(s/h)	3.63	24.28	159.89	4.44	8.40	83.45	17.87	57.67	145.31
Ex Post Forecasting Relative MSE – Informational Gain (%)									
R(ml/s)	7.63	12.86	19.98	14.73	39.78	60.79	15.17	61.42	73.27
R(ml/h)	15.14	24.69	37.02	30.97	81.40	143.57	31.51	124.65	148.13
R(s/h)	6.99	10.48	14.20	14.16	29.78	51.48	14.18	39.17	43.21

Korea

For Korea, *ex post* three year ahead forecasts of investment and output growth (from 1982 to 1984) gain by 9.55% and 9.75% respectively between the OLS and the Stein, 17.21% and 17.76% between the OLS and the 2SHI, and 6.99% and 7.30% between the Stein and the 2SHI.

Also, *ex post* three year ahead forecasts of investment and output growth (from 1988 to 1990) gain by 21.92% and 23.94% respectively between the OLS and the Stein, 45.34% and 48.95% between the OLS and the 2SHI, and 19.21% and 20.18% between the Stein and the 2SHI.

Table 8.8 Forecasting Investment and Output Growth in some Asia Pacific Economies: Results of Stochastic Simulation

Thailand: 1970 to 1992 Output Growth									
Average R^2									
	0.973	0.939	0.936	0.881	0.744	0.684	0.882	0.714	0.675
OLS-based disturbance variance $\{\sigma 1^2\ \sigma 2^2\ \sigma 3^2\}$									
	0.413154E-03	0.413154E-02	0.413154E-01						
Estimation period									
	1972 to 1981			1972 to 1987			1972 to 1987		
Forecasting period									
	1982 to 1984			1988 to 1990			1988 to 1992		
	$\sigma 1^2$	$\sigma 2^2$	$\sigma 3^2$	$\sigma 1^2$	$\sigma 2^2$	$\sigma 3^2$	$\sigma 1^2$	$\sigma 2^2$	$\sigma 3^2$
Ex Post Forecasting Relative Mean Error (%)									
OLS	17.37	13.85	57.12	11.15	13.49	23.56	14.52	9.70	−6.09
STEIN	15.86	11.45	52.72	9.31	8.30	17.44	12.18	3.88	−9.47
2SHI	14.48	9.51	48.47	7.66	4.38	11.78	10.10	−0.45	−11.78
Ex Post Forecasting Relative RMS Error (%)									
R(ml/s)	1.79	3.76	17.51	1.19	2.55	14.49	1.24	2.03	5.94
R(ml/h)	1.69	3.51	16.05	1.05	2.10	11.44	1.08	1.56	4.51
R(s/h)	1.61	3.32	15.00	0.95	1.84	9.30	0.96	1.36	3.77
Ex Post Forecasting Relative MSE – Informational Gain (%)									
R(ml/s)	12.13	14.21	19.72	27.53	48.62	60.45	30.08	66.72	70.82
R(ml/h)	24.03	26.97	36.97	58.64	93.03	143.55	63.89	119.25	145.00
R(s/h)	10.62	11.17	14.41	24.39	29.88	51.79	25.99	31.51	43.43

Finally, long-term (five year ahead) *ex post* forecasts of investment and output growth (from 1988 to 1992) gain by 18.16% and 20.18% respectively between the OLS and the Stein, 36.71% and 38.80% between the OLS and the 2SHI, and 15.70% and 15.49% between the Stein and the 2SHI.

As in the case of Indonesia above, the use of longer historical sampling sizes would produce better *ex post* forecasts, and, as expected, longer-ahead forecasts that are based on the same historical dataset will lose some efficiency. The dominance, however, retains the same sequential hierarchy $MSE(b) \geq MSE(\beta s) \geq MSE(\beta h)$.

Malaysia

For Malaysia, *ex post* three year ahead forecasts of investment and output growth (from 1982 to 1984) that are based on the 1970 to 1981 dataset gain by 6.94% and 11.58% respectively between the OLS and the Stein, 13.40% and 20.49% between the OLS and the 2SHI, and 6.04% and 7.98% between the Stein and the 2SHI.

Short-term *ex post* forecasts (1988 to 1990) for Subsample 2 that are based on more information or longer datasets (from 1970 to 1987) of investment and output growth in Malaysia improve by 15.35% and 15.55% respectively between the OLS and the Stein. However, between the OLS and the 2SHI, the improvement is 31.37% and 31.93%. The gain between the Stein and the 2SHI is 13.89% and 14.17%.

Based on the same historical dataset (from 1970 to 1987), long-term (five year ahead) *ex post* forecasts for Subsample 3 (from 1988 to 1992) of investment and output growth in Malaysia improve by 22.42% and 21.91% respectively between the OLS and the Stein. However, between the OLS and the 2SHI, the improvement is 43.34% and 41.94%. The gain between the Stein and the 2SHI is 17.09% and 17.27%.

We also note that, in the case of forecasting investment and growth for Malaysia, using more data would produce better or more accurate forecasts. An interesting finding is that larger measurement errors on the data may reduce the accuracy of our predictions. This is not true with static linear regression models. The informational gain hierarchy remains, however, valid in all cases of different sample sizes and different measurement errors.

Thailand

Ex post three year (1982 to 1984, and 1988 to 1990) and five year (1988 to 1992) ahead forecasts of investment and growth for Thailand appear to follow the same pattern of dominance as observed above with data from Indonesia, Korea, and Malaysia.

For investment and for the three forecasting subsamples (1970 to 1981 plus *ex post* 1982 to 1984 forecasts, 1970 to 1987 plus *ex post* 1988 to 1990 forecasts, and 1970 to 1987 plus *ex post* 1988 to 1992 forecasts), *R(ml/s)* is 19.98%, 60.79%, and 73.27% respectively, *R(ml/h)* is 37.02%, 143.57%, and 148.13%, and *R(s/h)* is 14.20%, 51.48%, and 43.21%.

For output growth and also for the three forecasting subsamples, *R(ml/s)* is 19.72%, 60.45%, and 70.82% respectively, *R(ml/h)* is 36.97%, 51.79%, and 145.00%, and *R(s/h)* is 14.41%, 51.79%, and 43.43%.

Here, larger measurement errors may increase the accuracy of our *ex post* forecasts of investment and output growth for Thailand. However, using more data to make forecasts would substantially improve the informational gain.

References

Allen, R. G. D., *Mathematical Analysis for Economists*, London: Macmillan, 1960.

Anderson, T. W., *An Introduction to Multivariate Statistical Analysis*, 2nd Edition, New York: Wiley, 1984.

Baranchik, A. J., 'Inadmissibility of Maximum Likelihood Estimators in some Multiple Regression Problems with Three or More Independent Variables', *Annals of Statistics*, Vol. 1, 1973, pp. 312–321.

Chaturvedi, A., Tran Van Hoa, and Shukla, G., 'Performance of the Stein-rule Estimators when the Disturbances are Misspecified as Spherical', *Economic Studies Quarterly* (Japan), Vol. 44, 1993, pp. 601–611.

Engle, R. F. and Granger, C. W. J., 'Co-integration and Error Correction: Representation, Estimation and Testing', *Econometrica*, Vol. 55, 1987, pp. 251–276.

Harvie, C. and Tran Van Hoa, 'Long Term Relationships of Major Macrovariables in a Resource-Related Economic Model of Australia: a Cointegration Analysis', *Energy Economics*, 1993.

Harvie, C. and Tran Van Hoa (1995a), 'Terms of Trade and Macroeconomic Adjustments in a Resource Exporting Economy: The Case of Australia', *Resources Policy*, forthcoming.

Harvie, C. and Tran Van Hoa (1995b), 'Long Term Relationship between Oil Production and Oil Price, and the Current Account, Real Exchange Rate, Capital Stock, Nonoil Output, Manufacturing Output and Growth: The UK Experience', *Journal of Energy and Development*.

Johansen, L., 'Econometric Models and Economic Planning and Policy: Some Trends and Problems', in M. Hazewinkle and A. H. G. Rinnooy Kan (eds), *Current Developments in the Interface: Economics, Econometrics, Mathematics*, Boston: Reidel, 1982.

Judge, G. G. and Yancey, T. A., *Improved Methods of Inference in Econometrics*, Amsterdam: North-Holland, 1986.

Pindyck, R. S. and Rubinfeld, D. L., *Econometric Models and Economic Forecasts*, Sydney: McGraw-Hill, 1991.

Pippenger, J. E., *Fundamentals of International Trade*, New York: Prentice Hall, 1984.

Tran Van Hoa, 'The Inadmissibility of the Stein Estimator in Normal Multiple Regression Equations', *Economics Letters*, Vol. 19, 1985, pp. 39–42.

Tran Van Hoa (1986a), 'The Inadmissibility of the Stein Estimator in Normal Multiple Regression Models: Analytical and Simulation Results', 15th Anniversary of the NBER-NSF Seminar on Bayesian Inference in Econometrics, ITAM, Mexico City, 16–18 January 1986.

Tran Van Hoa (1986b) 'Effects of Monetary and Fiscal Policy on Inflation: Some Evidence from the J-Test', *Economics Letters*, Vol. 22, 1986, pp. 187–190.

Tran Van Hoa (1987a), 'Some Dominance Theorems on the Double k Class Estimator in Linear Models', *Economics Letters*, Vol. 22, 1987, pp. 237–240.

Tran Van Hoa (1987b), 'Improved Finite Sample Estimators in Linear Models: Generalized Ridge and Positive Part Stein', *Economics Letters*, Vol. 22, 1987, pp. 241–245.

Tran Van Hoa and Chaturvedi, A., 'The Necessary and Sufficient Conditions for the Uniform Dominance of the Two-Stage Stein Estimators', *Economics Letters*, Vol. 28, 1988, pp. 351–355.

Tran Van Hoa and Chaturvedi, A., 'Further Results on the Two-Stage Hierarchial Information (2SHI) Estimators in the Linear Regression Models', *Communications in Statistics (Theory and Methods)*, Vol. A19, No. 12, 1990, pp. 4697–4704.

Tran Van Hoa (1992a), 'Modelling Output Growth: A New Approach', *Economics Letters*, Vol. 38, 1992, pp. 279–284.

Tran Van Hoa (1992b) 'Energy Consumption in Thailand: Estimated Structure and Improved Forecasts to 2000' (in Thai), *Thammasat Economic Journal* (Thailand), Vol. 10, 1992, pp. 55–63.

Tran Van Hoa (1992c), 'A Multi-equation Model of Energy Consumption in Thailand', *International Journal of Energy Research*, Vol. 16, 1992, pp. 381–385.

Tran Van Hoa (1992d), 'A New and General Approach to Modelling Short-Term Interest Rates: With Application to Australian Data 1962–1990', *Journal of Economics and Finance: Proceedings*, Vol. 16, 1992, pp. 327–335.

Tran Van Hoa, Chaturvedi, A., and Lal, R., 'Improved Estimation of the Linear Regression Model with Autocorrelated Errors', *Journal of Quantitative Economics*, Vol. 8, 1992, pp. 347–352.

Tran Van Hoa (1993a), 'The Mixture Properties of the 2SHI Estimators in Linear Regression Models', *Statistics and Probability Letters*, Vol. 16, 1993, pp. 111–115.

Tran Van Hoa (1993b), 'Effects of Oil on Output Growth and Inflation in Developing Countries: The Case of Thailand 1966:1 to 1991:1', *International Journal of Energy Research*, Vol. 17, 1993, pp. 29–33.

Tran Van Hoa (1993c), 'Foreign Investment, External Debts, Growth, and Inflation in Thailand: Does a Long Term Relationship Exist?' (in Thai), *Thammasat Economic Journal*, Vol. 11, 1993, pp. 29–38.

Tran Van Hoa and Chaturvedi, A., 'Asymptotic Approximations to the Gain of the 2SHI Estimator over the Stein Estimators in Linear Regression Models When the Disturbances are Small', *Communication in Statistics*, Vol. 22, 1993, pp. 2777–82.

Tran Van Hoa, 'How to Make Better Forecasts to Better Formulate Forward Planning Business Policy', *Thammasat Economic Journal*, Vol. 15, 1995, pp. 41–55.

Ullah and Ullah, 'Double k-class Estimators of Coefficients in Linear Regression', *Econometrica*, Vol. 46, 1978, pp. 705–22.

World Bank Database 1994 DX Package, Melbourne 1994.

9 Health Care in Thailand: Present Systems and Future Trends with Applications to Other Developing Economies

Sirilaksana Khoman

1 INTRODUCTION

Economic development and advances in medicine have resulted in unprecedented improvements in the general health of the world's population in the last few decades. But wide variations between countries exist in terms of health expenditures, health outcomes, and the mechanisms through which health care is provided. Vigorous debate has ensued over the appropriate health care system. Indeed health care reform has been on many nations' agenda, and health care systems have come under much public scrutiny in recent years.

In many societies, health care is considered a basic human right, access to which in principle is not limited by ability to pay. However many states that have traditionally shouldered the responsibility for health care are moving towards introducing or expanding market discipline to shift the burden from the public sector to private individuals. Such rethinking has generally been necessitated by the increasingly onerous burden of public provision. Societies all over the world are in fact grappling with a range of problems with respect to the amount of resources to be devoted to health care, the appropriate type and quality of care that should be provided, inefficiencies and cost escalation, as well as problems of inequitable access.

The objective of this chapter is to examine the health sector in Thailand, the role of the public sector in the provision of health services, the various financing schemes that exist, and the efforts made to reform the current system. As a developing country that has made some strides in health care, with several innovative programmes in place and continuing efforts at further fine-tuning, Thailand's problems and dilemma can be of value to other developing countries, and especially to transition economies in the process of devising their own health care systems.

Section 2 reviews the conceptual foundation that provides the principal guidelines and direction for reform. An overview of Thailand's health sector is presented in Section 3 and the major health schemes examined. It reviews the experience of Thailand in developing, implementing, and at times experimenting with various financing schemes. The main problems of each scheme are presented, and adjustments and experimentations are analysed, particularly in terms of coverage, health care delivery, and financing mechanisms. The benefits of shared experiences are discussed with possible application to transition economies in Section 4.

2 CONCEPTUAL FOUNDATION

Much of today's concern over the appropriate health care system for any country involves asking what the appropriate role of the public versus the private sector should be. This question has troubled policymakers for centuries. This is because public participation in production carries with it both risks and opportunities. The risks arise from the tendency to use public resources inefficiently where personal accountability is the exception rather than the rule. The opportunities arise from the government's ability, in principle, to improve resource allocation when markets fail, and from its capacity to provide relief to the needy, and work towards achievement of society's goals.

Different countries make very different choices about the public versus private provision of social services like health. The choice of system is by no means a random event, but reflects the underlying economic, social and political forces and their interaction. Private sector growth is often a response to government decisions about the amount and type of health services, and government production often depends on what is happening in the private sector.

The health care system can be broadly viewed as a subsector in society shaped by historical circumstances and evolving in response to economic, social, and political influences. The diversity of health care systems existing in different countries reflects the varying (and perhaps constantly changing) strengths of the public sector, the constraints on governments, the capacity of the private sector, the nature of consumer demand, the diversity of policy objectives, political orientation and philosophical inclination. Consequently the design of policy options has to take these circumstances into account.

A holistic representation of the health care system is presented in Figure 9.1. Health needs and a country's economic condition are given as the setting that influences the direction of policy. Several 'production relationships' are postulated. First the philosophical inclination and the political power structures combine to 'produce' society's objectives. The power structure may consist of voters, interest groups, legislators, bureaucrats, autocrats and/or elitist groups, and the political process may or may not involve representative decision-making. Whether decisions are made through median voter preference, by autocratic rule, or somewhere in between, these decisions will determine how the health resources are produced, managed, and organized, and how production is financed. Health outcomes are then determined by how resources are utilized and translated into outcomes via distribution and delivery.

Because the resulting configuration is the outcome of balancing these various forces, the existing health care system may or may not achieve efficiency in resource allocation or attain the other goals of society. Should the government step in to address these issues? Does the government have a mandate to do so, given that the configuration is itself an outcome of government activity? Determining the desirable public/private mix in health care involves examining the underlying nature of the health services themselves. It is therefore necessary to explore the nature of the problem and the appropriate government responses, bearing in mind that government is also an entity with its own objectives and constraints.

2.1 Rationale for State Intervention in Health

There are two main reasons for state[1] intervention: (i) market failure or inefficiency, and (ii) the pursuit of other (non-efficiency) goals.

2.1.1 Market Failure or Inefficiency

In the field of health, the largely uncoordinated interaction of demand and supply within the market system will not normally achieve an efficient level of output because of the following problems: a) imperfect consumer information (asymmetry of information), b) uncertainty of demand,

Figure 9.1 Holistic Representation of the Health Care System

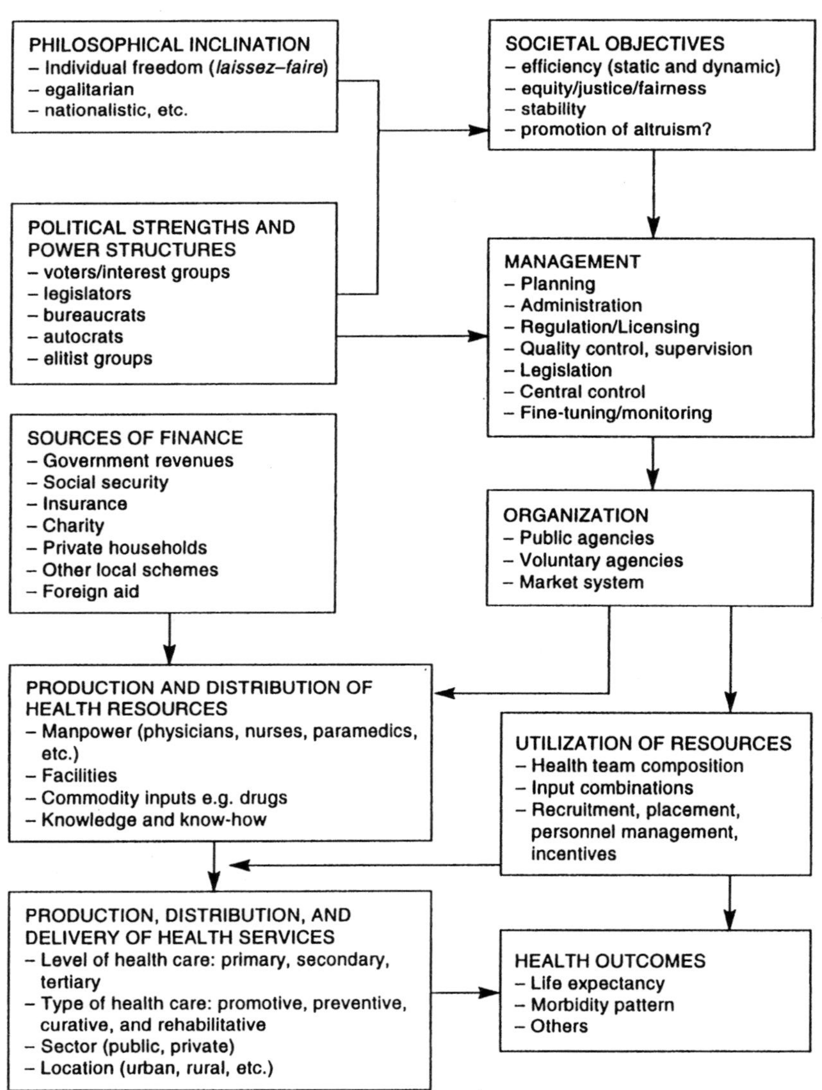

c) 'convexities' such as decreasing costs and monopoly, d) externalities, and e) public goods. These problems obstruct the efficient functioning of the market system, so that efficiency is left unattained and 'market failure' occurs.

(a) Imperfect Consumer Knowledge and Information

Unlike most other commodities, a typical consumer's knowledge of his state of health or the type of treatment to be applied in the event of sickness is limited. More importantly, such knowledge is not easily acquired either through self-study or repeat purchases. This imbalance (or asymmetry) of information between consumer and supplier puts consumers at a disadvantage, and their ability to 'pick and choose' suppliers is thus reduced. Suppliers (doctors and/or hospitals) can over- or under-supply treatment without the consumer's knowledge. Thus the built-in self-regulating mechanism of the market that safeguards the consumer's interest is not present. Suppliers of health services can exploit consumers, resulting in loss of benefits to society.

For other commodities, such as high-technology products like microwave ovens, computers or automobiles, consumers may also have limited knowledge, but brand names and repeat purchases have informational content and provide useful guides. Moreover products of the same make and model are more or less identical. Warranties are usually offered. Sampling and demonstrations are usually possible. Such is not the case with health care. The consumer may base his choice of doctor or hospital on reputation, but since few cases are exactly the same, dissatisfied patients cannot readily complain about treatment outcomes, without being faced with the argument that their case is different from others.

Such practices as getting second opinions which help patients get information about correct diagnoses, may not be culturally acceptable in some societies. There is therefore no *market mechanism* to induce doctors and hospitals to provide good or even appropriate service. Knowledge confers power, and by limiting the extent of competition, the imbalance of information and knowledge makes it possible for suppliers of medical care to exercise monopoly power, detrimental to allocative efficiency.

(b) Uncertainty of Demand

In general, people cannot predict when, or what kind of, sickness would arise. Statistical evidence and risk factors are often not heeded because of large inter-personal variations. And when treatment becomes necessary, it may involve large outlays. The market institution that helps consumers deal with uncertainty is insurance.[2] However the market may not work well due to problems of *adverse selection* and *moral hazard*.

Adverse selection occurs because of another kind of asymmetry of information: that between the consumer and the insurance company. Because an individual may have more information regarding his own susceptibility to ill health which the insurance company may not have access to, the latter may not be able to distinguish between high-risk and low-risk individuals. Since high-risk individuals would have a higher tendency to buy insurance policies, the premium charged would have to be high to cover the payments that are paid out. This further drives out low-risk individuals, requiring further escalation of premiums, so that the market for some kinds of insurance would not exist.

Moral hazard confounds risk and behavioural factors. That is, the fact that insurance is bought actually increases the likelihood of illness, due to intentional or unintentional increases in illness-inducing behaviour such as carelessness. In addition, if the doctor is paid according to actual services rendered (on a fee-for-service basis), then neither doctor nor patient has any incentive to economize on visits or treatment, because once insured, payment (by the insurance company) is assured. This would lead to utilization of services beyond the efficient level.

(c) Decreasing Costs and Monopoly

In many production processes, increasing returns to scale prevail over some range of output. This is part of what economists called 'non-convexity'. To supply additional units of output or services, average costs decline over this range. Thus, a single supplier may capture a significant portion of the market by being able to drive out competitors because of their low average cost arising from size. If a supplier is able to capture a sufficiently large share of any market they can, by restricting their output, increase the price to consumers. In many hospital services that require large investments, the average cost of servicing an additional patient may decline as the cost of those investments are spread over a larger number of patients.

In such cases, even though it may be feasible to ensure competitiveness by dividing production up into smaller units through government coercion, this would not be efficient as average costs would be driven up. These are 'natural monopolies', where production is efficient only with one or a few suppliers. The market 'fails' in this case to produce efficiency.

Examples abound in the health field of seemingly competitive behaviour such as the purchase of high cost equipment like CT scans, often more for their prestige value, resulting in clearly underutilized resources. This may seem to go against the above arguments since wasteful competition seems to be fostered by decreasing unit cost situations rather than the creation of monopolies. But it is precisely because the market is not perfectly competitive that costly behaviour is able to occur, since efficiency (and cost containment) would have to be rigorously pursued to survive in a truly competitive world. A combination of non-competitive elements combine to make 'wasteful' behaviour possible.

(d) Externalities

Externalities occur where the economic actions of individuals and/or producers affect others directly, that is, not through the price system. Because only the effects on themselves are taken into account, the decisions made will not be 'efficient'.

Individual action with respect to, for example, immunization and disease control reduces the risks to others, thereby producing positive returns (external benefits or positive externalities) that spill over to the rest of the community. Individual action is based on individual benefit, and therefore would result in under-investment in health, causing welfare loss to society.

Under these circumstances the attainment of efficiency in resource allocation cannot occur solely through reliance on market forces in the private sector.

(e) Public Goods

Public goods are those goods for which the externalities or spillover on the rest of the community is complete in the sense that no one is, or can be, excluded. Once the good or service is produced, it becomes available to everyone and each person consumes an equal amount of that good or service. Examples include malarial eradication through aerial spraying – a local public good, in the sense that the benefits accrue to the sprayed area. Research and development and the knowledge created also falls under this category. Planning and forecasts of manpower requirements also generate knowledge, and such knowledge is also a public good.

Because the benefits fall on everyone (or the cost of supplying an additional person is zero), consumption is said to be 'non-rival', and the free market would have no incentive to provide public goods. No individual would have any incentive to pay for the good, but will have strong incentives to become a 'free-rider'. Without state initiative, public goods would probably not be produced, unless a managed incentive system (such as patents for inventions) exists. This would have to fall under the realm of state legislation.

2.1.2 Other Goals of Society

Society may have other goals in addition to efficiency, such as equity, civil liberty and freedom, and the promotion of altruism or 'moral' behaviour. These goals can be considered 'merit goods' that society would like to have for their intrinsic or aesthetic value. The market system does not have any built-in mechanisms to achieve these objectives or produce a pattern of resource allocation that is desired by society.

The non-efficiency objective that is most commonly set in the field of health care is equity. Indeed one of the primary activities of government is distribution. But interpretations of equity vary.

One is the concept of full equality: every one should have equal treatment for equal health care needs. Another interpretation is in terms of minimum standards: no person should be denied a socially specified minimum level consumption (of health care services, or any other good or service).

A further interpretation of equity relates to health care organization and the costs incurred to receive medical care. These include any fees or charges that may be levied, any income lost through taking time off work, and the cost of travelling to the medical facility. If for example some people have to travel further than others, then this would constitute inequality of access. Equality of access therefore implies equality of cost, and geographical distribution becomes an issue.

The market system which operates efficiently for *a given distribution of income and wealth* would probably not achieve equity no matter which interpretation is used, if income and wealth distribution is unequal.

Another type of 'merit good' occurs where the state makes a judgement, different from private assessment, that certain goods are 'good' or 'bad', and attempts to encourage the former (such as yearly medical check-ups) and discourage the latter (such as alcohol consumption). This is of course the 'father knows best' argument, whereby state judgement supersedes individual preferences. This may provide a basis for public spending on merit goods or taxing of 'demerit' goods.[3]

2.1.3 Caveat

Given the above arguments about the imperfections or shortcomings of the market system, the reasons for state intervention can be summarized as follows: to counteract asymmetry of information, create systems to handle uncertainty, to deal with situations of natural monopoly, externalities and public goods, and to bring about situations conducive to the pursuit of other goals such as equity, freedom, altruism and morality.

The fact that the market system cannot be relied upon to produce efficiency in resource allocation or to distribute goods and services equitably in accordance with society's goals offers a reason for governments to intervene. Ideally this would be achieved through measures that would not destroy the efficiency properties of the market through what are called 'non-distortionary' measures. However such instruments may not be available in sufficiently flexible form for the government to employ, so that trade-offs between efficiency and equity become typical.

An additional caution is that government intervention *per se*, may not provide a panacea to cure all of the market ills, and inappropriate forms of intervention can actually exacerbate the situation.

The government is an institution, just like a firm or a household. Policies are formulated and executed by individuals whose actions depend on rules, customs and incentives just like firms and households. Decisions are made on the basis of imperfect information and subject to a variety of constraints. It is not inconceivable that those who control the government (politicians) and those who administer it (bureaucrats) are guided by their own preferences, and what they do may conflict with the welfare of individual citizens.

The government may act to preserve the interests of certain sections of the population, so that decisions reflect the relative power of different interest groups and lobbyists. Democracy does not ensure that the interests of society will be protected. Policies designed to achieve electoral success or to further the goals of an established bureaucracy, may indeed not lead to maximum social benefits, especially when the benefits of future generations are also included.

Policy options must be considered against the backdrop of the process by which decisions get translated into actions in each society. This depends on the internal organization of the agency, typically hierarchical in structure, and the ways in which the incentives faced by individuals within that organization influence their behaviour. Pertinent questions include: what latitude do bureaucrats have in exercising discretion? What is the impact of special interest groups, the strength of consumer movements, welfare rights activists, and others?

The desirability of government action therefore depends on how government is motivated. The fact that the market outcome is inefficient or inequitable does not mean that government intervention will necessarily lead to an improvement. Nevertheless it is useful to determine whether policies exist that will solve, or at least, alleviate the problems. The best system – whether it is private, public, or mixed – for each situation can only be determined by a careful analysis of the theoretical and empirical evidence.

2.2 Forms of State Intervention in Health

Within the framework of a mixed capitalist economy, the government has a wide range of instruments at its disposal. State provision is the most common type of instrument used in many developing countries. That is, the government may seek to achieve the desired allocation of resources through direct provision or state participation in production which replaces the market system. Common examples of state participation in production include public enterprises, utilities, and government hospitals. Specific health programmes are also often undertaken by developing country governments such as immunization and maternal health, nutritional improvement, sanitation, and health education.

In most of these cases, economic reasoning would justify intervention on the grounds of externalities and/or equity considerations, which would not necessarily imply or justify production by the state. If externalities are present and/or certain services are desirable because they better target the poor, then fiscal measures can be used. A government may use tax or subsidy policies to deter those activities it wishes to restrict, and to encourage those activities it wishes to expand. Examples of the use of tax/subsidy policies are research grants, tax concessions, congestion and pollution taxes, and taxes on scarce energy resources. Immunization, maternal and child health, nutrition, family planning, health education, waste disposal, water supply, and other forms of preventive care all contain elements of positive externalities that warrant subsidy, but not necessarily production by the state.

In addition, the state may rely on regulation of the market system, depending on the nature of the problem. Regulation involves specifying, via law, what activities may, or may not, or must be undertaken. Examples of regulation include direct controls (such as rationing and central planning), legislation (for example, anti-trust laws, pollution control, zoning, licensing, accreditation, safety and quality standards, certification, and property rights, rent control restrictions, compulsory immunization, and various kinds of public health directives such as the requirement to report all communicable diseases). In the case of natural monopoly, the threat of competition, the requirement of bidding for concessions, and so on, can be used to create 'contestable markets', that do not involve state production. 'Networking' and sharing of facilities and equipment in the case of decreasing unit costs can be encouraged.

Where problems of imperfect information abound, information dissemination can be undertaken by the state. Information dissemination is akin to state participation in production with the product being knowledge and information. Examples include public awareness programmes regarding disease prevention, use of drugs, preventive behaviour and so on. On the other hand, the mere fact that information imperfections exist does not necessarily mean that information must be produced by the state. Stakeholder awareness can be promoted, the practice of acquiring second and third opinions can be encouraged, and incentives can be offered for professional associations to undertake the information dissemination role.

Combinations of instruments are also possible. For example, in the case of disease-causing water pollution, the government may choose to impose taxes on the amount of pollution generated or subsidize research on pollution-free modes of production. It could also set emission standards, effluent limits, or standards for the manufacture of pollution-free inputs, or raise the price of pollution-generating fuel. For the positive externalities generated by immunization, the government could offer the services at government hospitals free of charge (state production), but could also pay private hospitals for each case immunized (subsidization).

The role of the government in health care varies from country to country. In the UK the government owns and operates most of the country's hospitals. Developing countries typically have a large public sector providing for the health needs of the population. In the US the system of allocating health care is more market oriented, but there is considerable state regulation and subsidy of medical expenses: Medicaid for the poor and Medicare for the elderly.

Often the role of the government is determined by historical factors, rather than economic rationale. But it is important to rationalize them and relate policies to market problems.

The case of public goods seems to be the only clear case warranting state provision, using general tax revenues, since the benefits fall on everyone. Any service provided by the state (free of charge at point of use) should at least have the characteristics of pure public goods, namely, costly exclusion and zero cost of additional supply. If the service has distributional value and/or generates externalities, these do not fall under the realm of this clear case for public provision, and are candidates for other forms of intervention such as taxes or subsidies. And even when state provision can be justified, the relative efficiency of public versus private sector provision would also have to be investigated to determine whether that service should actually be *produced* by the state. A public good can be provided free of charge at point of use, but could still be contracted out to private producers.

It is clear that many kinds of health services provided by the state in many countries do not pass the criteria that would warrant public sector production. To further complicate matters, even where the characteristics of public goods are present, there may still be debate about the desirability of the good itself. Defence expenditure, for example, is the subject of considerable controversy. Even scientific research can raise arguments about the appropriate size of public funding. Private police forces exist in some countries and examples abound of private funding of research. Malarial spraying is a local public good, but the state may undertake the spraying itself, or contract out the production of the service, even though retaining responsibility for its *provision.*

3 HEALTH SCHEMES AND HEALTH CARE IN THAILAND

3.1 Government Role in Health Care

During the past two decades, Thailand has been among the fastest growing economies in the world. But there is evidence that although absolute poverty has declined, the distribution of income has not improved (Krongkaew, 1995). In spite of government efforts in providing health and other social services, pockets of malnutrition and other eradicable diseases remain and inequity of access to health services abounds. Added to this is the alarming spectre of an AIDS-induced public health crisis. As of October 1991, the total number of confirmed AIDS and AIDS-related cases were 177 and 487 respectively, and positive HIV cases were estimated at around 300,000 cases (Nitayarumphong and Pannarunothai, 1996).

Table 9.1 Government Budget by Type of Spending

Government Budget	1995 Baht	%	1996 Baht	%
1. Agriculture	69,942,072,100	9.78	78,293,833,500	9.29
2. Industry and Mining	2,266,849,400	0.32	2,663,606,600	0.32
3. Transportation and Communication	64,549,888,900	9.03	88,488,527,200	10.49
4. Commerce and Tourism	5,365,024,900	0.75	6,835,675,300	0.81
5. Science Technology Energy and Environment	10,944,795,900	1.53	15,109,757,300	1.79
6. Education	137,273,464,700	19.20	171,914,096,400	20.39
7. Public Health	52,596,063,000	7.36	64,938,251,200	7.70
8. Social Service	84,801,136,900	11.86	117,705.130,700	13.96
9. Defence	99,986,043,800	13.98	108,015,611,700	12.81
10. Internal Society	31,771,378,900	4.44	40,549,627,100	4.81
11. General Public Administration	110,921,017,700	15.51	100,482,830,300	11.92
12. Debt Payment	44,582,263,800	6.24	48,203,052,700	5.72
	715,000,000,000	100.00	843,200,000,000	100.00

In Thailand approximately 7% of the national budget is allocated to health care each year. This forms about 1.2% of GDP. It can be seen from Table 9.1 that government spending on health will total almost 65 billion Baht (USD 2.6 billion) in 1996,[4] and the proportion of the government budget allocated to public health is steadily rising.

The rising trend of all health expenditures in Thailand, public and private, is also striking. The proportion of GDP spent on health is projected to rise dramatically in the year 2000 to 8.1% of GDP, with total per capita health expenditures growing faster than GDP (NESDB, 1990).

In terms of health care provision, the government is the country's major provider through the Ministry of Public Health (MOPH), which has a nation-wide network of hospitals at the regional, provincial, and community levels, and health centres at the subdistrict level, constituting a three-tiered health delivery system. The 8,202 health centres are staffed by health workers, nurses and midwives serving a population of 5,000 to 10,000 people, in every subdistrict in the country. Each of the 679 district hospitals have up to 100 beds, serving a population of 20,000 to 100,000. The district hospitals have two to five general practitioners in residence. The 92 secondary- and tertiary-care hospitals (86 of which are regional and general hospitals in the provinces) each have up to 1,000 beds, and are fully staffed with specialists. Table 9.2 presents the range of services that exist in the provincial areas.

Table 9.2 Hospital and Medical Establishments and Beds in Provincial Areas

Category of Establishment	1993 Number	Number of Beds
Regional Hospital	17	12,023
General Hospital	69	21,393
District Hospital	628	15,989
Extended OPD	3	30
Health Centre	8202	–
Community Health Center	540	–

Source: Ministry of Public Health, *Public Health Statistics 1993*

The MOPH plays a major role in providing primary health care, and most of these services are located in rural areas, as well as in non-Bangkok urban centres. The MOPH spends almost half its annual budget in the rural and non-Bangkok urban areas, with an increasing share (about 25%) going to primary health care, as opposed to secondary and tertiary care. The trend is towards the MOPH spending an increasing share of its budget on promotive and preventive rather than curative services, on rural areas relative to urban areas, and on primary health care relative to other levels of care (Khoman and Mongkolsmai, 1993). Such allocation is in line with the externalities argument and the equity argument earlier discussed.

However it can be seen that whether we consider the overall supply of physicians, hospitals, or hospital beds, rural–urban differentials are strikingly apparent. Even the regional breakdown which actually obscures the bias in favour of urban centres, shows marked disparity between Bangkok and the rest of the country. The latest statistics in Table 9.3 show that one physician serves 958 people in Bangkok, while in the Northeast the population served per physician is greater by more than ten times. Khoman (1992) also shows that physician services are much less accessible to the rural people than to urban dwellers. Such disparities together with the problem of inequitable income distribution (again in favour of urban dwellers) require specific targeting of vulnerable groups, and government efforts in initiating financing schemes intended to assist financially vulnerable groups are reviewed in the next section.

Table 9.3 Population per Medical and Public Health Resources, 1992

Region	Physician	Dentist	Pharmacist	Nurse	Hospital Bed*
North	1: 6,316	1: 41,176	1: 24,910	1: 964	
Northeast	1: 10,970	1: 78,211	1: 45,020	1: 1,606	
Central	1: 5,804	1: 29,181	1: 25,854	1: 815	
South	1: 6,079	1: 31,574	1: 21,143	1: 806	
Bangkok	1: 958	1: 4,599	1: 2,142	1: 363	1: 260
Regional average excluding Bangkok	1: 7,326	1: 42,811	1: 29,608	1: 1,050	1: 800
Whole Kingdom	1: 4,425	1: 23,530	1: 13,076	1: 885	1: 666

*Beds in government hospitals for general services only

Source: Ministry of Public Health, *Public Health Statistics 1993*

3.2 Government Expenditures and Major Schemes

Several health financing schemes are initiated by the government, ostensibly to assist disadvantaged groups. The main problems that arise here relate to coverage, inappropriate subsidy, and the management of health care delivery.

Health financing schemes in Thailand can be divided into four main types as shown in Table 9.4. These are (1) voluntary health insurance, (2) mandatory schemes, (3) social welfare schemes, and (4) fringe benefit schemes such as health coverage for government officials and state enterprise employees. For some types, however, the division has not always been clear cut over the years, as Thailand experiments with ways and means to provide its population with security and access to health care. These schemes covered about 59% of the population in 1992, and coverage is expected to increase, social security coverage having doubled in a period of three years. In addition about half of the uninsured population actually receive free medical care at government hospitals, but there is no system that guarantees that all the needy people receive appropriate care. Each of the formal schemes will be discussed in turn.

Table 9.4 Coverage of Health Schemes in Thailand

Scheme	Target Population	Population covered in 1992	%	Source of finance	Subsidy per head 1992
1. Voluntary Health Insurance					
1.1 Health card	mainly rural	1.3 million	2.3	Card holder and govt. (MOPH)	63 Baht
1.2 Private insurance	mainly urban	0.9 million	1.6	Insurer	–
2. Mandatory schemes					
2.1 Workmen's Compensation	Formal sector employees	1.8 million	3.2	Employers and govt. (MOLW)	–
2.2 Social Security	Formal sector employees	2.5 million (1992)	4.4	Employers, employees, and govt. (MOLW)	541 Baht
		4.5 million (1995)	7.56		
3. Welfare*					
3.1 Low income support	Low income mainly rural	11.7 million	20.7	Government (MOI)	214 Baht
3.2 Support for the elderly	Population over sixty	3.5 million	6.2	Government (MOPH)	72 Baht
3.3 School children	Primary school children	5.1 million	9.0	Government (MOE)	
4. Government fringe benefits					
4.1 Government reimbursement	Government official/emp. and families	5.6 million	9.9	Government (various agencies)	916 Baht
4.2 State enterprise benefits	State enterprise employees and families	0.8 million	1.4	Government (various enterprises)	815 Baht
Insured Population		33.2 million	58.7		
Uninsured Population		23.3 million	41.3		

* Other welfare recipients include veterans, monks, and those deemed truly needy
MOPH: Ministry of Public Health MOI: Ministry of Interior
MOLW: Ministry of Labor and Welfare MOE: Ministry of Education

Sources: MOPH (1992), Social Security Office (1995), calculated from Hsiao (1994), Mongkolsmai (1993), and Khoman (1995a)

(1) Voluntary health insurance

Voluntary health insurance consists of private commercial insurance that covers a population of about 0.9 million, almost exclusively in the formal sector. Also classified here as voluntary health insurance is the Health Card Program, which was implemented in the rural areas in 1983 as a voluntary scheme.

However the Health Card project has evolved over the years, and can now also be considered a kind of social welfare programme as well, since implicit subsidy from the government was never purposely withheld, and the current form of the project now receives an explicit contribution from the government equal to the contribution of the card purchaser. Its coverage however is still fairly limited and has fluctuated between 2.7 and 1.3 million people, mainly because of lapses in policy direction, and the often *ad hoc* nature in which it is implemented.

The Health Card Program was started in 1983 primarily to promote maternal and child health. It was an innovative programme since it involved selling health cards to villagers who had hitherto been accustomed to receiving free care. Purchase of the card meant prepayment of a certain fixed premium in return for free services over a period of one year. Proceeds from card sales were placed in the health card fund in each community, and were managed by a village committee.

Right from the outset, the health card fund was designed to be a village-level fund, so that grass-roots participation and management skills could be fostered. Out of this fund, 75% was allocated to the health providers in the following proportion: 15% to the health centre, 30% to the community hospital, and 30% to the regional or provincial hospital, reflecting the pattern of utilization in the referral system and the severity of illness and cost to the provider. The remaining 25% was apportioned as follows: 10% to personnel in the provider institutions, and 15% was used as operating expenses of the fund. Thus the programme familiarized the rural population with concepts of preventive behaviour, insurance, risk pooling, fund management, and community self-help, though initial emphasis was placed on improvement of health. Self-help and communal participation was also fostered by recruitment of Village Health Volunteers and Village Health Communicators who would liaise with health personnel at the village health centre regarding the health conditions of the villagers. From the 1970s there were more than 70,000 people serving as health volunteers in villages, overseeing basic primary health care, such as sanitation and nutrition, and surveillance of disease incidence. More than 25,000 revolving drug funds were set up, stocking common drugs for minor diseases, managed at the village level. This was designed to improve accessibility to those left out of insurance schemes.

The Health Card project began in 18 villages in seven provinces. Upon inception, the primary objective of the programme was to improve health among the rural population, with emphasis on primary health care – including health education, environmental health (sanitation and water supply), maternal and child health, family planning, nutrition, immunization, prevention and control of locally endemic diseases, treatment of common ailments, and provision of essential drugs. In addition, the programme incorporated a referral system, whereby card holders were required to visit primary care centres, namely the village drug fund as the initial point of contact, and had to be properly referred to higher levels, namely the subdistrict health centre, the community hospital, and finally the general or regional hospital. This was aimed at promoting greater efficiency in the use of different levels of health services, since over-utilization of high-level hospital care was occurring, as villagers routinely by-passed the health centres in favour of physician services. Initially, in return for observing the referral system, hospital users could use the 'green channel' and avoid the long queues at the provincial hospitals.

Because of the problems encountered, and the lack of a clear policy, the features of the Health Card Program were constantly being adjusted, and sometimes policy-makers vacillated over time. This was principally because many provincial hospitals saw the programme as a burden, both financial and administrative. In many provinces, adverse selection resulted in high cost, and the programme had to be subsidized from general hospital revenues as the project could not break even. In others surplus funds were generated and profitably re-invested. The features often at issue were the number of free episodes allowed, the coverage ceiling per visit, the number of family members included, the types of diseases covered, the price of the card, and the renewability. Confusion also arose because of erroneous expectations of improved services after purchase of the card. This however did not materialize. Table 9.5 presents an overview of the evolution of the benefit structures over time.

Between the years 1985 and 1990 some health card funds were initiated at the district and subdistrict levels (rather than the previous village-level management), with three types of cards: a family card of 300 Baht, a maternal and child card of 100 Baht, and an individual card priced at 200 Baht, with the number of episodes reduced from eight to six.

Various problems arose due to confusion with the different types of cards, the terms and conditions of use, the losses incurred due to the inability of hospitals to recover costs from the health card fund contribution, and the problems with the strict referral system that tended to disregard geographical proximity. Tantiserani (1988) found that the Health Card Program was active in about 33% of the villages and 70% of the subdistricts in 72 provinces, with about 2.7 million people holding about 550,000 family cards. A subsequent MOPH survey in 1992 found that coverage had extended to 36% of the villages, but the population covered was reduced to only 30% of the subdistricts in 68 provinces, and 1.3 million persons holding 260,000 family cards.

Table 9.5 Development of Health Card Program Benefit Structures, 1983–95

	1983–84	1984–85	1985–90	1991–present
Scheme offered Price Benefit	MCH (blue) 100 Baht MCH/immunization	MCH (blue) 100 Baht MCH/immunization	MCH (blue) 100 Baht MCH/immunization	–
	Family (red) 200 Baht Medical care MCH/immunization	Family (red) 200 Baht Medical care	Family (green) 300 Baht Medical care	Family 500 Baht Medical care
	Individual (yellow) 100 Baht Medical care	–	Individual (red) 200 Baht Medical care	–
Insured period	One year, unused cards renewable twice for one year	One year, unused cards renewable once for one year	One year, not renewable	One year, not renewable
Conditions	'green channel', 8 free episodes, 4 family members, not for chronic diseases, cancer, etc., 500–1,000 Baht coverage of accident-caused illness; 10% discount for accident-caused treatment cost and other medical costs exceeding 1,000 Baht	'green channel', 8 free episodes, 4 family members, not for chronic diseases, cancer, etc., 2,000 Baht coverage of accident-caused illness; 10% discount for accident-caused treatment cost and other medical costs exceeding 1,000 Baht	6 free episodes, 2,000 Baht coverage (except for cosmetic surgery, dentures, and optometry)	unlimited free episodes, no limit on number of family members, no ceiling on coverage, not for chronic diseases, cancer, and 'self-inflicted' diseases
Subsidy	Implicit cross-subsidization from other sources of hospital revenue	Implicit cross-subsidization from other sources of hospital revenue	Implicit cross-subsidization from other sources of hospital revenue	Explicit budgetary contribution of 500 Baht per card sold

Source: Information from Tantiserani (1988) and Mongkolsmai *et al.* (1994)

This reduction in coverage has been attributed to the lack of policy direction on the part of the MOPH during this period (Kiranandana, 1990). The programme was implemented in an *ad hoc* manner and thrived only in provinces that most actively encouraged villager participation. The programme never represented a lucrative activity for the large hospitals in any case, and implicit subsidy to the programme had to be drawn from other sources of hospital revenue.

In 1990 the health card scheme was modified and called the 'New Health Card Approach', with the concept of risk-sharing featured prominently. Price restructuring (ranging from 200 for the individual card, and from 300 to 500 Baht for the family card, covering up to three generations) was experimented with in five provinces (Manopimoke, 1995). In addition the referral system was relaxed, and coverage expanded with unlimited numbers of free visits and no coverage ceiling per visit. About 20% of the population in the selected areas participated in the project.

In 1991 the various different card types were discontinued, with only family cards priced at 500 Baht offered. A major change in the programme since 1994 is the explicit contribution of the Ministry of Public Health: an equal contribution of 500 Baht per card. No limits were imposed on the number of episodes or the cost coverage per visit. Moreover more flexibility was built into the referral system, and each province could impose any conditions deemed appropriate for the particular situation. Some provinces like Rachaburi allowed card purchasers to pay in instalments (Mongkolsmai, *et al.*, 1994). Administrative changes were also implemented, with the Health Card fund managed by a committee at the district level in coordination with village-level bodies. This was aimed at expanding the enrolment base to the district level, instead of the village as had previously been the case. As for the share of funds, 80% of the card price would go to providers of medical care, while the remaining 20% would be retained for marketing and sales incentives.

The health card may be a candidate for use in expanding coverage of those currently without insurance, and studies are being undertaken to ascertain its feasibility in urban areas as well.

(2) Mandatory schemes

Mandatory schemes include the Workmen's Compensation Scheme and the Social Security Scheme. Both schemes are managed by the Ministry of Labour and Welfare and at present cover workers in firms employing ten or more employees. These schemes require extensive record-keeping on employment to verify eligibility, and are thus confined to formal-sector employees.

The Workmen's Compensation Fund covers job-related injuries, and theoretically sicknesses that are work-induced. The latter however is difficult to prove particularly if adverse health effects are only evident after many years, such as the case of manganese poisoning, silicosis, lead poisoning, and others. Even job-related injuries, particularly if they are perceived to be minor, are allegedly under-reported (Kultap, 1983), if workers are not assertive or well-informed, and the employer is concerned with loss of work-time or the hassles of the required paper-work. All employers hiring ten or more workers are required by law to contribute to the fund.

Various problems are being encountered with the administration of the Workmen's Compensation Fund. In particular, the fact that medical providers are paid for whatever services they provide (the fee-for-service method of payment), there is a tendency towards cost escalation and excessive treatment. Experience with this scheme led to greater cautiousness in implementing the Social Security Scheme.

The Social Security Scheme, implemented under the Social Security Act of 1990 was designed to provide security to populations not covered under other benefit programmes. However its implementation is currently confined to the most manageable group, namely employees in formal-sector establishments. In the first three years of its inception, the scheme covered employees in firms employing 20 or more employees. The coverage is now extended to firms employing ten or more employees, expanding the population covered to 4.5 million or 7.56% of the population in 1995.

Under the Social Security Scheme, health insurance is provided as part of an overall package of seven benefits, namely for illness unrelated to work, maternal benefits, disability unrelated to work, death, child benefits, old-age, and unemployment. Employers hiring ten or more employees, and employees themselves are each required by law to make monthly contributions of 1.5% of the employee's wages to the Social Security Fund, with an equal 1.5% contribution provided by the government. Since the contribution is based on income and not the expected risk or incidence of illness, risks are pooled and benefits are skewed in favour of high-risk individuals.

Out of this tripartite contribution, 2.45% has been used to provide medical care for the insured for illness and maternity, and 2.05% for disability and death. It is expected that in 1996 benefits will be expanded to include child and old age benefits, requiring an increase in the contribution. Unemployment benefits, however, will be implemented at a later stage for fear of the problem of moral hazard, that is, providing unemployment benefits could induce unemployment as is suspected in some countries.

The Act also provides for expansion of the scheme on a voluntary basis to include the self-employed, such as farmers, own-account workers, and other uninsured groups. However this provision was probably included for political expediency at the time that criticism was levied against the scheme for providing protection only to the relatively well-off. Even if the self-employed were eligible to participate, the problem remains of how to deal with the 'third' party's contribution. The Health Card Program has therefore been proposed as a more practical form of coverage for the self-employed, but Thailand is still experimenting with this idea.

A more immediate concern is the present system of providing medical care. Current practice requires the insured worker to register at a specified hospital, called the 'main contractor', where he can receive free medical care in case of illness. Certain types of services, such as cosmetic surgery and optometry, are excluded. These restrictions are similar to those under the Health Card Program. The main contractor receives an annual prepayment or capitation fee from the Social Security Fund, initially equal to 700 Baht per insured person registered, regardless of actual utilization. Capitation was chosen over fee-for-service as a method of payment to providers, for its administrative simplicity, and to prevent the cost escalation that invariably occurs with the latter form of payment. The Workmen's Compensation Scheme, for example, pays hospitals on a fee-for-service basis, and has resulted in substantial cost escalation, as well as the administrative burden of dealing with massive claims documents. The capitation method of payment, however, may not be attractive enough to induce medical providers to enrol in the scheme. The relative merits of alternative payment methods are summarized in Table 9.6.

The main contractor is able to recruit 'sub-contractors' providing lower levels of care, as well as 'supra-contractors', providing higher levels of medical services. Participating in the scheme are both public and private hospitals. One main problem in implementing the scheme was the confusion with respect to insured persons receiving care in hospitals in which they are not registered. Accident victims, for example, made headlines when allegedly denied treatment by non-contract hospitals.

Initially the main contracting hospital was chosen by the employer and this may partly be responsible for the low utilization in the first

Table 9.6 Strengths and weaknesses of alternative methods of paying health providers

Payment method	Strengths	Weaknesses
Fee for service	Provider's reward closely linked to level of effort and output	Creates incentives for excessive and unnecessary treatment, tending to cause cost inflation
	Allows for easy analysis of provider's practice	Administrative burden of validating massive claims documents
Per case (for example, using diagnostic-related groups)	Provider's reward fairly well tied to output	Technical difficulty of forcing all cases into standard list can lead to mismatch between output and reward
	Gives provider incentive to minimize resource use per individual treated	Providers may misrepresent diagnosis in order to receive higher payment
Capitation (per patient under continuous care)	Administratively simple; no need to break down physician's work into procedures or cases	Gives provider incentive to select patient based on risk and reject high-cost patients
	Facilitates prospective budgeting	May create incentives for provider to underservice accepted patients
	Gives provider incentive to minimize cost of treatment	Difficult to analyse provider's practice
	Allows for consumer clout if patient can select own provider	
Salary (straight payment per period work)	Administratively simplest	Loss of patient influence over provider behaviour unless patient choice links provider salary to patient satisfaction
	Facilitates prospective budgeting	Can easily create incentives for provider to underservice patient and to reduce productivity

Source: Adapted from *World Development Report*, 1993, p. 124

year of implementation of the scheme. In 1991 the rate of utilization for out-patient care was 0.32 visits per insured person per year, and in 1992 the rate dropped to 0.22. In calculating the capitation fee, it was estimated that there would be three visits per insured person per year. Similarly in-patient utilization was lower than expected; in 1991 and 1992 the rate of utilization was respectively 0.016 and 0.012 visits per insured person per year. The estimated utilization rate was 0.05.

Apart from the inconvenience of receiving care at the designated hospital, which workers were not able to select for themselves, and the limited number of participating hospitals to choose from, several other problems emerged. Many workers were ignorant of their rights, some were not aware of the contributions they made to the Social Security Fund because of automatic deductions from their wages, and many lacked understanding of the procedures that had to be followed to obtain medical care (Patichon, 1995). Further, providers of medical care were ill-prepared in managing the scheme in terms of health care delivery. Attempts have therefore been made to improve the delivery system and the quality of care, so that insured persons may have better access to the medical care to which they are entitled.

Specifically, the Social Security Office issued a policy directive in 1992 to grant insured persons the right to choose their own hospital. This policy was implemented in one province in 1992 and expanded to 19 and 44 provinces in the following two years. The policy is being implemented in 60 provinces at present. The proportion of insured persons choosing their own hospital has therefore increased from 2% in 1992 to 36.6% in 1995 (Social Security Office, 1995).

In addition, the Social Security Office has adopted a policy of encouraging formation of provider networks, to increase efficiency in health care delivery, to improve accessibility of services, particularly if network members are well distributed geographically, and to pool risks. Moreover, additional payment is also given to the main contractors in proportion to the in-patient and out-patient care that they provide. This is intended to foster competition and give incentives to medical providers to increase their market share and engage in their own marketing for contracts with workers. Consequently the number of main contractors increased from 137 in 1991 to 1,879 in 1995. Among private providers, the number of network members increased by about ninefold in three years: from 69 in 1992 to 620 in 1995. In the public sector, the increase has been more moderate: from 671 in 1991 to 1,257 providers in 1995. The switch from public to private hospitals has also been dramatic. In 1991 only 16% of the insured persons chose private hospitals, whereas in 1994 the proportion increased to 58.8%. A system of 'managed competition' was envisaged.

At the present time two patterns of network formation are being tried out. First is the direct contract network, whereby the main contractor would contract directly with network members, and assume responsibility for management of the capitation fee received from the Social Security Office and act as a 'secondary medical care provider'.

Figure 9.2 Social Security and Medical Care Network

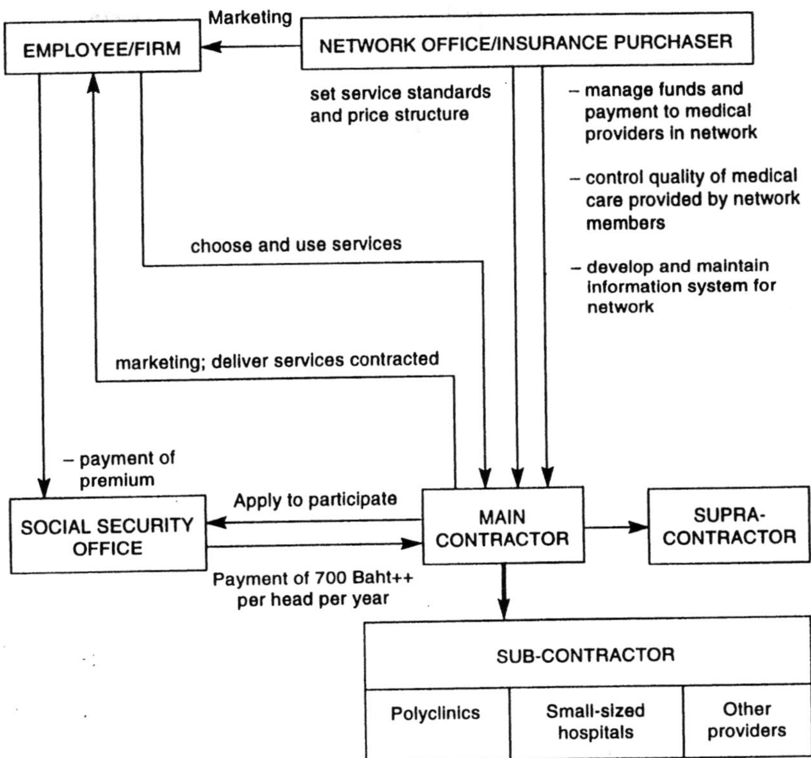

The second pattern is the indirect contract network, whereby the main contractor would transfer the capitation fee to a Network Office whose responsibility would be to manage the pool of funds received from several main contractors. The Network Office would also assume responsibility for marketing and recruiting network members. In the second case, the main contractor would be responsible for medical services only. The situation is summarized in Figure 9.2.

In practice there is much confusion in the system with great variation between networks with respect to: (i) network coverage of the three levels of care: the sub-contractor, the main contractor and the supra-contractor; (ii) the ability to manage funds and the payment mechanism that would encourage cost containment and foster financial feasibility for the network; (iii) the quality and standard of medical services provided by the networks; and (iv) coordination between networks and network management at the national level.

There is also some evidence of abuse.[5] That is, medical providers that some networks have recruited are so far apart geographically, that the opportunity for insured persons to benefit from such location is almost nil. Some network members are in provinces several hundred kilometres apart. They are entitled to obtain the additional payment which is calculated on the basis of services provided, but these services are provided to different people and the insured person does not benefit from the apparently wide range of providers available. These problems are currently being studied and further adjustments made to the system.

(3) Social Welfare Schemes

Several welfare programmes exist in Thailand. First, the Low Income Support Program gives free medical care in government health facilities to poor rural families whose income falls below a defined poverty line.

Government policy towards providing free medical care to the low-income population was initiated in 1975. The objective was to reduce the prevailing inequity of access to health services. Known as the low income support scheme, it offers free medical care at government hospitals to the low-income population and this has become the main health scheme for the rural population.

Initially those eligible were identified as persons with monthly incomes below 1,000 Baht and the target low-income population was set at 7-8 million people. However up until 1980 no identification cards were issued, and free care was given at the discretion of the health facilities' staff. Since 1981 low-income cards have been issued to those eligible, redefined as families with incomes lower than 2,000 Baht per month, or individuals with monthly incomes below 1,500 Baht. Currently the cut-off income is 2,800 Baht for families, and 2,000 Baht for individuals. The cards entitle holders to free medical care at all government health facilities operated by the Ministry of Public Health, the Bangkok Metropolitan Administration, the Red Cross Society, Pattaya City and municipalities. Each card is valid for three years.

The government provides bloc grants to health facilities based on the expected distribution of the eligible population and past records of service to patients. Specifically, budgetary allocation is based on the number of low-income people living in the designated less-developed villages defined by the National Economic and Social Development

Board (NESDB). In addition, the number of users of health care facilities is taken into account, and the number of veterans and their families.

The free medical care budget for the low-income population has increased in real terms from 521 million Baht in 1982 to 1,911 million Baht in 1993.[6] As a percentage of the health budget, the low income budget has varied over a narrow range of 7.7% in 1980 to 7.9% in 1993. This has actually declined from 12.5% of the health budget in 1976. In real terms, the budget per patient has declined from 155 Baht in 1976 to 45 Baht in 1980, stabilizing at around 50 Baht in the past 10 years. In terms of the budget allocated per card holder, this has shown a rising trend, increasing substantially in real terms from 68 Baht in 1984 to 163 Baht in 1992.

However, the budgetary allocation is invariably insufficient to cover the cost of providing services. Satsanguan and Leopairote (1992) report a unit cost of 85 Baht for an out-patient visit and 1,200 Baht per case or 360 Baht per day for in-patient care at district hospitals in 1991. Thus hospitals routinely cross-subsidize this group from other sources of revenue, such as reimbursements for government officials and hospital fees. The extent of cross-subsidy varies from hospital to hospital. For example, Nan Provincial Hospital in the North reported that during the six-month period between October 1992 and March 1993, the costs of providing care for low-income patients amounted to 1.4 million Baht per month, while the budgetary allocation was 10.5 million Baht for the year, or just 0.87 million Baht per month. In this particular hospital the cross-subsidization was thus about 6 million Baht per year (Mongkolsmai, 1993). In the province of Samutsakorn, the budget allocation was 2.3 million Baht while actual expenditures were 5.8 million Baht.

This scheme does not require cost-sharing on the part of the eligible population, and has been subject to much criticism since its inception, particularly with respect to the distribution of the card. A 1980 study by the Rural Health Division of the Ministry of Public Health revealed that out of a sample of 4,269 patients in health facilities in nine provinces, and 513 providers of free medical care for the low income population, 12% of the beneficiaries using provincial and district hospitals and 9% of card holders visiting health centres, had monthly incomes of greater than 2,000 Baht. Another study (Rural Health Division and Mahidol, 1988) found that, using a sample of 14,400 households, about 20% of the card holders were found to be non-poor. Mongkolsmai and Khoman (1993) also report that some non-poor families, possibly with connections to officials, also possess the card.

The cut-off level used for eligibility is almost four times higher than the poverty line defined as the minimum income required for subsistence.[7] Thus judging from this criterion, at least the population below the poverty line should be covered. Mongkolsmai (1993) however shows that although the population below the poverty line in 1988/89 constituted about 29.4% of the rural population, the low-income support programme covered only 7.65 million people or 19.87% of the rural population. In terms of the poor, the card coverage was limited to only 28.3% of the low-income group defined by the cut-off income level, and 49% of the poor as defined by the poverty line. In 1990 the coverage improved as a result of expanded efforts to reach the target groups, and increased screening of card recipients. Nevertheless coverage of the card remains low as up to 20% of those below subsistence are still left out.

However, even with low coverage of the poor, Thailand still possesses a safety net that protects the needy. That is a large number of low-income people routinely receive free medical care even without any card. These patients are called low-income Type B patients.[8] In 1987 there were 13.7 million people receiving free medical care, but out of these only 7.6 million were low-income card holders. The proportion is believed to be roughly the same at present, so that those seeking health care in Thailand can possibly have access to health facilities without income being a constraint.

The problem that remains is the difficulty of reaching those who do not seek care, and properly identifying eligibility. Given that much of the rural population is engaged in agricultural activity, with a substantial proportion of income received in kind, assessing and imputing income is a difficult task. The definition of a household is also problematic where family members work in the cities and remit earnings.

Another scheme that provides free medical services is the scheme that covers the elderly. In 1992 the population covered by the scheme was about 3.5 million, and this is likely to expand considerably in the future due to population ageing. The Ministry of Education also provides free medical care to primary school children in schools under its jurisdiction. This benefits children in both urban and rural areas, but provides proportionately higher benefits for the rural population who are less likely to have other coverage. Over 5 million children or approximately 9% of the population are covered under this scheme.

Other welfare recipients include veterans and monks. In addition, those who are considered needy (as determined by social workers attached to government hospitals) are routinely given free care. In addition, the Ministry of Interior also offers free care cards to urban dwellers who apply as low income families.

Another major form of health coverage is offered as fringe benefits in large private companies, government agencies and state enterprises. In the government sector, some 5.6 million government officials and their families are covered, and close to one million state enterprise employees and dependents. These two groups make up about 11% of the population. Mongkolsmai and Khoman (1993) found that among the users of public hospitals, government officials tend to fall in the medium- to high-income groups. Examination of the subsidy per head in the last column of Table 9.4 further shows that in fact this group of beneficiaries receives the highest subsidy from government expenditures on health.

Altogether some 58% of the population are protected by some kind of coverage in Thailand. This however still leaves about 42% of Thailand's population or 24 million people unprotected by any kind of scheme. This group includes subsistence farmers, self-employed people, rural workers, as well as urban dwellers engaged in informal sector activity such as street vending and small-scale commercial undertakings. Those living on the fringes of society such as slum dwellers and homeless migrants into the city also typically have to fend for themselves. An interview survey of Bangkok transients (Khoman, 1996b) who dwell in makeshift accommodation of grass mats and mosquito nets, under bridges and at railway stations, shows that none of these transients are covered by any health scheme. But they say they are fit and well.

Attempts are now under way by the Ministry of Public Health to expand insurance coverage to slum dwellers, the self-employed, and highly mobile groups such as construction workers, service workers, and prostitutes. Some studies undertaken (Mongkolsmai *et al.*, 1994), however, reveal that construction workers and prostitutes have little interest in purchasing any form of health card. Prostitutes already visit the 'V.D. clinic', a service provided by most government provincial hospitals as the need arises. The construction workers surveyed also showed little interest, partly due to the complicated nature of health coverage and the low perceived need.

3.3 Pricing and its Effects

Another major form of government intervention in health is to provide health services at highly subsidized prices, independent from any of the above schemes.

Government hospitals in less-developed countries tend to have fees that are 'too low', and Thailand is no exception. Mongkolsmai and Khoman (1993) found that fees are invariably set at a substantially lower level than the costs of provision, and there are few conscious attempts to align social costs and benefits. Pricing policy is obscure and often based on arcane if not archaic price lists. There are no incentives for cost containment, let alone cost recovery, due to lack of financial accountability on the part of hospital administrators.

Medical practitioners in Thailand frequently argue that the pricing of government hospital services should not be based on any economic criteria because it is essentially a public service, and profit or loss should not be a consideration. It is also often argued that in government hospitals, the salaries of medical and paramedical staff are paid from the government budget, capital expenditures are usually financed from tax revenue and/or donations, and that only operating costs should be covered by patient fees. This kind of argument fails to capture the opportunity cost concept that must be applied to the use of all resources in order to achieve efficiency in resource allocation.

The issue is whether such subsidy is appropriate, and whether the subsidy influences utilization behaviour in an undesirable direction. Khoman (1995b) reports that the pricing of public hospital services is often not consistent with the equation of social costs and social benefits. Many low-income groups rely on self-financing or are more responsible for their own health needs through purchase of the health card. On the other hand, many groups of beneficiaries receive subsidized service disproportionate to their economic status. While welfare programmes appreciably benefit the lowest income groups, this is not exclusively so, and many beneficiaries fall into the medium and even high-income categories. Notably, government officials, most of whom are classified in the middle to high-income groups turn out to be most heavily subsidized through the civil service reimbursement of medical expenses.

Pricing is intimately linked to how health care is financed and thereby involves broader concerns of determining how much of the economy's total resources are devoted to health services, how much is spent by the government, and how much burden non-government sources bear. Low cost recovery means that the burden is passed on to non-users through reliance on general tax revenues. Stark differentials between costs and fees also lead to misleading signals to both provider and user. Low fees result in long waiting time which then acts as an allocative device instead of the price mechanism. Users begin to seek preferential access to services through personal connections, position and clout, leading to greater inequity. In addition, the quality of the services tends to be driven down due to the lack of resources.

In Thailand, estimates of demand elasticities (Mongkolsmai and Khoman, 1993) show that the demand for in-patient and out-patient care is in general not sensitive to changes in price, money income, or total household income. Thus a restructuring of fees appears to be a feasible policy option.

3.4 Private Health Expenditures

In spite of the many government-initiated programmes, private households, in both rural and urban areas, have invariably been the major source of finance for health services in Thailand. In recent years, over 70% of the total health expenditure is made by households and private companies (Khoman and Mongkolsmai, 1993). This percentage has increased over time from 63% in 1977 to 72% in 1986 and almost 74% in 1992 (Table 9.7).

This is partly the result of greater awareness about health in the general population and particularly among the higher-income groups, able and willing to consume high-priced health services, often at private facilities. But part of this increased reliance on the private sector may exacerbate inequalities.

Because private households already shoulder much of the responsibility for health care, it is important not to pursue policies that place a disproportionate burden on the disadvantaged groups. Out of these private expenditures, there is evidence (Khoman, 1992) that a large percentage of the poor resort to self-prescription, and purchasing drugs from local drug stores. Thus these people receive only a small portion of public spending on health in the form of subsidized hospital care or even the specific schemes earlier discussed. A more rational pricing policy is therefore not likely to hurt the poor, particularly if the resources so mobilized could be used to reach out to the most vulnerable groups.

In terms of private sector providers, these still constitute a small part of the health sector in Thailand, although they are rapidly gaining more prominence as health care turns into a thriving industry. Private providers are typically concentrated in urban areas and mainly in Bangkok.

Table 9.7 National Health Expenditure Account: Thailand (1992 Prices in Baht)

	1978	1980	1982	1984	1986	1987	1988	1990	1992
MOPH	7,661.6 19.9%	7,683.7 17.2%	9,552.6 20.5%	11,867.6 17.4%	12,249.1 15.3%	12,277.9 14.1%	12,867.7 13.5%	17,286.4 15.0%	24,904.1 16.8%
Other Ministries	3,265.1 8.5%	3,894.6 8.7%	4,081.5 8.8%	4,730.7 6.9%	5,176.1 6.5%	5,203.4 6.0%	5,326.5 5.6%	5,020.1 4.4%	4,836.5 3.3%
Civil Servant Benefits	760.8 2.0%	1,117.1 2.5%	1,741.9 3.7%	2,444.2 3.6%	3,386.5 4.2%	3,610.6 4.1%	3,915.3 4.1%	4,799.0 4.2%	5,182.3 3.5%
Workmen's Compensation	140.0 0.4%	168.1 0.4%	217.3 0.5%	340.4 0.5%	288.6 0.4%	345.5 0.4%	430.5 0.5%	492.7 0.4%	753.0 0.5%
Social Security	–	–	–	–	–	–	–	811.9	1,823.0
State Enterprise Benefits	165.4 0.4%	316.6 0.7%	447.5 1.0%	523.7 0.8%	685.3 0.9%	727.1 0.8%	733.2 0.8%	691.8 0.6%	652.0 0.4%
Private Insurance	476.9 1.2%	401.9 0.9%	458.1 1.0%	514.4 0.8%	556.3 0.7%	573.9 0.7%	570.7 0.6%	576.1 0.5%	560.0 0.4%
Foreign Aid	376.5 1.0%	642.6 1.4%	547.0 1.2%	536.8 0.8%	660.4 0.8%	644.5 0.7%	390.8 0.4%	87.9 0.1%	362.8 0.2%
Private Household Expenditures	25,721.8 66.7%	30,461.6 68.2%	29,503.3 63.4%	47,296.4 69.3%	56,934.4 71.2%	63,974.4 73.2%	71,413.7 74.7%	85,258.1 74.1%	109,381.4 73.3%

Total	38,567.9	44,686.3	46,549.0	68,254.4	79,936.6	87,357.2	95,648.3	115,023.9	148,455.14
(% of GDP)	3.4	3.8	4.5	5.1	5.5	5.6	5.8	5.7	5.9
Total per Capita Expenditures									2,474.0
Per Capita Expenditures from Insurance Plans/Govt.									645.0
Per Capita Expenditures by Private Household									1,823.0

Source: Hsiao (1994)

4 CONCLUSIONS AND POSSIBLE APPLICATIONS TO TRANSITION ECONOMIES

Thailand's example demonstrates the need to identify the objectives of society with respect to the provision of health care, and the overall impact of different schemes before implementation. Transition economies are faced with many challenges, but can take advantage of many opportunities as well. In setting up the machinery to put into place a more market-oriented economy, transition economies have a chance to lay the correct foundation from the start. The advantages and disadvantages of the market system in allocating health care can be seen from other countries, so that various forms of public intervention can be designed in the light of known market shortcomings.

In health, the potential functions of the state can be seen to lie in the areas of distribution, correction of market failures, counteracting the absence of futures and insurance markets, dealing with externalities, public goods, and merit wants. Any services provided by the state have to meet these criteria. Apart from that, cost-based criteria should be used, regardless of who the provider may be.

These issues are intimately related to the issue of financing. The financing of health care has indeed become the subject of global interest and concern in recent years, as capitalist and socialist countries alike grapple with problems of cost escalation, dwindling resources, inadequate quality of care, inefficiency in resource use, and unequal distribution of services. Transition economies in Indochina, Eastern Europe, and China, as well as capitalistic strongholds like the United States all face formidable challenges in trying to answer the question of who should pay for health care, and how health care should be managed.

In developing countries, the rural areas are of particular concern, given the regional disparities in incomes that typically place the rural population at a disadvantage in terms of general living conditions and access to health care. Moreover, the weak administrative framework that typifies rural areas creates added difficulties for managing whatever financing scheme is implemented, especially where large proportions of the population are engaged in subsistence activities, cut off from the formal sector. These areas have to be targeted for government assistance.

A starting point could be to rationalize services as well as fees. User fees for curative services should be closely aligned with cost, with provision for subsidization of preventive services and low-income groups. Prices should be based, in part, on cost-based principles, with allowance for subsidy of needy groups, and subsidy of services that have large externalities, such as preventive care. Attention has to be paid to the proper targeting of beneficiaries.

Generous subsidies for non-critical services should be avoided, and user fees be more closely aligned to costs. Unlike taxes, these fees can be earmarked to finance the expansion of priority services, while increasing rather than decreasing efficiency. Publicly provided goods and services will be used efficiently if they are priced to reflect the cost of production as well as externalities and other market imperfections. In contrast, subsidized (or underpriced) services result in excessive consumption and excess demand, and the taxes needed to pay for such subsidies often create distortions elsewhere in the economy.

Charging cost-based user fees for public facilities that have large private benefits, such as curative care of non-communicable diseases and private in-patient rooms, results in efficiency in both production and consumption. In addition, it also mobilizes resources to finance the expansion of priority services, many of which are used primarily by the poor. Subsidizing mobile rural services, for example, is one way to give the poor access to health care, with at least part of the cost borne by others. Such fees lead to gains on all fronts: the supply of publicly provided goods and services is allocated more efficiently, the reliance on fees also avoids the need for distortionary taxes, and at the same time equity goals are served.

Incentives for cost containment, reduction of the incentive towards over-utilization, and so on, should also be built into the system, through for example, capitation for insurance-type schemes, provisions for co-payment, and cost-sharing schemes for high-cost elective treatment, chosen beyond the basic level. In addition, accountability should also be fostered.

Charging fees based on costs need not reduce the poor's access to health facilities. If spending on services used by the poor is expanded concurrently with increased fees for services used by the rich, the distribution of subsidies could be substantially improved at no additional cost. If for example a large percentage of the poor resort to self-prescription their share of public spending would rise if user fees were used to cover the public cost of high-level curative care and the savings then used to finance additional services for those who may now be denied access.

These principles do not preclude safeguarding the poor's access to health services, or the access of the very poor, who cannot afford even modest fees, to services at every level. Differential pricing is needed and clearly focused targeting.

If target groups are to be identified, screening methods need to be devised. Identifying individuals or households that are 'poor' can be an onerous task, given subsistence activities and under-reported incomes. Moreover even as statistical records improve, there is always the tendency for some groups to pass themselves off as 'poor'. Other targeting methods include (i) geographical demarcation, whereby poor areas are defined for coverage, (ii) self-targeting, using variations in the cost and quality of services to induce self-selection in participating in various schemes, (iii) targeting the diseases of the poor to be included in the benefits covered, based on the epidemiological assumption that the poor and non-poor are afflicted with different diseases, and (iv) targeting based on socio-demographic characteristics such as age, sex, occupation and ethnicity if health problems and financial vulnerability are believed to be based on these characteristics.

However in designing policies, one also needs an understanding of what functions governments have assumed in the past, and why. An understanding of the behaviour of the state is also relevant in determining the desirability of government action. In addition, the appropriate form of intervention also depends on the instruments available to the government, such as what taxes and expenditure policies are feasible, what kinds of information is available to the government, what incentives there are for individuals to reveal information (such as about their endowments or their preferences for public goods), and the constraints on the government's actions. In addition, the incentives of the government itself have to be taken into account, such as whether there is a tendency to favour certain segments of the population, and tax some groups of the population more heavily to subsidize others.

Public provision, the nature and type of financing schemes, the level of fees, all affect the behaviour of producers and consumers and influence the distribution of wealth and income in the economy. If the beneficiaries are not the truly needy, then public provision can be distortionary. Whether a disproportionately heavy burden is placed on the poor depends on how spending is allocated and revenue raised. If wealth taxes such as property taxes, capital gains taxes, and inheritance taxes are low or non-existent, then public provision of health, could have regressive elements. All these considerations have to be dealt with, if long-run benefits are to be reaped, and sustainable development accomplished.

Notes

1. The term 'state' is used to emphasize the 'generic' sense, distinct from particular governments.
2. Technically, market efficiency requires a full set of markets for all relevant dates in the future and for all risks. Typically, a full set of futures and insurance markets does not in fact exist.
3. The ethical basis for such judgements is subject to dispute, and attempts have been made to include such objectives in the framework of individualistic judgements, by extending the latter to include views about the desirable state of society.
4. Approximate exchange rate in 1996: USD 1:25 Baht.
5. This information was obtained from private discussion with top-level personnel in the Ministry of Public Health.
6. Using constant 1986 prices (Rural Health Division, Ministry of Public Health).
7. For a single person, the cut-off point was 1,500 Baht per month or 18,000 Baht per year, whereas the poverty line in 1989 was 4,141 Baht per year for the rural population, and 6,324 Baht per year for the urban population (Hutaserani, 1992).
8. Those with the low-income support card are classified as low-income Type A patients.

References

Atkinson, Anthony B. and Joseph E. Stiglitz, *Public Economics*, Singapore: McGraw-Hill, 1987.

Hsiao, William C., 'Health Care Financing in Thailand: Challenges for the Future', Paper presented at a seminar at the College of Public Health, Chulalongkorn University, 1994.

Khoman, Sirilaksana, *Household Choice of Health-Care Provider in Thailand*, Research Report No. 92–02 submitted to the International Health Policy Program, 1992.

Khoman, Sirilaksana, 'Mechanisms of Socio-Economic Change in Rural Areas: The Case of Education and Health in Thailand', *Review of Marketing and Agricultural Economics*, 61:2, 1993.

Khoman, Sirilaksana (1995a), 'Rural Health Financing: Thailand's Experience', Paper presented at the International Seminar on Financing and Organization of Health Care in Poor Rural Population in China, organized by the China Network for Training and Research in Health Economics and Financing, Harvard School of Public Health, and the Ministry of Health, P.R. China, in Beijing, October 8–11, 1995.

Khoman, Sirilaksana (1995b) 'Equity and the Pricing of Government Health Services in Thailand' Paper presented at the Second International Conference on Health Reform Around the Globe, organized by the Canadian Society for International Health, in Ottawa, November 12–15, 1995.

Khoman, Sirilaksana (1996a) 'Social Security in Thailand: Issues and Policy Options' Paper presented at the Senior Policy Forum on Social Reform and

Social Development Policies in Asia-Pacific Region, organized by the China (Hainan) Institute for Reform and Development, in cooperation with the German Corporation for Technical Cooperation (GTZ), at Haikou, Hainan, P. R. C., February 6–8, 1996.

Khoman, Sirilaksana (1996b) 'Urban Poverty and Access to Health Care: Insights from Bangkok Slums' unpublished manuscript, 1996.

Khoman, Sirilaksana and Dow Mongkolsmai, *Public-Sector Health Financing in Thailand: A Synthesis of Findings,* Research Report No. 93–04 submitted to the International Health Policy Program, 1993.

Kiranandana, Thienchay, *Evaluation of the Health Card Project,* Ministry of Public Health, Bangkok, (in Thai), 1990.

Krongkaew, Medhi, 'Thai Society and the Distribution of Opportunity and Income', Paper presented at the Annual Symposium XVIII, organized by the Faculty of Economics, Thammasat University, Bangkok, 1995.

Kultap, Praneet, 'A Study of Industrial Injury: A Case Study of the Textile Industry', unpublished M.A. Thesis, Faculty of Economics, Thammasat University, Bangkok, 1983.

Manopimoke, Supachit, 'Voluntary Health Insurance in Thailand: Development and Achievement', Paper presented at the Regional Conference on Health Sector Reform in Asia, held at the Asian Development Bank, Manila, Philippines, May 22–25, 1995.

Mongkolsmai, Dow, 'The Social Welfare for Health Care', Paper presented at the National Workshop on Health Financing in Thailand, at Phetburi, November 12–13, 1993.

Mongkolsmai, Dow and Sirilaksana Khoman, *Study of Beneficiaries of Public Hospitals in Thailand,* Research Report No. 93–02, submitted to the International Health Policy Program, 1993.

Mongkolsmai, Dow, Plearnpit Satsanguan, Anong Rojvanit, Sirilaksana Khoman, Praphatsorn Leopairote, and Thanakorn Ungswad, *Features of Voluntary Health Insurance: Case Study of the Health Card Project for Selected Population Groups in Rachaburi Province,* Research Report submitted to the Office of Health Insurance, Ministry of Public Health, 1994.

Nitayarumphong, Sanguan and Supasit Punnarunothai, 'Thailand at the Crossroads: Challenges for Health Care Reform', Paper presented at the Workshop on Health Care Reform: At the Frontier of Research and Policy Decisions, organized by the Ministry of Public Health at Nakorn Rachasima, January 22–24, 1996.

Patichon, Preeya, 'Choice of Hospital and Utilization of Medical Services Among Insured Persons Under the Social Security Scheme in Nonthaburi Province', unpublished Master of Economics Thesis, Faculty of Economics, Thammasat University, Bangkok, (in Thai), 1995.

Population Studies Institute, Chulalongkorn University, *Thailand Demographic and Health Survey,* Bangkok, 1988.

Satsanguan, Plearnpit and Praphatsorn Leopairote, *A Study of Unit Costs in Public Hospitals in Thailand,* Research Report No. 92–02, submitted to the International Health Policy Program, 1992.

Tantiserani, P., 'Health Card in the Rural Areas', Paper presented (in Thai) at the Workshop on Health Insurance System for Thailand, Pattaya, August 18–19, 1988.

Thailand, Ministry of Public Health, *Rural Health Division Survey Report*, Bangkok, (in Thai), 1980.

Thailand, Ministry of Public Health and Faculty of Health Sciences, Mahidol University, *A Study of the Coverage of Free Medical Care Services for the Low Income People in Thailand*, Bangkok, (in Thai), 1988.

Thailand, Ministry of Public Health, *Evaluative Report on Social Security*, Office of the Permanent Secretary, Bangkok, (in Thai), 1992.

Thailand, Ministry of Public Health, *Public Health Statistics 1993*, Bangkok, 1995.

Thailand, National Statistical Office, *Survey of Population Change, 1987–88*, Bangkok.

Thailand, Office of the Prime Minister, *Government Budget, 1996.*

Thailand, Ministry of Labour and Welfare, Social Security Office, untitled report, 1995.

Index

add-factors, 203
advantages, 46
adverse selection, 228
agricultural reforms, 49
agriculture, 31
aid, 44–5
AIDS, 234
anti-competition, 75
applications to transition economies' health care system
  charging fees, 257
  incentives, 257
  pricing, 251–3
  subsidies, 257
ASEAN, 47–8, 51
Asia Pacific, 200
Asian, 49, 50
asymmetry of information, 227

benefit structures, 241
BHP, 28
BOT, 68, 103, 106–7
broadcasting, 38
budget deficit, 45
business, 27
  classification of, 127
  cooperation, 141–6
  expectations, 119
  experience, 128
  size, 120–3, 139
  survey, 117–19

centrally planned economy, 7
characterizing scalar, 205
Chaturvedi and Tran Van Hoa, 206
cointegration, 180
comovement, 195
communication, 33
construction, 30–1, 128
contestable markets, 233
convertible currency, 84
cooperation, 27
cost-based criteria, 256–7
cost-benefit analysis, 182
cost-sharing schemes, 257
credit resources, 44–5
crisis, 7–10
CT scan, 229

data-based, 203
Doi Moi (Renovation), 9–13
dominance, 205, 211
dynamic elasticities, 202

econometric models, 195
Economic Assistance Committee, 44
economic development, 5–17
economic renovation *see* Doi Moi
economic tigers, 200
education, 35–6
education and training, 35
electronics, 146
empirical Bayes, 200, 207
employment, 17
energy, 29
environmental health, 239
EPZ, 68–9, 103
equity, 230
error correction models, 184
ex ante forecasting, 211
exchange rate management, 73
export, 26, 73
export oriented, 48
ex post forecasting, 200–1
external debts, 180
externalities, 229, 234

financial systems, 84
fisheries, 32
flexible accelerator investment, 202
flexible modelling approach, 200
flying geese pattern, 179
foodstuffs, 31
forecasting, 198
forecasting error, 201
foreign debts, 45
foreign direct investment (FDI), 39, 40, 46, 52, 53–7, 68, 70–1, 73–5, 78, 83, 99, 100–1, 103
  amount of, 57
  by investment category, 60, 67, 102,
  by investor, 58, 63, 64, 178
  orientation of priority, 108–9
foreign exchange, 81

foreign investment, *see* foreign direct investment
Foreign Investment Law, 45, 65, 67, 92–7
forestry, 32
form of investment, 94
free rider, 230
free-trade policy, 489
fringe benefits, 237

gas, 28–9
GDP, 69
General Department of Tourism, 171
general tax revenue, 233
Geneva Convention, 87
government role, 234
growth, 18–9, 70, 201–3

Harvie and Tran Van Hoa, 203
Health Card, 239
health care, 223
health education, 239
health insurance, 237
health provider, 245
health schemes (coverage of), 238
human resources, 36

identifiability, 202
IMF, 114
implementation, 171
imports, 26
import substitution, 47
Indonesia, 190, 215–18
Industrial Zone Regulation, 68
industrialization, 7
inflation, 45
information technology, 39, 198
infrastructure, 142
integrated of order (0) and (1), 83–5
international capital mobility, 195
international finance, 181
investment, 27, 40, 47 *see* also foreign direct investment
investment laws, 132
Investment Rules (1977), 88

Johansen-class, 203

Korea, 192, 218–20

labour supply, 141
land management, 33
legal systems, 89–90
life cycles, 202

loan, 45
long-term relationships, 183, 199
low income support scheme, 248
low risk, 228

macroeconomic performance, 5–10, 13, 14
Malaysia, 190–1, 220
management, 33, 171
mandatory scheme, 237, 242
manufacturing, 128
market failure, 225–7
maximum likelihood, 201, 204
mean squared error, 203
measurement errors, 209
Medicaid, 233
Medicare, 232
merit good, 230
micro and macroeconomic reforms, 13
MIGA (Multilateral Investment Guarantee Agency), 81
mining, 28–9
Ministry of Planning and Investment (MPI), 110
Ministry of Public Health, 233–6
misery index, 180
moral hazard, 228
multinational companies, 75

nationalization, 81
National Party Congress, 44
neoclassical 201–2
network formation, 246
New Health Card Approach, 242
NGO, 115
NIC, 52–3
non-distortionary measures, 231

obstacles to economic development, 16–8
ODA, 41, 45
OECD, 186
oil, 28–9, 110
open door policy, 12–13
opportunity costs, 252
ordinary least squares (OLS), 198
overseas countries, 123–4
ownership, 81

Pac Po, 167
partial adjustment, 202
policy, 192
policy objective, 225
pollution-free modes of production, 233

pollution tax, 232
prior information, 207
private health expenditure, 253
private ownership, 12
product differentiation, 172
prospects, 24–42
public administration, 18
public administration reform, 19
public awareness programmes, 233
public good, 229
public provision, 223

quadratic loss, 205

random walk, 184
rationing, 232
reduced form, 202
resource allocation, 231

science, 37
Social Security Scheme, 243
Social Welfare Scheme, 237
SPCC-PC, 113, 222
Standardized National Accounts (SNA), 114, 186, 200
standard of living, 198
state intervention, 231
state-owned enterprises, 19
state production, 233
Stein, 198
stochastic simulation, 203, 210
stock market, 210
strategies, 18, 173
Strawderman, 208
structural change, 203, 210
sub-factors, 203
suboptimal forecasts, 205
survey, 117–26, 150–2
  business experience with Australia, 128
  income distribution, 129, 131
  infrastructure, 142, 144, 146,
  labour supply, 141–2

tax
  incentive, 83
  priorities, 79, 80
technology, 37
technology transfer, 98
telecommunication, 34–5
telephone interviews, 118
Telstra, 28
textiles, 128
Thailand, 191, 220
Thong Nhat (Reunification), 6
tourism, 38, 159–60
  in South-East Asia, 163–5
  in Vietnam, 161–3, 165–70
  strategies, 172–6
trade, 24–7
training, 35–36
transition, 199
transport, 33
two stage hierarchical information (2SHI) estimator, 198, 206–7
types of business, 127

Ullah-Ullah double k-class estimator, 208
uncertainty of demand, 227
unemployment, 17
unit roots, 184
USSR, 124

value added, 50
VD clinic, 251
Vietnam Business Directory, 118
Vietnam Post, 34
village health communicators, 239
village health volunteers, 239

Wald risk, 201, 205
Workmen's Compensation Fund, 242–3

Champika 074 292 90 361

Dilshan 07840311112